AF266851

EXPANDED LEADERSHIP EDITION

PTCD

POST-TRAUMATIC CHURCH DISORDER

ADDRESSING THE ELEPHANT
IN THE SANCTUARY

AARON D. DAVIS

For more information, or to book an event, contact :
Aaron@TattooPreacher.com
http://www.tattoopreacher.com

Book design by Aaron D. Davis
Cover design by Aaron D. Davis

ISBN - Paperback: 978-1-947837-18-8
ISBN - Hardcover : 978-1-947837-20-1

DEDICATION

To the love of my life, my wife Lisa—
This book is dedicated to you. The insights within these pages and the path to healing they represent came at a great cost, and I wasn't the only one who had to bear the weight of it. Through every mountaintop and every valley, you have stood faithfully by my side—my greatest support, my constant encourager, and my unwavering champion.

Thank you for loving me so deeply and so well. I'm eternally grateful to share this life with you. I love you more than my words could ever express.

I would also like to dedicate the message of this book to my son, Rocky. Son, everything I write, I write with you and your future in mind. I fully expect to have many years to pass on my life's lessons and experiences to you—long into the season when we both are sporting gray hair. But if, for any reason, that time were cut short, I want you to know there are truths and insights in these pages that I believe are vital for your journey. Many of them were learned through pain and perseverance, and it's my hope that by sharing them with you, you can gain wisdom without having to endure the same struggles.

This book speaks to leadership, character, and godly principles. My prayer is that you will embrace these Kingdom truths—learn them, live them, and eventually pass them on. May the ceiling of my experience truly become the floor of yours.

I love you, son. I hope you always know it…

CONTENTS

	Preface	i
	Part 1 – Laying the Groundwork	v
	Introduction	ix
1	The Pain Is Real	1
2	Trauma Doesn't Have Me	7
3	The Mirror of the Word	13
4	Kingdom Perspective	19
5	The Kingdom Leadership Model	25
6	The Standard	35
7	Discontentment Deception	51
8	Charisma VS. Character	57
9	Trauma Lenses	77
10	Victim Or Victor	83
11	The Strength of the Wolf	93
12	Leaders Eat Last	103
13	Grace in the Mess	109
	Part 2 – Leadership Paradigms	119
14	Pastoral Lenses	125
15	Staff Lenses	135
16	Member/Volunteer Lenses	145
17	Member/Volunteer Lenses Part II	151
18	PK (Pastor's Kid) Lenses	161
	Part 3 – The Path to Healing	169
19	Consumerism	171
20	When A Leader Fails When a Leaders Falls	179
21	Judged	195
22	Where Was God?	205
23	God Isn't Done	217
24	It's A Choice	227
25	It's A Choice Part II	235
26	All Things New	247
	About The Author	261
	Bibliography	265

ACKNOWLEDGMENTS

Over the years, I've been blessed by so many leaders who have guided, challenged, and stretched me—pushing me to grow and persevere through some of life's toughest seasons. I'm grateful for each one of you. But I want to take a moment to specifically honor my parents, Larry and Rene' Davis. More than anyone else, you have modeled godly leadership and shaped the way I view and live out leadership today. Thank you, Mom and Dad, for every sacrifice, every lesson, and every word of encouragement along the way. I understand what godly leadership looks like because of your example.

Shortly after I got married in 1996, my dad gave me a Bible and wrote something inside the cover. Those words captured the heart and legacy of leadership that both he and my mom poured into me throughout my life. I would like to share a portion of what he wrote here with you:

"Aaron, there is so much I want to say, but it seems impossible to do. But I will say, saturate yourself in the love of God – Guard the words of your mouth and let integrity precede you always, and as God told Ezekiel, "...all my words that I shall speak unto thee, receive in thine heart and hear with thine ears. And GO GET thee to them of the captivity...and speak unto them and tell them. 'Thus saith the Lord God...'
I love you so much, Son - Dad"

I love you both—so very much. Thank you for always pointing me toward God's way of living and for teaching me to understand and apply *Kingdom* principles as defined by Him and His Word.

Preface
Starting with "Why?"

After releasing this book in the spring of 2025, Steve—one of my closest friends and a pastor of more than forty years—called to congratulate me and commend me on a job well done.

"Aaron, I read your new book, PTCD, and I couldn't put it down. I finished it in two days… you did a great job."

We've been friends for a long time, and based on his tone, I could tell there was something he was holding back. So I pressed with a single word:

"…but?"

He paused for a few seconds before continuing.

"Well… I haven't been able to sleep for two days since reading it. And when I do, I'm having dreams about leadership. I guess I'm troubled because after reading your book, I realize there are a lot of things I should have done differently. We were taught to lead differently back then. At this point, I can't go back and fix it… I just feel troubled."

PTCD was written as a tool for instruction and healing across multiple demographics—those who have been hurt by the church, those aspiring to lead, and those currently leading who may have inherited or implemented questionable leadership structures modeled for them by others who likely inherited them as well.

But as I listened to my friend—who I know loves people deeply and has given his life to ministry—I realized something. I had always intended for *PTCD* to function as a leadership guide, particularly for *"MIT's"* (Ministers in Training). What surprised me was how many seasoned senior leaders—and even business leaders—have reached out to tell me how deeply the leadership applications resonated with them.

If a seasoned leader walked away from the book feeling anything close to regret or failure, then perhaps I had not been clear enough in how I addressed the leadership audience. My only desire in writing *PTCD* was healing and empowerment—not unintended discouragement.

A few weeks later, I sat down with another longtime friend, Daniel. Daniel has the reputation of being a brilliant marketer and was responsible for the syndication of three of the most popular television shows of all time. He hadn't yet read the book, but as a seasoned television and radio personality, he began interviewing me about it.

He asked what I hoped readers would walk away with after finishing PTCD.

We talked about the millions worldwide who have been wounded in their church experience. We discussed my passion for healing, restoration, and reconciliation between people and God—between Christ and His Bride. As I spoke, he listened, nodding, flipping the book over in his hands and studying the cover.

Then I said something that made him stop and look me directly in the eyes.

"It's also a book on Christian leadership from a biblical perspective— whether you're leading a family, a business, or a church."

He paused.

"Aaron, that subject appeals to a much larger audience than just those who have been hurt or experienced inconsistency in church," he said. *"And I don't get that from looking at the cover or hearing the title."*

He continued, *"If leadership is a major theme in this book, you should consider releasing an expanded leadership edition—one that provides additional leadership content and makes it clear that it's directly applicable to those who lead."*

I had already been considering a leadership edition after my conversation with Steve. But after sitting with Daniel, I knew it wasn't just an idea to be pondered—it was necessary for me to see it through and write it. Because while we definitely need to talk about how leadership should function, we also need to address what happens when it doesn't—and why so many carry wounds they were never meant to carry.

Leadership is a calling that carries considerable weight. In this book, we will address that weight and how God expects more from those who answer the call to lead. Some of that weight comes from God's prerequisites and standards. Some comes from people and their expectations. And some comes from the expectations we place upon ourselves.

In this expanded leadership edition of PTCD, my desire is to bring healing to leaders who have been wounded as well. I'm convinced that leadership is a high calling. As you read this book, I challenge you to weigh everything through the lens of God's Word. If something creates defensiveness in you, pause and ask yourself why. In my experience, many of us who lead others have not had our leadership paradigm *challenged* often. Yet some of our most significant growth happens when our beliefs or practices are tested and we are willing to see ourselves honestly in the mirror of that challenge.

None of us are too seasoned, too established, or too set in our ways to learn something new—if we are willing to allow God to examine our hearts, systems, assumptions, and leadership constructs.

After reading PTCD, a senior pastor in Michigan left a review on Amazon stating that he planned to purchase a copy for every member of his staff. I believe many of you in leadership will likewise find confirmation in these pages for areas where you have led well. You may also recognize patterns of failure you have observed in others and feel compelled to sow this book into the next generation of leaders as a tool for their own growth.

But like my friend Steve, some of you may discover opportunities for personal growth in your own leadership systems. If that happens, give yourself grace. It is God who called you to leadership, and it is God who is faithful to complete the good work that He began in you. There is therefore now no condemnation for those who are in Christ Jesus.

In the midst of your own processing, don't forget that Scripture is filled with stories of leadership shortcomings followed by restoration. Many of the leaders highlighted in the Bible experienced seasons of oversight—or even outright failure.

Take, for instance, 2 Samuel 11 and 12. King David, a man described by God as *"a man after His own heart,"* succumbs to covetousness, lust, adultery, and ultimately orchestrates the death of Uriah the Hittite to conceal his sin. Many of you know the story. Nathan the prophet confronts David with a rebuke from the Lord. He presents a hypothetical case and asks David what judgment should be rendered against the guilty man. David responds with a severe sentence. Then Nathan delivers the piercing words: *"You are the man."*

David is exposed.

But David also repents.

Though there was significant fallout from his failure, God provided restoration. From the union that began in failure, Solomon was eventually born—the next king of Israel.

I share this story for a reason. When you read this book through leadership lenses, some of the content may feel confronting—like Nathan standing before David. But how you respond determines what happens next.

What if David had refused to repent? What if he had allowed shame to silence him? What if he had withdrawn from God instead of worshiping through the pain? What if he had chosen bitterness over humility?

Solomon may never have been born. Legacy would have been altered. The next generation would have suffered.

The wages of David's sin produced a season of death and loss. But once he received correction and course-corrected, future legacy was secured. 2

Samuel 12:24–25 tells us that God even sent Nathan back to give Solomon a special name: *Jedediah*— *"Beloved of the Lord."*

What a turnaround in leadership legacy.

David had personality flaws and leadership flaws, and I'm convinced that we can all be thankful that God uses flawed people. Like most of us, some of David's insecurities were probably formed through failed leadership experiences and unhealthy environments in his own life—his mother possibly not being recognized as a *"lawful"* wife of Jesse and David feeling alienated as a result, his father overlooking him, his brothers diminishing him, Saul attempting to kill him and treating him with contempt. Those experiences undoubtedly shaped him.

Yet David was also a brave warrior. Full of faith. A worshiper. A man who returned to God again and again with repentance and humility.

David's story is really every leader's story.

We've all been shaped by experiences—some healthy, some not. We've all navigated serving imperfect or even absent leadership. We've all learned hard lessons. And some of us have developed unhealthy patterns along the way.

But we also serve a God who is faithful to complete what He begins in those who love Him and are called according to His purpose. When we approach His correction with humility and embrace His grace, He restores. He refines. He secures legacy. He makes all things new.

So, as we embark on this journey together, let's be clear about how we're going to approach this conversation. Church hurt and leadership failure aren't abstract ideas—they're real. They affect our emotions. They linger in our memory and shape our thinking. They influence how we process our own leadership responsibilities. And if we're not careful, those experiences can quietly shape the way we implement our leadership paradigms and model leadership for future generations.

Leaders reading this book need to understand something clearly: conversations like this demand courage. They demand humility. And they demand structure. If we are going to examine leadership honestly, to evaluate our models, our patterns, and the weight that comes with leading others, we must begin in the only place that keeps us anchored. That place is Scripture. And the goal is not reaction, but restoration.

Writing a book on *Post-Traumatic Church Disorder (PTCD)* can take many different directions, largely shaped by an author's personal leadership experiences, the pain they've encountered, and the degree of healing they've experienced. Even the tone of the writing, depending on the words chosen, has the power to sway readers toward either hope or cynicism.

With that in mind, I approached this project with a deep sense of responsibility. I knew I wasn't just telling stories—I was guiding people through an often emotionally charged and deeply personal subject. It was important to me that this journey be one marked by honesty, grace, and a genuine desire to help others find healing.

In recent years alone, we've witnessed some of the most extreme cases of leadership failure in the church. Prominent ministers have made headlines after being accused of misconduct ranging from sexual assault, rape, and child abuse coverups, to adultery, fraud, embezzlement, physical abuse, and even suicide—some tragically taking their own lives in the very pulpits from which they once preached.

Even in what might be considered "less severe" examples, it's no secret that church drama can be some of the most intense. Just keeping it real—sometimes events that I have experienced in church felt like an episode of *Jerry Springer* broke out. I've personally witnessed things in ministry settings—especially funerals—that most wouldn't believe unless they saw it with their own eyes.

So, it's no surprise that even the title of this book stirs emotion and evokes curiosity as it instantly triggers memories, assumptions, or expectations about what this book might explore—and why it matters.

As you've probably gathered, *Post-Traumatic Church Disorder (PTCD)* isn't a clinical diagnosis. It's a phrase I coined that is a play on the widely recognized term *Post-Traumatic Stress Disorder (PTSD)*—to describe the emotional, spiritual, and even physical trauma some people have experienced in church environments.

As a former law enforcement officer, I personally walked through the effects of post-traumatic stress after surviving an attempt on my life in the line of duty. That experience gave me a unique lens through which I began to recognize similar patterns of trauma, not just in myself but in others who had been wounded by their church experience.

Much like PTSD was once misunderstood and dismissed, trauma stemming from harmful church experiences has often been downplayed or ignored—even though it's been widely reported and deeply impactful for those who have experienced it. In writing this book, I hope to bring light to a very real issue that has quietly disrupted people's faith journeys—and, in some cases, even their eternal trajectory.

The root of the problem often lies in unhealthy leadership models, flawed paradigms, and improper responses to people within the church. And the truth is, I don't believe all of it is necessarily malicious. In many cases, I believe church leaders simply haven't been equipped with the right tools to recognize or address the damage being done. They're repeating the patterns they had modeled for them—never fully realizing those patterns may be causing more harm than good.

One of the most interesting parts of writing this book was observing how people responded when I told them the topic I was addressing was *Post-Traumatic Church Disorder* (PTCD). Almost every time, the reaction was nearly identical: a nervous laugh, a slow shake of the head, eyes drifting up and to the left, as they recalled a specific memory relating to their own PTCD experience, followed by something like, "That's a book that *needs* to be written," or "I *need* to read that book."

From my experience, PTCD is far more common among believers than we may realize—or want to admit.

In fact, out of probably a hundred conversations I had on the topic while writing, only one person told me, "I'd like to read that—not because I've experienced it myself, but because I haven't, and I want to understand what others have gone through."

Writing on the subject of PTCD comes with its fair share of hurdles. One of the biggest is recognizing how trauma can shape the lenses through which we see the world—often leaving us blind to our own biases and assumptions born out of those experiences.

Throughout my conversations with people who have walked through their own PTCD journeys, I've noticed a wide range of reactions. Some who were hurt in large or mega-church environments have developed a deep distrust of big churches altogether. Many of them now advocate strongly for the home-church model, believing it to be the only *truly biblical* way to experience God and community. On the other hand, I've observed others—those wounded in smaller church environments—who now avoid intimacy like *the plague* and choose only to attend large congregations where they can blend in, check off the "weekly church" box, and slip out unnoticed.

I've spoken with women who were deeply hurt by male pastors and now will only sit under strong female leadership. I've watched men who grew up under spiritually abusive matriarchs now cling to a doctrine that silences or suppresses women. And I've had countless conversations with PKs (pastor's kids) who still long to walk with Jesus but wrestle with painful memories of church people who treated them more like targets of judgment than children of God.

So, as I sat down to write this book, I had to ask myself the hard question: *Have my experiences created my own blind spots?* It became clear that if I wanted to do justice to this subject, I'd have to continually weigh my perspective against other viewpoints, acknowledge the possibility of my own biases, and go deeper—beyond the lenses of my own pain-filled experiences—to address this subject fairly.

Who Am I Writing To?

After 50 years of growing up in the church and 30 years in ministry, I have a lifetime of experiences to draw from. I've served in and attended churches ranging from small congregations to mega-churches across a wide range of denominational backgrounds: Baptist, Nazarene, Assembly of God, Church of God, and various independent or non-denominational churches. I've pastored in churches of under 100, a church that grew to 500, and served on the pastoral team of a church of well over 1,000.

At the time I am writing this book, my son is a young adult who will inevitably, at some point in his life, experience letdowns in church leadership. With those years of experiences in mind, I asked myself a simple but powerful question: *If I weren't here to walk with my son through his own potential leadership wounds or Post-Traumatic Church Disorder experience one day, what would I want him to know? What wisdom, insight, or balance would I hope to pass on?*

Additionally, while it would be important for me that my son would have the benefit of learning from my experiences, I know that there are also countless numbers of others who could benefit from those lenses. As a result, I believe this book will serve as a meaningful tool for:

1. **Those who've experienced PTCD (*Post-Traumatic Church Disorder*) firsthand** and need a fresh perspective to help process the pain, understand what happened, and move toward healing.
2. **Aspiring leaders, believers, or Ministers in Training (MITs)** who

are still forming their understanding of leadership—how to lead well, follow wisely, and discern what the Bible teaches about Godly leadership versus what may simply be tradition or culture.

3. **Established leaders** who are beginning to question the leadership models they were modeled—or perhaps the ones they've replicated—that don't align with the Kingdom principles outlined in Scripture. This book offers perspective for those wrestling with the tension between a systemic, corporate-style leadership model that often fails to consider its broader impact on the church and the biblical blueprint for servant leadership in God's Kingdom.

While I genuinely believe the content of this book can benefit *any* leader with an open mind, I've also found that many seasoned leaders have already settled into the belief that they've already become *"the leader"* they were meant to be. As a result, they feel little need to seek additional insight or a fresh perspective. Different views often stem from diverging values. Unfortunately—and especially when it comes to the topic of PTCD (*Post-Traumatic Church Disorder*)—those same leaders are often the ones causing the deepest wounds in the very people they are called to serve. I'm convinced that a leader who stops learning is a leader who stops growing.

As you continue reading, I want to invite you to take a deep breath and lean in. This book is not about pointing fingers or keeping score—it's about healing, understanding, and reclaiming what may have been lost as a result of your own PTCD experience. Whether you're still raw from a recent wound or trying to make sense of hurts from decades past, this journey will help you unpack the pain, confront the causes, and—most importantly—discover what the Bible actually says about leadership, restoration, and the path forward. There is healing on the other side of pain, and on this journey, we're going to chase after it together.

Introduction

The year was 2010. Leading up to that point, I had personally seen a significant online influence develop through platforms like YouTube and various social networks, where I shared topical video blogs from a bold, unapologetic Christian perspective. One of those blogs even ranked in the top 10 out of over 260 million on a major platform. That exposure opened doors to minister to people from all walks of life—rock stars, porn stars, worship leaders, pastors, prostitutes, addicts, witches, Satanists, tattoo artists. The reach was wide, and the impact was incredible.

Around that same time, the pastor of the church I had been attending for seven years approached me with a vision to launch an online ministry for our church. Given the momentum I was already experiencing with my personal online reach, he asked me to help lead the initiative as the online campus pastor. This was during the early wave of online ministry—before it became mainstream and accessible to any church with a camera and Wi-Fi. Fortunately, our church already had a television studio equipped with HD cameras and a dedicated live sound mix, which allowed us to deliver a high-quality, forward-thinking production right out of the gate. As a result, we saw rapid growth and significant impact early on.

One day, I received a message from a woman named Nora. Nora and I had corresponded off and on for several years. She lived in the Netherlands, was heavily tattooed, had multiple facial piercings, and often reached out to me with questions about the Bible. Over the years, Nora explained that she didn't know any Christians in her area who were willing to talk with her about her questions—largely due to the cultural and religious divide between those who identified as Christians and people who looked like her. When I encouraged her to try visiting some churches locally, she shared that she already had—and was rejected—multiple times.

Having pastored in a small Southern town in Tennessee, I understood some of what she was describing. I had experienced my own share of judgment and prejudice from Christians who couldn't reconcile the idea of a pastor with tattoos and earrings. Ironically, the harshest criticism I've ever faced hasn't come from the self-proclaimed Satanists or witches who occasionally messaged me online with strong opposition to Christianity—though some of their comments were certainly disturbing. No, the most hateful, aggressive responses I've received have come from people who identified as Christians, accusing me of being a *false prophet* simply because of how I looked or that I dared to call myself a pastor.

Still, as frustrating as those encounters were, I've never lived in a place where I truly felt there was *no one* I could turn to—to ask questions, to find acceptance, or to pursue Jesus if I were in her shoes as something of a religious *"pariah."* Yet that's exactly what Nora was describing. She was searching, reaching out for truth, and all she encountered was the rejection of an outcast.

One day, while I was at church, Nora reached out to me with a heavy request—she was about to undergo surgery that carried potentially life-threatening risks. Fear had gripped her, and like so many of us who grew up under the weight of religious pressure, she was battling questions about her salvation. You know, the kind—those deeply ingrained fears that had us running to the altar every Sunday, wondering if our mistakes of the last week might send us to hell if we didn't repent. Nora wanted to be sure she was right with God before going under anesthesia. She asked if I would pray for her, and more than anything, she wanted to be baptized.

We had talked a lot over the years about salvation, and I had no doubt she was saved. I explained to her what baptism symbolized and encouraged her to visit a few local churches to let them know she was ready to be baptized. I thought that surely, among the churches in her town, someone would see her through God's eyes of compassion and be willing to embrace her and baptize her regardless of her appearance.

A week later, she messaged me with very disappointing news. She had visited three different churches, and all of them turned her away. One even went so far as to call her *a child of Satan* because of her tattoos. Devastated but still searching, she asked if she could mail me a cross necklace—if I would bless it and return it to her so she could wear it during surgery, just in case she didn't survive.

My heart broke for her. I was stunned that after all the rejection she had faced from people claiming to represent Jesus, she was still willing to pursue Him. The compassion I felt for her was overwhelming—this young woman clinging to faith in the face of rejection, trying to patch together whatever pieces of hope she could find, even hoping that having me *bless* a cross necklace would benefit her. I was the only pastor she'd ever met who welcomed her, and I was furious at the self-righteous judgment that had pushed her away when all she wanted was to know Jesus more.

I sat there for a moment, stewing in my emotions, and I had an idea. I'd never heard of anyone else doing it; there was no chapter and verse substantiation to justify it, but I was not willing to not be there for this young lady when her heart was so pure in her request to follow our Lord Jesus in water baptism. So, I messaged her and instructed her to fill her bathtub with water while I set up a camera and web link in my office and to message me back to let me know when her tub was full.

When she messaged me back, I instructed her to make sure her computer was nowhere near the bathtub (I definitely wanted her to see Jesus face to face ONE DAY, but not THAT day). I then asked her to turn her volume all the way up, click on the video link, and message me to let me know when she could see me on her screen. When she told me she could see and hear me, I instructed her that we would probably conduct the first online baptism in the history of the world and most certainly the first international one. I then instructed her to go and sit in her bathtub while I prayed over her and then asked her to plug her nose and dunk herself as I baptized her online in the name of the Father, Son, and Holy Spirit and according to Acts 8:32 in the name of Jesus! It was a life-changing moment for her. At the time that this book was written, that was 15 years ago, and Nora still occasionally reaches out to me when she needs a pastor.

I chose to open this book with Nora's story because, while everyone's experience may look a little different, the deeper truth remains the same: many have been deeply wounded by people who were supposed to represent Jesus but failed. The circumstances vary, but the disappointment, the rejection, and the lingering effects of *Post-Traumatic Church Disorder* (PTCD) feel strikingly similar for so many.

Nora didn't fit the image of what the Christians in her town believed a *"believer"* should look like. But that's the irony—from Genesis onward, most of the heroes in Scripture wouldn't have measured up to the religious expectations of today's modern-day *"Pharisees."* Yet, God continually chose the broken, the unlikely, and the overlooked to carry out His purpose. He is a restorer of the broken, and He has commanded us, as His people, to carry out that same work of restoration.

Galatians 6:1-5
1 My beloved friends, if you see a believer who is overtaken with a fault, the one who is in the Spirit should seek to restore him in the Spirit of gentleness. But keep watch over your own heart so that you won't be tempted to exalt yourself over him. 2 Love empowers us to fulfill the law of the Anointed One as we carry each other's troubles. 3 If you think you are somebody too important to stoop down to help another (when really

you are not), you are living in deception.
4 Let everyone be devoted to fulfill the work God has given them to do with excellence, and their joy will be in doing what's right and being themselves, and not in being affirmed by others.

Moses was a murderer. David committed adultery and arranged a man's death. Paul persecuted and killed Christians. Peter denied Jesus in His most vulnerable moment. Rahab was a prostitute. Samson was impulsive, prideful, and reckless. Jonah ran from God's calling. Jacob was a manipulative deceiver. King Manasseh was one of the most evil rulers in Israel's history. Mary Magdalene was tormented by demons. Gideon was insecure and unsure of his worth. And what about the disciples? They were often self-centered, fearful, and spiritually immature. Yet, every single one of them was handpicked by God—not because they were perfect, but because He saw something in them worth redeeming.

God didn't disqualify them based on their worst moments. Instead, He extended mercy, brought transformation, and fulfilled His purposes through them. Moses led a nation. David became a man after God's own heart and a forefather of Jesus. Paul became a pillar of the early church. Peter helped birth the Church after Pentecost. Rahab was grafted into the lineage of Christ. Samson, despite his failures, delivered Israel. Jonah led a revival. Jacob became the father of a nation. Manasseh found forgiveness. Mary Magdalene was the first to proclaim the resurrection. Gideon led a miraculous victory. And Jesus poured into His flawed disciples until they became the very ones who turned the world upside down.

These stories remind us that God specializes in redemption. No sin, failure, or painful past is too great for His mercy. If He could use them, He can absolutely use you.

Unfortunately, painful experiences are not uncommon in a believer's life and development. No matter what you've been told, who turned their back on you, how you were treated, or whether your circumstances seemed justified or not—you need to know this: you are still a vital and irreplaceable part of God's plan. Even when His people have failed you, or your own decisions have left you questioning your worth, God has not changed His mind about you.

In the chapters ahead, we're going to unpack the inconsistencies, toxic systems, flawed leadership models, and misguided mechanisms that have led so many to develop *Post-Traumatic Church Disorder* (PTCD). But this isn't a book aimed at attacking the Church or demonizing leadership. My heart in writing this is to shine a light on the areas where church culture has fallen out of alignment with God's heart and—more importantly—to explore how we can heal, grow, and move forward in freedom after a painful church experience.

So I invite you to open your heart and your mind. We're going to talk about something that's often avoided or buried in silence—yet for so many, PTCD is a deeply painful and lingering reality. The very fact that you're holding this book now is a confirmation—it's time to address the elephant in the sanctuary.

Chapter One
The Pain is Real

As we begin to unpack the topic of *Post-Traumatic Church Disorder* (PTCD), often referred to as *"church hurt"* and recognize the very real trauma it can cause, it's important to confront a widespread misconception. Far too often, I've heard church leaders brush off someone's painful or even traumatic experience within a church setting, reducing it to a personal weakness. They imply that the individual was *too sensitive* or *lacked the emotional maturity* to properly process the situation, and they just flippantly move on. This kind of dismissal not only invalidates the pain but also shuts the door to meaningful healing and restoration for someone who has been wounded.

Several years ago, I had the privilege of walking closely with a young man—we'll call him *"Chris"* to protect his privacy. During his adolescence, Chris suffered a devastating betrayal at the hands of his youth pastor. The abuse was so severe it landed Chris in the hospital and the pastor with a very lengthy prison sentence. The trauma left him with deep physical, emotional, and spiritual scars. Over time, Chris began to trust me enough to share the truth about what happened to him, a secret steeped in pain and shame that shaped his view of himself, church leadership, and even God.

As he began making progress in his healing journey, he came into contact with another friend of mine, Mike, through our shared circles. Because of my connection to Mike, Chris extended a cautious level of trust to him, even though he wasn't ready to share his full story. One day, Chris confided in Mike—just enough to say he had been hurt badly by the church and that it still affected how he felt. He was very cautious and uncomfortable in church and around Christians.

Instead of responding to that moment with empathy or even respectful curiosity, Mike made a careless and damaging remark: *"Well, whatever happened to you took place a long time ago, and you just need to get over it."*

That one sentence unraveled years of hard-earned spiritual and relational progress that Chris and I had made together. Whatever Mike assumed or thought he understood, his flippant response invalidated the weight of Chris's pain. He had no way of knowing the depth of the trauma Chris had endured or the miracle it was that Chris was even still alive after such a brutal violation, let alone him even being willing to talk to someone who called themselves a *"Christian."*

Chris's wounds were real and went far deeper than Mike could comprehend. Unfortunately, his comment didn't just fall flat—it cut deeply. In a single moment, he reminded Chris exactly why trusting people— especially church people—was an unacceptable and unsafe option for him.

Rotten Lemons

I liken it to the old cliché: *When life deals you lemons, make lemonade.* I don't believe a person who uses that analogy has ever been dealt a truly rotten lemon. Those who have, know that there are some tragedies that are so rotten and so disgusting that no amount of sweetener could ever make it palatable.

Those who have been dealt that *"rotten lemon"* wish they could *"just get over it."* Many have cried more tears than they could ever count. They wish things could go back to how they were before they were so wounded, but their trauma has placed them in a constant catch-22 where they have built walls around themselves to keep from ever being hurt on that level again. Their *rotten lemon* experience changed them, and they don't know how to function anymore outside of the lenses that their trauma has produced. This is why it is so important that people know that they can turn to God with pain that would otherwise seem impossible to overcome.

I firmly believe that no trauma is too great for God to redeem—when we begin to grasp the depth of His love, grace, and power to restore, healing becomes possible. In the pages ahead, we will absolutely explore how to begin the journey of healing from these painful and often hidden wounds. But first, it's important to recognize this truth: when someone experiences trauma at the hands of spiritual leaders or within a church context, it is a very real, valid form of trauma—one that has too often been dismissed, ignored, or buried. Tragically, many who have been wounded in this way have quietly slipped out of the church and into obscurity, with their pain never acknowledged or addressed.

Only in recent decades has the medical community begun to meaningfully recognize, diagnose, and treat trauma. While science had long acknowledged that traumatic events could leave lasting effects, it struggled for years to define how best to respond to them. One key discovery that I came to understand after navigating my own *post-traumatic stress* event after an attempt on my life is this: trauma is deeply personal. Two people can experience the same event and be impacted in vastly different ways. This insight is crucial as we approach spiritual trauma—what breaks one person might not affect another the same way, and that difference is not a sign of weakness but a reflection of their unique story, makeup, and even previous compounding wounds.

Dead Bodies and Cheeseburgers

When I worked as a detective, I used to joke that I could *"investigate a murder scene while eating a cheeseburger"*—and honestly, it wasn't far from the truth. For whatever reason, I often seemed emotionally detached from the violence and tragedy unfolding before me. I witnessed scenes so graphic and disturbing that simply viewing the photographs could send someone else into a spiral of sleepless nights, nightmares, or psychological trauma. Yet somehow, I experienced those moments in 3D seemingly unaffected. It's a strange phenomenon how the exact same event can leave one person shattered while barely making a dent in another, simply based on how each of us is wired.

But that contrast became even more apparent to me on the day my law enforcement career ended. I was attacked on duty by two men who tried to kill me. In hindsight, it was what I'd personally call a pretty decent butt-kicking—I sustained injuries, and I still carry some of the physical scars today. It hurt, of course, but strangely, even more than a decade later, when I look back, I don't emotionally register the experience as *"deeply traumatic."* On a personal trauma scale, I'd give it maybe a 2 or 3 out of 10. And yet, not long after the incident, I started having severe panic attacks. It didn't make sense to me. I wasn't reliving the event in my head or dwelling on it with fear. But something beneath the surface had clearly been triggered—whether it was the accumulation of years of unprocessed stress or the body finally catching up with what the mind had brushed off. Either way, it confirmed to me that trauma doesn't always hit the way we'd expect it to—and that even when it feels like we're fine, there can be wounds that go much deeper than we realize.

Confronting and Processing the Pain

Before I experienced it firsthand, I was like the *"make lemonade"* guy I mentioned earlier—I assumed people who struggled with anxiety, depression, panic attacks, and the like were just mentally or emotionally weaker. I thought they simply needed to toughen up, shift their mindset, and choose to *think happier thoughts*. The truth is, I didn't know what I didn't know. Looking back now, with the clarity of hindsight, I understand that trauma doesn't always follow logic. It's not always about how intense the event was—sometimes trauma sneaks in, settles deep, and disrupts your life in ways you never saw coming. That season sent me on a long road of healing that took years to walk through.

You must realize that any wound or hurt you receive (emotional or physical) is some form of trauma to your system.[i] Whenever you are physically or emotionally hurt, there is always an emotional reaction (or emotional trauma). You can feel shock, hurt, sadness, fear, anger, and agitation as a result of the event. The more hurtful sensations during or after the event, the greater the trauma imprint that is burned into your memory, and the more fears you will have of being harmed in future incidents.[ii]

I share this with you so that you understand—regardless of what others may have said or assumed about your pain—your experience is valid. If you've picked up this book, chances are something real and painful has impacted you somewhere in your church experience. Whether it makes perfect sense or not, acknowledging what happened and the toll it's taken on you is a necessary step toward healing. But let me emphasize this: the goal isn't just to acknowledge it—it's to move forward and heal. What I've learned through my own battle with trauma is that if we don't confront and process our pain, it has the power to rob us of the future God intended and the destiny He's still calling us to fulfill.

Halted in Haran

Genesis 11 offers a brief account of Abraham's father, Terah. Known as the father of both the Christian and Jewish faiths, Abraham's story begins with this important family background. In verse 28, we learn that Terah's eldest son, Haran—Abraham's brother—died while his father was still alive.

Genesis 11:28b (TPT – Emphasis by the author)
*…Terah was the father of Abram, Nahor, and Haran, and Haran was the father of Lot. 28 **Haran preceded his father, Terah, in death** in the land of his birth, in the Chaldean city of Ur.*

Then, when we read on a few lines later, verses 31-32 state:

Genesis 11:31-32 (AMPC – Emphasis by the author)
*31 And Terah took Abram his son, Lot the son of Haran, his grandson, and Sarai his daughter-in-law, his son Abram's wife, and **they went forth together to go from Ur of the Chaldees into the land of Canaan**; but when they came to Haran, **they settled there**.*
*32 And Terah lived 205 years; and **Terah died in Haran**.*

What stands out to me in this chapter is that Terah gathers his family and possessions and sets out for Canaan—the land that Abraham would eventually inherit, often referred to as *"the promised land."* But when Terah arrives at a city called *Haran*, he stops and settles there. Interestingly, this city shares the same name as his son, who had died.

We don't know whether Terah's son was named after the city or if the city was named after his son, but what we do know is this: when Terah reached the place that bore the name and memory of his deepest relational wound, he stopped. Though he had set out for Canaan, the place God would later give to Abraham, Terah halted his journey in a place that reminded him of his deepest, darkest pain—and as Genesis 11:32 states, Terah died there, in Haran.

Terah's story only spans a few verses, centered around personal tragedy. But it makes me wonder—what might have happened had he continued on to Canaan as he originally planned? Scripture often refers to God as *the God of Abraham, Isaac, and Jacob*. Could it be that Terah was also meant to be part of that legacy? Perhaps he was intended to be remembered as a man of great faith—but the weight of trauma caused him to settle short of his destiny. It's speculative, but more than just possible, I think it's probable.

I believe that, just like Terah, God is leading each of us toward our own *"Canaan"*—a place of promise and purpose. But I can't help but wonder how many believers around the world have missed out on that promise because they stopped short, settling in their own personal *"Haran"*—a place marked by pain and trauma—before ever reaching their intended destination.

I'm convinced that God's promises are, more often than not, manifested just beyond our pain. But the enemy is always nearby, urging us to stop and settle in our sorrow, convincing us that we can't go any further. In my experience, that temptation to give up is frequently rooted in the trauma caused by our personal *Haran*, where something deeply painful tried to rewrite our story and redefine our future.

Over many years in ministry, I've walked through my own *Haran* experiences. I'm intimately familiar with the similarities between PTSD (*Post-Traumatic STRESS Disorder*) and PTCD (*Post-Traumatic CHURCH Disorder*) because I've lived through layers of both. I know what it's like to want to give up. I've felt the sting of heartbreak caused by people I loved and trusted. I've experienced the betrayal of leaders—being misused, misjudged, lied to, and feeling left behind.

Though my story is personal, it's far from rare. Over the years, I've spoken with countless others who've shared similar wounds—stories of church-related trauma and disillusionment. One thing I've learned is this: when the pain is inflicted by a spiritual leader that we looked up to and trusted, the impact can run deep and be long-lasting. That kind of disappointment has the ability to shake our foundation of faith in a way few other things can.

The pain is real—but so is the hope. Unlike Abraham's father, Terah, you haven't died yet while having settled for less, and there is healing for your *Haran* experience. If you've felt the sting of betrayal, the weight of spiritual trauma, or the ache of being wounded in the place where you expected healing, you are not alone—and your story is not over. This chapter laid the groundwork by acknowledging your experience, but as we continue this journey together, we will begin to confront the roots of that pain, expose the leadership failures and broken systems that have contributed to it, and—most importantly—rediscover the God who still sees you, still calls you, and still has a *Canaan* waiting for you. Healing isn't just possible—it's God's heart for you. And the journey toward that healing has begun.

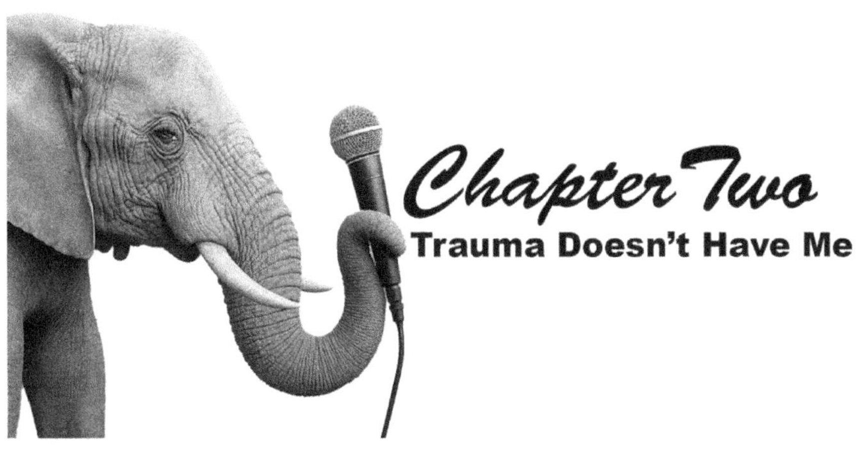

While some of my church experiences have been incredibly painful and haven't always ended the way I would've hoped, it's only fair to acknowledge both the good and the bad. The reality is that many seasons (even the ones that ended badly) were genuinely wonderful—until they weren't. There were years filled with laughter, healing, personal breakthroughs, battles fought and won together, and powerful moments in worship where God's presence was so tangible that no one wanted to leave, even long after the service was supposed to end.

Ironically, those beautiful memories often make the painful ones hit even harder. That contrast is what cuts so deep. So, as I write this book, please know—it's not my intention to paint an unfair or one-sided picture. I'm not here to justify a narrative that only focuses on the negative when, in many cases, one painful event has the power to overshadow years of positive experiences.

This is especially true when the wound comes from someone we love and trust. In so many *Post-Traumatic Church Disorder* (PTCD) stories, a single act of betrayal or abuse can unravel decades of growth and connection. It doesn't erase the good—it just makes it sometimes harder to remember.

After spending my entire adult life in pastoral ministry, I've walked with more than one church through seasons of intense trauma and helped countless individuals process deep, personal pain. Just recently, an evangelist friend relayed to me a conversation he had with another pastor. My name came up, and the pastor said, *"Aaron Davis is the reason our church is still here today."*

I don't share that to pat myself on the back or seek any recognition—it's about perspective. The only reason I've been able to help others through their darkest moments is because I've had to navigate so many of my own. The truth is, there were times when I personally didn't have a friend to walk with me through it—or even a resource like this book to offer some guidance or additional perspective. It was just me and God, figuring it out as I tried to navigate it.

It's never easy. But I can confidently say it's especially difficult when you feel like you're walking through it alone. That's why I believe this book matters, particularly in the season the church finds itself in today. I'm here to let you know that you're not alone in the pain you have experienced and that healing is possible.

Honorable Reflections

As I began writing this book, I found myself reflecting on decades of ministry and personal experiences—many of which could easily be categorized as PTCD moments. Truthfully, if my goal were to prove that I understand the depth and complexity of this topic, I could realistically fill an entire book just recounting those stories and detailing how I navigated them. And while there might be an element of value in sharing those experiences in full, I don't actually spend time dwelling on those negative events. I've addressed them in my heart and now choose to leave them in the past. Not to mention, sharing unnecessary details would also risk casting others—some of whom cannot share their side of the story—in a negative light, and I would never desire to do that.

My intention is not to harm reputations or stir controversy. I believe in protecting honor, even for those who may not have extended that same grace to me. So, throughout this book, the few stories I do share will be intentionally vague. The focus won't be on the specifics of what happened but rather on the wisdom, healing, and growth that came as a result. The lessons are what matter most—and it's those lessons I want to pass along to you.

In this next example, I'm going to share with you how Church relationships can sometimes become complicated and why it is important to still maintain a standard of personal integrity in spite of offenses.

God, Do I Have to Keep Putting Up with This?

Our church had endured a series of difficult trials in recent years. Tensions were high, and leaders were walking on edge. Somehow, I found myself in the middle of what felt like a no-win situation. Because of my unwavering commitment to integrity, honesty, and honor—along with my background in law enforcement and the strong relational equity I had built with the pastor, staff, board, and congregation—I became a kind of liaison between them all. Each group trusted me to respond with wisdom, balance, and respect, especially when emotions flared, or people failed to acknowledge their own blind spots. In this case, I became the sounding board for nearly everyone involved.

Truthfully, I was emotionally and physically drained. Years of carrying the weight of tension while trying to keep the scales balanced had taken a toll on my own peace. In this particular moment, I found myself unsure of how to move forward. I asked God on multiple occasions for clarity or direction, but His answer never changed. Time after time, I heard the same quiet response He had spoken to me for years: *"Aaron, man your post."*

I knew exactly what He meant. When God told me to "man your post," He wasn't just urging me not to quit—He was giving me a clear assignment in language I understood. He was letting me know that I was a watchman on the wall. My role was to stay alert, to stand strong for those on the inside, to guard the perimeter, and to ensure that no enemy slipped in unnoticed. It meant being a pillar of protection and a source of stability for everyone involved. And while I accepted that responsibility, the truth was... I had been at that post a long time, and I was tired.

By the time I walked into the board meeting, I already knew what we were about to face. The pastor had shared his perspective with me in advance, and the staff had discussed their concerns with me. Several board members had also pulled me aside, relaying their unease. I felt the weight of every conversation.

While these meetings were intended to be a safe space for open dialogue, several individuals had expressed hesitation, unsure of how their concerns would be received if they voiced them publicly. We weren't all on the same page, and the weight of everyone's expectations felt as though they rested squarely on my shoulders. Each group assumed I'd stand with them.

Once the presentation was made, the room fell into a thick silence, and all eyes were on me.

I took a slow breath, sat in the tension for a moment, and then broke the silence by opening Pandora's box—not with confrontation, but with a calm, respectful question that addressed the obvious issue hovering in the room. With grace and honor, I asked, *"Given everything you've shared, how do you envision us, as a church, accomplishing this goal?"*

Eyebrows raised, jaws tightened, and grimaces appeared as one board member—predictably—did not appreciate what I'd asked. I'm not sure if they assumed I would automatically side with them or simply remain silent, but it was clear my question hadn't landed well.

Having spent years as a detective, I was no stranger to confrontation. I'd sat on witness stands while lawyers attempted to rattle me—demeaning me, talking down, even yelling in an attempt to break my composure. Intimidation doesn't easily shake me. Still, I've always made it a point to honor leadership, whether they were pastors, board members, or staff. But that day, this board member tried to assert dominance through condescension, raising their voice and attempting to *put me in my place.* I didn't flinch. I simply looked them in the eyes and quietly, calmly, and respectfully stood my ground as they unleashed their frustration in front of the entire room.

After letting him take his shots at me in front of the room, I stayed quiet for a moment. I took a deep breath, rested my elbows on the table, leaned forward, lowered my head, and brought my hands together over my mouth and nose in a quiet posture of prayer. With my eyes closed, I whispered under my breath, *"God, do I have to keep putting up with this bull crap?"* For the first time in years, His response wasn't the usual, *"Aaron, man your post…"* Instead, it was a clear and resounding *"No."* I knew with that response that my role was no longer simply to be a trusted peacekeeper or a *watchman,* but I was being released to help bring change to what was out of alignment.

Though I was deeply frustrated by how I'd been addressed, I chose not to respond and remained silent at that moment. I didn't want to escalate the situation or allow another's disrespect to fuel my reaction. But in the days that followed, I addressed the incident directly—and ultimately, that board member was removed from his position.

I share this story because I truly believe that how we respond in challenging moments with difficult people is one of the most critical tests we'll ever face in our spiritual journey. That board member was clearly out of line—but had I allowed my emotions to take over and responded poorly, I likely would have forfeited the very influence that gave my voice weight in that room. And without that influence, any role I might have played in guiding positive change in the future could've been sacrificed by an improper response. And truthfully, I believe that is exactly what the enemy would have wanted.

Yes, I had every reason to be offended—what happened was undeniably disrespectful. In fact, one of the staff members who was present came to me afterward, tears in their eyes, and apologized on behalf of everyone present for how dishonorably I had been treated. I could have lashed out, but I chose to hold my peace until the right moment came to address the issue appropriately.

While I can't claim to have always responded properly in every situation I've encountered over the course of my professional career, this time, I did, and because of that, the enemy's ability to sow more serious damage was limited. There was still fallout, of course, but wisdom and restraint helped preserve key relationships and stability that might have otherwise been lost had I reacted differently.

After a lifetime spent in church leadership—from volunteer roles to executive pastor positions—I've witnessed the best and worst of what leadership can look like. I've sat in boardrooms where wisdom and humility guided the room, and others where egos and broken systems left lasting wounds. These experiences, both the victories and the failures, have given me a front-row seat to the beauty and the brokenness that often coexist in ministry.

When I first began to consider writing this book, my initial response to God was a firm, *"Let someone else take that on."* But then came that still, small voice asking me a question that stopped me in my tracks: *"Who's MORE qualified than you to write and publish a book on this topic—and to lead people to a place of healing and wholeness?"* The weight of that question made me pause and truly consider it.

Over the years, I've joked during sermons that I hold an honorary doctorate in church trauma from *"Manure Occurreth University."* The truth is, though—it's not just me. A lot of people could claim the same. But what may set my perspective apart is this: *I'm no longer living in or with the pain.* I've processed through it. I've come out on the other side. There's a big difference between having trauma and allowing trauma to have you. I've experienced trauma, but I've also learned how to overcome it. As a result, this book isn't being written from a place of bitterness or brokenness but as a guide for victory, restoration, and hope.

So, while I can think of many others who might be just *"AS"* qualified to lead others through their healing journey for *Post-Traumatic Church Disorder,* I have to admit— I don't personally know anyone *"MORE"* qualified than me to take on this assignment.

Alright, God... challenge accepted.

Chapter Three
The Mirror Of The Word

I clicked on an audio file circulating on social media titled *"Pastor Shreds Team Member in Staff Meeting."* The moment it started playing, my heart sank. I instantly recognized the voice—it was a pastor whose ministry I've long respected and gleaned wisdom from over the years. From the sound of it, someone had discreetly recorded a staff meeting in which this pastor was confronting a subordinate who had apparently fallen short of meeting his expectations. And he was clearly *not* happy.

At first, I felt a wave of shock listening to his tone—yelling in intense frustration—as he reprimanded the staff member, even referencing how much he paid him to do his job. I couldn't help but feel compassion for the employee, who remained calm and respectful throughout the exchange, continually addressing his pastor with seeming respect.

"Yes, Pastor... I understand, Pastor... I'm not sure, Pastor..."

As I listened, I felt defensive for the employee when, at one point, the pastor questioned him about how many hours he had spent in preparation for the project he was being reprimanded about. When the staff member calmly answered, citing the exact start and end times that he worked, the pastor then accused him of "clock-watching" when he said something to the effect of, *"So, now you are keeping a count of every hour...?"* I thought to myself it was unfair for the pastor to ask him what hours he worked and then reprimand him for answering his question. From an outsider's perspective, the initial impression of the entire exchange came across as combative, unfair, and unbecoming of a godly leader. It was a tough listen—and frankly, not a good look.

Then, I paused and reminded myself that there's often more to a story than what's captured in a single recording or moment. So, I began to process the situation through a broader lens—one shaped by my own experiences as a leader. In doing so, a different set of questions and perspectives came to mind.

I thought back to a personal encounter I had with this same pastor years ago. I was just a teenager at the time, standing quietly off to the side of a crowded hallway filled with hundreds of people. He didn't know who I was. I watched him as he walked past me, seemingly very focused on where he was going—but then, after about ten steps, he suddenly stopped, turned around, walked straight back to me, and without saying a word, gave me the hugest, most heartfelt hug. What he didn't know was that I needed that hug that day, and I never forgot it.

So, as I listened to this difficult audio clip, I also held onto a very different memory of the same man—one that didn't align with what was being so negatively portrayed. I didn't have all the details of what took place in that meeting, but I had encountered a version of him that showed a very different side, and I began to ask myself some questions.

Regarding the Employee:

How many times has this pastor depended on the man in question, only to be disappointed by unmet expectations or missed deadlines?

Has he consistently arrived late to mandatory meetings, offering unreasonable excuses for poor time management?

How often has this pastor had to confront him about these patterns?

Could the employee simply lack initiative—or worse, is lazy?

Is he known for stretching tasks, working slow or lazily to fill the time rather than delivering results?

Does he have a habit of overpromising and underdelivering?

Is it possible that the pastor has repeatedly covered for this staff member after being let down in front of others?

Regarding the Pastor:

How critical was the project or event in question, and how clearly did the pastor. communicate his expectations?

Was he under intense pressure that day, and this particular failure just happened to be the breaking point?

Had he tried multiple approaches with this employee and, after seeing no improvement, was resorting to a firmer confrontation out of frustration?

Is it possible that the employee responded with disrespect before the recording began and only shifted to a calm, respectful tone after the pastor's reaction—or once the recorder was turned on?

And in the world we live in now, I even had to ask myself something that would have sounded absurd not long ago: *is it possible this audio clip was fabricated or manipulated using AI voice cloning technology to damage the pastor's reputation?*

To every one of those questions, my answer was the same: *I don't know.*

There's always more than one side in a confrontation or disagreement. While I feel like my questions were perhaps more gracious than the confrontation appeared to superficially deserve, as I put on different lenses and viewed the same scenario through them, I found that I had more questions than I had answers. Even more so, all of my questions created a possible perspective that went much deeper than what may have been apparent on the surface.

What I can say with certainty is that, as a leader, there have been times when my own responses have fallen short—moments where I didn't handle things in the most honorable way, and I've had to come face to face with moments in my own journey that were far more complex than they appeared on the surface. In most trauma stories, there's typically a *victim* and a *perpetrator*—a *hero* and a *villain*, so to speak. And I'm fully aware that in someone else's narrative today, I may be the *"villain"* in their story.

I'm not saying that the pastor wasn't in the wrong—based on what I heard, he probably was. But I also know how many times I've personally dropped the ball as a leader, even within my own home, where I can vividly recall moments where my emotions got the best of me and I responded unfairly to my son. I remember the look in his eyes—confused, afraid, and trying to make sense of why I was yelling.

Some of those moments came from a place of fear—fear that if he didn't take me seriously, his choices could lead him down a hard road. Sometimes I was trying to protect him. Other times, I was trying to protect myself. And, honestly, there were moments when I was just being a jerk.

And all of that happened in the context of my most important leadership assignment—fathering my own son. There is not another person in the world that I love like I love that kid, and there is not a more important leadership assignment that God has given me than my assignment to lead him in becoming a godly man. Yet still, I know that at times I've failed to lead well while raising him.

Whether you're a senior pastor, a department head, a Sunday school teacher, a youth trip chaperone, a business owner, a manager, or a parent—at some point in life, you will find yourself in a leadership position. And when you're *a believer* in Christ, your leadership should be shaped by Scripture. Above all else, you're a Christian first, and the Bible is the written will of God that should guide the way you lead.

The Mirror of the Word

The Bible has a remarkable way of revealing where we're succeeding and falling short. Someone once said, *"We don't read the Bible—the Bible reads us."* When it comes to leadership, I've found that to be absolutely true. God's Word has served as a mirror in my life. When I look into it, I don't just see words—I see my reflection. I recognize the areas where I'm growing, but I also see the flaws and weaknesses that still need work because Scripture gives me a standard for what that reflection should look like.

So, if we're all called to lead from a godly perspective, we need to ask ourselves: *If the Word of God is the will of God, then what is the biblical standard for how I should lead others?*

As I researched this topic, I made it a point to reread the entire New Testament and the book of Proverbs—chapter by chapter—through the lens of one central question: *What is the biblical standard for leadership?* What I discovered was a clear, consistent direction on what it means to lead as a follower of Christ.

In today's culture, it's become almost cliché to blame experiences of PTCD (*Post-Traumatic Church Disorder*) on what people vaguely label as *"institutionalized religion"* or *"the corporate church."* And while there have certainly been moments where authority has been misused, or people have been harmed in the name of religion, I've found that most of what gets chalked up to being a *church issue* is actually a *leadership* issue—more specifically, a *leadership mentality* issue.

If we want to move forward, we need to correctly identify what's actually out of alignment. Only then can we confront those inconsistencies head-on and begin to understand what has caused the painful experiences that contributed to PTCD and the expectations we hold for godly leadership.

What we harvest is always a result of the seeds that are planted. So if we see that we are producing harvests in our church and leadership experiences that do not reflect the nature and image of Christ for His bride, then we must certainly evaluate the seeds we are planting.

When our church experience falls short of our expectations—or even what God intends—it's essential to identify the root of the issue. Just because something happens within the walls of a church doesn't automatically mean the entire institution is to blame. Misplaced blame leads to misguided solutions. For example, if someone is hurt in a large church, they may assume a smaller church is the answer. But the issue isn't about congregation size. A church of thousands is not inherently better or worse than one of hundreds or tens. The problem often isn't institutional at all—it's individual. More specifically, it's often ungodly leadership, pride, arrogance, selfishness, or manipulation being exercised by individuals within the institution. Those are not systemic flaws but personal flaws that manifest in leadership roles.

A respected leader once said, *"A true leader questions everything— seeking out truth to ensure they aren't leading others down the wrong path."*[iii] If we accept that the Word of God is the will of God, then it's worth asking: Could the painful experiences many identify as PTCD *(Post-Traumatic Church Disorder)* actually be the result of a failure to apply the biblical model of leadership that God already laid out? If God has established a Kingdom leadership model, shouldn't we want to discover it, understand it, and implement it—especially in the very organizations we claim are founded on His Word?

As we move forward, the goal is not to shame or assign blame—but to illuminate the truth and bring clarity to the root causes of so much pain in the Church. If we're willing to let Scripture serve as the mirror it was always meant to be, we'll begin to see with greater clarity not only where others have missed the mark but where we ourselves need refining. God isn't calling us to leadership rooted in tradition, ego, or performance—He's inviting us into leadership modeled after Christ: selfless, humble, and transformational. If we truly believe the Church belongs to Jesus, then our leadership must reflect His heart. Let's press into that standard together in the chapters ahead, where we're going to explore exactly that: what Kingdom leadership looks like from God's perspective—and how it contrasts with the paradigms that have left so many wounded.

But seek (aim at and strive after) first of all His kingdom and His righteousness (His way of doing and being right), and then all these things taken together will be given you besides.
Matt 6:33 AMPC

Doing church is not the same as being the church. Too often, Kingdom leaders fall into the trap of believing that building *their* church is the mission God has called them to fulfill. While that passion is understandable, we have to remember: *the church* (the roof, four walls, programs, and Sunday morning experience) *was never meant to be the mission—it was meant to be the vehicle for the mission.* " [iv] The church is not a holy building that houses the Spirit of God—you are.

The true mission is to advance God's Kingdom. It's about strengthening the faith, knowledge, and resilience of believers through discipleship. It's about equipping and empowering the saints to lead from a Kingdom mindset. The church is the means, not the end. When we confuse the two, our focus can shift from God's Kingdom to our own kingdom, and that misdirection can cost us the very purpose we were called to fulfill.

In every area of life, if we don't intentionally pursue God's way, we'll naturally default to responding from our flesh—our emotions, impulses, and ego. The more we indulge our flesh, the more we amplify its consequences. That's why Matthew 6:33 urges us to seek *the Kingdom of God* first— His Kingdom represents His way of doing things and living rightly. Prioritizing His way realigns us with purpose and keeps us from being led astray by our own nature.

Leaders often default to the models we've seen and experienced. Parents tend to raise their children in ways that mirror how they were raised.

Teachers often reflect the style of a professor who impacted them. Pastors frequently adopt the leadership structures and paradigms of those they were mentored by. This isn't inherently negative—after all, as the saying goes, "*If it ain't broke, don't fix it.*" But problems arise when the examples we replicate aren't healthy—or worse, aren't godly.

In observing and studying various church leadership models, I've found that many of them are simply duplicates of systems other leaders have used. And while these churches may appear successful, it can be dangerous when leadership foundations are built on corporate ideologies and human reasoning rather than biblical truth.

If a leadership model isn't grounded in godly, biblical principles, it will inevitably produce fruit that reflects its flawed foundation.

Don't Believe Your Own Hype

Years ago, I asked a friend who was experiencing explosive growth in his organization and rising influence—right before it all collapsed—what he would say to himself if he could go back ten years. His response was both simple and profound: "*The second you start believing your own hype, you're on your way out.*"

Galatians 6:7-8 (AMPC – Emphasis by the author)
*7 Do not be deceived and deluded and misled; God will not allow Himself to be sneered at (scorned, disdained, or mocked by mere pretensions or professions, or by His precepts being set aside.) [He inevitably deludes himself who attempts to delude God.] **For whatever a man sows, that and that only is what he will reap.***
8 For he who sows to his own flesh (lower nature, sensuality) will from the flesh reap decay and ruin and destruction, but he who sows to the Spirit will from the Spirit reap eternal life.

One of the greatest obstacles I've seen among Christian "*leaders*" is the assumption that they already know how to lead. Maybe they've been praised by peers, read all the top leadership books, and even gained a following. But it's important to recognize that these external markers—titles, influence, and popularity—are not an absolute standard for what defines a good or godly leader.

When you let comparison set the bar for you, mimic the leadership style of someone you admire, or interpret *growth* as *success* or an automatic validation of your methods, you risk being misled and settling for something far less than what God intended. False confidence can blind you to needed growth. That's why it must be said again: when it comes to building the church and advancing God's Kingdom, the Word of God must be the foundational standard.

Creating Children Does Not Make You a Father

In a physical/sexual sense, we are living in a fatherless generation. Far too many men use the seed to create life as a byproduct of self-serving pleasure, with no intention of stepping into the role of a father. It's a narcissistic, irresponsible distortion of something God designed to be sacred. God intended fatherhood to take place within the covenant of marriage—where intimacy leads to children, and those children are raised by a father who serves as an instructor, protector, and encourager. That's how legacy is built, and the next generation is equipped.

But sin and selfishness have eroded that design. Too often, children are born into homes without present fathers—homes shaped more by abandonment and indulgence than by purpose and responsibility. As a result, many grow up with a distorted understanding of identity, authority, and what it means to be led or what it means to be a father themselves.

Unfortunately, I've witnessed a spiritual parallel in the church that mirrors the fatherlessness we see in the natural. Leaders, called by God to raise and empower the next generation, have sometimes sacrificed their spiritual sons and daughters on the altar of self-interest. Their leadership becomes more about advancing their own platform and reputation than creating a legacy by pouring into others. Rather than nurturing those under their care to step fully into their God-given identity and calling, the focus shifts toward how those individuals can elevate the leader's own status.

But that's not *Kingdom* leadership.

True spiritual leadership isn't about self-promotion—it's about empowerment. It's about helping others become all God has called them to be. As John C. Maxwell puts it, *"Leading well is not about enriching yourself. It's about empowering others."*[v]

Real leaders are able to take ordinary, overlooked people and help draw greatness out of them. They can see diamonds in the rough—where others might see nothing more than a chunk of coal—and call forth their potential instead of discarding them as problems. That's the kind of leader God is looking for. That's the kind of leader we're called to be.[vi] That is what a real father does.

Creating followers does not make you a good leader any more than creating children makes you a good father. A strong leader is intentional about raising up and empowering the next generation of leaders—just as a good father prepares his children to become strong fathers themselves. Don't be misled by inflated numbers, impressive titles, or growing follower counts—these things don't automatically mean someone is leading well.

Throughout the years, I've seen many charismatic men and women elevated to positions of influence who, truthfully, had very little understanding of how to lead others from a Kingdom-centered perspective.

Their popularity often stemmed from charm, personality, or an ability to teach on certain topics, but those traits alone don't equal leadership. Sometimes, being a captivating communicator draws praise from others with similar personalities, leading them to affirm someone's leadership potential. But as we will lay out in much detail in the next two chapters, charisma is not the biblical standard for leadership—character is.

It's also worth noting that simply serving under a respected leader and adopting their leadership style or model doesn't automatically mean someone possesses true leadership capacity or effectiveness. I've seen it time and again—ungodly or unbalanced leadership approaches being passed down and replicated within church structures, often under the assumption that they are healthy or even biblical. Sometimes these systems appear successful because the organization continues to grow, which can be both deceptive and affirming. But while numerical growth can be a visible and encouraging metric, it should never be the primary measure of whether a leader is truly succeeding. Real leadership is about more than numbers—it's about the health, integrity, and impact of the model being lived out.

"Having followers doesn't make you a leader. It means you've captured attention. Narcissists build themselves up for personal glory. Servant leaders build others up for a shared mission. Leadership is not about gaining an audience. It's about guiding a group to meaningful goals."[vii]

Healthy Things Grow

I've often heard leaders say, *"Healthy things grow,"* using it as a justification for the growth of their church and as evidence that they must be leading well. Growth becomes a badge of honor—something they wear with pride, assuming it's a clear sign of healthy success or even God's endorsement of their leadership. But here's the truth: weeds and cancer grow too.

If your primary measure for effective leadership is physical growth, you're setting yourself up for a flawed and potentially misleading conclusion. Let's take the example of parenting: children will grow physically whether or not their father is actively involved in raising them—it's hardwired into their DNA and purpose by God as He still molds them through a process to become who He intended them to be. Similarly, 1 Corinthians 3 reminds us that it is God who brings the increase and causes growth in the church.

Some might argue, *"If God is the one growing it, then He must be affirming what I'm doing—otherwise, why would He bless it?"* While that sounds reasonable on the surface, it overlooks a few important truths:

1. Followers aren't always Spirit-led in the decisions they make or

what they choose to attach themselves to.

2. Yes, God may be growing the church—but it might be happening in *spite* of your leadership, not *because* of it.
3. God, who sees the end from the beginning, may be more committed to fulfilling *His* purpose than aligning with *your* plans. He may still choose to use you—not necessarily to accomplish your goals, but to fulfill His.
4. Sometimes, God gives people grace, allowing them time to submit and get things right before He addresses the issues more directly.
5. God still has the ability to work things together for the good and for His purposes, even if He determines that you don't have the capacity to carry that thing into the next season.

Over the years—both in the public eye through news stories and in our own personal experiences—we've seen leaders act in ways that were clearly ungodly, and yet, for a season, their ministries still grew and their influence continued to expand. Those fleeting successes may have given them a false sense of validation—perhaps even the illusion that they were above correction. But growth is never a substitute for obedience. When results are used to justify rebellion or a lack of submission to God's Word, it becomes a dangerous form of self-deception. And Scripture leaves no doubt: accountability will always come.

Numbers 32:32b (AMPC)
...be sure your sin will find you out.

Galatians 6:7-8 (AMPC)
7 Do not be deceived and deluded and misled; God will not allow Himself to be sneered at (scorned, disdained, or mocked by mere pretensions or professions, or by His precepts being set aside.) [He inevitably deludes himself who attempts to delude God.] For whatever a man sows, that and that only is what he will reap.
8 For he who sows to his own flesh (lower nature, sensuality) will from the flesh reap decay and ruin and destruction, but he who sows to the Spirit will from the Spirit reap eternal life.

Each of us has been uniquely called by God to fulfill a specific role within His Kingdom and the body of Christ. No calling is greater or lesser than another—they're simply different. Just as legs and fingers are designed to be different lengths and serve distinct functions, so too are our callings uniquely measured for God's intended purpose. If a finger grew to the length of a leg—or a leg only reached the length of a finger—our body would be functionally impaired. In the same way, God has anointed each of us for a specific purpose, but walking in that calling requires submission to His authority and alignment with His Word. That submission is the true standard by which our leadership should be measured.

Consider King Saul. God chose and anointed him to lead Israel, yet his pride and insecurity ultimately derailed him. Instead of submitting to God's will, Saul let these internal struggles govern his actions—and God anointed another to replace him as King.

Saul's story stands as a sobering warning: when pride and insecurity are left unaddressed, they distort our perspective, poison our leadership, and become tools the enemy can use to orchestrate our downfall. Had Saul surrendered those strongholds to God, his story might have ended very differently. Pride and insecurity both sabotage faith—each in their own way. Pride puts confidence in self, while insecurity is driven by fear. Whether through arrogance or anxiety, both hinder a leader's ability to fully trust in God and walk in obedience.

When these internal struggles are paired with a faulty metric for success—namely, using the number of followers as a measurement of affirmation or rejection—leaders set themselves up for failure. That's because pride or insecurity inevitably responds to the numbers, allowing them to feed the very strongholds that should have been surrendered to God.

Leadership is never an easy assignment. I firmly believe that leaders are targeted more intensely than most because when they fall, the impact is widespread. Our humanity, spiritual baggage, and a very real enemy constantly seek to exploit our weaknesses—many of which are rooted in how we've processed our own personal pain or trauma. Whether it's pride, insecurity, shame, fear, or doubt, every leader faces internal battles that challenge their faith and threaten to place a ceiling on their growth. That's why it's absolutely vital, even in the face of those attacks—and often in direct defiance of them—that leaders must ground their strength, identity, and leadership standard in the wisdom and instruction found in God's Word.

As we wrap up this chapter, one truth rises to the surface: leadership that is not rooted in God's Word and Kingdom perspective will fall short of God's standard for a leader—no matter how impressive he looks on the outside. The PTCD pain, confusion, and disillusionment so many have experienced under flawed leadership paradigms often leaves real scars. But our journey doesn't have to end there. God has already provided a better way. Kingdom leadership is not about hierarchy, ego, or institutional success—it's about serving, empowering, and reflecting Christ.

In the next chapter, we'll begin to explore exactly what that model looks like—what leadership grounded in the *Kingdom* principles really entails. You'll see how it contrasts sharply with many of the systems that may have left you (or those you may encounter) wounded and how God's way offers a blueprint for restoration, alignment, and authentic spiritual leadership.

In the modern church, leadership styles have often drifted far from the example set by Christ and the teachings of Scripture. Many leaders have unknowingly adopted secular, corporate blueprints to guide their ministries without recognizing their spiritual consequences. This drift has contributed significantly to the pain of *Post-Traumatic Church Disorder* (PTCD). Before we can embrace a Kingdom leadership model, we must first confront the reality that some of our long-held assumptions and practices may be out of alignment with the heart and Word of God. This confrontation, however, is not without emotional resistance. This emotional and psychological struggle is known as *cognitive dissonance.*

Cognitive dissonance occurs when one holds conflicting beliefs, values, and ideas or when their actions go against what they say they believe. For example, a person who claims to believe the Bible is absolutely true yet actively engages in behaviors or holds beliefs that contradict specific biblical teachings would likely experience *cognitive dissonance*, especially if they were not previously aware they were wrong but presented evidence to the contrary.

When someone experiences cognitive dissonance, *no matter what you say to them or what evidence you present to them, if it goes against their beliefs, then you will be wrong 100% of the time. Even if they haven't got the slightest clue, you will still be wrong...*[viii]

Cognitive dissonance goes even deeper when it comes to those who have been indoctrinated to believe a certain way. Where *a smart person will change their view if new information contradicts their belief, an indoctrinated person lacks this ability, as they are conditioned to dismiss facts.*[ix]

Where the rubber meets the road, as it pertains to leadership, PTCD, and the cognitive dissonance that some may experience when reading this chapter, I think most people simply haven't been properly taught what *leading* within the parameters of the *Kingdom of God* looks like. Subsequently, they are left to their own assumptions and interpretations of the leadership models they have observed, studied, or been indoctrinated with from unbiblical representation, and the overall experience is then a result of a flawed model instead of Godly instruction.

Cutting the Ends Off

I heard a story years ago about a woman who learned to cook from her grandmother. She noted that every time her grandmother baked a ham, she would cut off the ends, place the ham in the roasting pot, and then put it in the oven.

When the young woman became an adult, she decided to cook Grandma's ham recipe for dinner when her grandmother was in town to visit. Grandma joined her in the kitchen to assist, and as her granddaughter proceeded to slice the ends off the ham, the grandmother asked, *"Honey, why are you cutting the ends off the ham"?* The granddaughter looked back confusedly and responded, *"Because that is what you always did when you baked a ham."*

Her grandmother laughed and responded, *"Oh, honey, the only reason I cut the ends off of the ham was because when you were growing up, my baking pan was too small, and back then, we couldn't afford to purchase a bigger one…not because that's the proper way to cook a ham."*

Of course, the leadership parallel for this story is that what is modeled for us is not always what's proper. Had the granddaughter not had this enlightening conversation with her grandmother, she may have likely taught future generations a silly misinterpretation as *"the proper way of cooking a ham."*

The Power Pyramid - When Kingdom Contradicts Corporate

First Corinthians 2:13–14 teaches that the wisdom of the Kingdom of God stands in complete opposition to worldly or secular ways of thinking, often appearing as foolishness to them. These Kingdom principles cannot be understood through natural reasoning alone; they are revealed by the Spirit of God and can only be discerned by the awakened spirit of a believer.

This is why it is so important that we, as believers, prioritize the foundation of biblical instruction above any other philosophy or teaching. Secular and corporate leadership structures can seem completely logical on paper and yet be completely unhealthy and antithetical to Godly perspective and instruction. As we have established in the previous chapters, the foundation for how we live and lead as a believer MUST BE THE WORD OF GOD.

Probably, more than any other unhealthy leadership model I have seen adopted by the church and church leaders from secular and corporate leadership models is what I call the *Power Pyramid.*

Simply illustrated, the *Power Pyramid* looks like an organizational chart where the CEO sits at the tip of a pyramid, his key leaders sit beneath him with their titles and responsibilities, and as you go further and further down the layers of the pyramid, the base gets wider and wider with the lowest level representing those with the least significance within the organization. In this model, everyone within the organization exists to lift up the vision of the leader, and in the leader's mind, everything flows downhill from them. It's not that there aren't aspects of this model that can relate to Kingdom leadership culture, there are mindsets often incorporated within it that create imbalance.

While the *Power Pyramid* leadership model is not always applied this way, in extreme cases, I have been made aware of more than one leader who, in an effort to assert their authority, has boldly declared, "*I am the voice of God for this organization.*" These leaders expected their instructions to be treated on par with *"divine commands,"* shaming those who did not comply and even accusing them of rebelling against God if they did not. While this may seem far-fetched or surprising, such behavior has been more common in ministry leadership than one might assume, and there have actually been entire denominational sects that have adopted this as a doctrinal leadership structure. But history and experience teach us a sobering truth: "Leaders who cannot be questioned, end up doing questionable things."[x]

Leaders who elevate themselves above their biblical or God-appointed authority do so at the cost of revelation and intimacy between God and His people. While it's true that God calls and equips leaders with vision and direction for the organizations they're entrusted to steward, trouble arises when those leaders are placed on pedestals meant only for God. Such misplaced exaltation inevitably leads to spiritual fallout.

Under the New Covenant, Jesus sent the Holy Spirit so that each believer could personally connect with God and hear His voice directly—without needing a liaison, pastor, prophet, or priest. While God certainly uses leaders to speak into our lives and provide instruction, when the Spirit of God dwells within us, external voices should offer confirmation of what God is already speaking to you internally. Healthy spiritual leaders should equip and encourage those they lead to discern God's voice for themselves, ensuring that personal guidance comes first and foremost from God, not from man.

The *Power Pyramid* fuels the pride of insecure leaders seeking exaltation and grants excessive influence to controlling and manipulative leaders—an influence that was never meant to replace God's authority. This model distorts leadership by elevating individuals to receive the honor, praise, and control in believers' lives that should only belong to God. When this model is embraced and replicated in the lives and leadership of well-intentioned future leaders, it can set them up for failure, exposing them to deceptive and unbiblical leadership practices that undermine their calling.

Certainly, I'm not saying that organizations do not need conventionally understood *leadership*. God undoubtedly calls and equips individuals to be leaders and fulfill a conventionally understood leadership role. The Bible affirms that God appoints leaders not only within the church but also in secular government, and strong, visionary leadership is essential—leaders who seek God's guidance, cast vision, and help implement His plans. The issue is not the necessity of leadership within an organization itself but the use of ungodly leadership models in carrying out that calling. Ultimately, it all begins with how a leader perceives leadership and the model they choose to follow within that perspective.

Most leaders who adopt the Power Pyramid model are not inherently bad people. In many cases, they are simply following the example set by those they have respected, implementing it in their own organizations as the standard way of operating. However, I believe the Bible presents a better model for leadership that might seem foolish through a corporate or secular lens.

I recently read this quote on the subject of leadership, and it is very relevant in comparison to the Power Pyramid model of church leadership:

The Fruit of the Spirit will always seem foolish if control is your idol. Love looks reckless if your highest goal is self-preservation. Joy seems naïve if you believe cynicism keeps you safe. Peace feels irresponsible if anxiety makes you feel in control. Patience seems passive if you've built your life around urgency. Kindness looks weak if you think hostility is the only way to win. Goodness feels unnecessary if your worth is tied to what you produce. Faithfulness seems boring if you think life is about chasing the next thing. Gentleness feels ineffective if you believe force is the only way to be heard. Self-control seems oppressive if you're convinced that freedom means indulging every desire. The way of Jesus will always seem foolish in a world obsessed with control, but control is an illusion. It keeps you striving but never arriving. What the world calls foolish, God calls freedom and the Spirit will grow what control never could.[xi]

All of us have been in situations where the Holy Spirit confronted us on something we were doing and then revealed to us through scripture a better way. When that happens, we are left with a choice to either *repent* (change how we think about what we are doing and change our actions) or continue without addressing the new revelation that the Holy Spirit has uncovered.

Secure leadership admits & owns when it's wrong and then rights the wrong.

The Godly Leadership Model – Protect & Empower

When we look to the wisdom of God's Word, we see that whether we are leading a family, a small group, a ministry team, an entire church, or an entire organization, effective leadership within the Kingdom consists of two primary instructions, to *protect* (1 Peter 5:1-5) and to *empower* (Ephesians 4:11-16) in love those we have been called to serve.

1 Peter 5:1-5 (TPT – emphasis by the author)
*1 Now, I encourage you as an elder, an eyewitness of the sufferings of Christ, and one who shares in the glory that is about to be unveiled. I urge my fellow elders among you 2to be compassionate shepherds who tenderly care for God's flock and who feed them well, for you have the responsibility to **guide, protect, and oversee**. Consider it a joyous pleasure and not merely a religious duty. Lead from the heart under God's leadership—not as a way to gain finances dishonestly but as a way to eagerly and cheerfully serve. 3 Don't be controlling tyrants but lead others by your beautiful examples to the flock. 4 And when the Shepherd-King appears, you will win the victor's crown of glory that never fades away. 5 In the same way, the younger ones should willingly support the leadership of the elders. In every relationship, each of you must wrap around yourself the apron of a humble servant. Because: God resists you when you are proud but multiplies grace and favor when you are humble.*

Ephesians 4:11-16 (TPT – emphasis by the author)
*11 And he has appointed some with grace to be apostles, and some with grace to be prophets, and some with grace to be evangelists, and some with grace to be pastors, and some with grace to be teachers. 12 And their calling is to **nurture and prepare** all the holy believers **to do their own works of ministry**, and as they do this they will enlarge and build up the body of Christ. 13 These grace ministries will function until we all attain oneness into the faith, until we all experience the fullness of what it means to know the Son of God, and finally we become one into a perfect man with the full dimensions of spiritual maturity and fully developed into the abundance of Christ.*
14 And then our immaturity will end! And we will not be easily shaken by trouble, nor led astray by novel teachings or by the false doctrines of deceivers who teach clever lies. 15 But instead we will remain strong and always sincere in our love as we express the truth. All our direction and ministries will flow from Christ and lead us deeper into him, the anointed Head of his body, the church.

*16 For his "body" has been formed in his image and is closely joined together and constantly connected as one<u>. **And every member has been given divine gifts to contribute to the growth of all; and as these gifts operate effectively throughout the whole body,**</u> we are built up and made perfect in love.*

Healthy, godly leadership—shaped by wisdom and experience—both *protects* emerging leaders from dangers they may not yet see and *empowers* them by intentionally recognizing their gifts and callings and equipping them with the training, guidance, and opportunities they need to grow into their God-given purpose.

I recently spoke with a young father and pastor about the difference between healthy and unhealthy leadership. He has a three-year-old daughter, so I asked him: *How broken would a father have to be to raise his daughter in a way that her entire purpose becomes serving, affirming, and empowering his calling—at the expense of her own?* He paused, visibly disturbed by the idea, and said he couldn't even imagine thinking that way.

Yet tragically, this is the very mindset many unhealthy Christian leaders have embraced—viewing leadership through the distorted lens of a Power Pyramid model, where others exist primarily to serve the leader's vision.

Don't use people to get to your destiny. Help them reach theirs and they will help you reach yours. The greatest, most valuable, eternal investment you can make, is in people.[xii]

As we discussed in Chapter 4 – Kingdom Leaders lead from a Kingdom perspective, a true leader doesn't just create more followers, they create more leaders, and a true father doesn't just create more children, they create empowered men and women. Godly fathers want their ceiling to be their children's floor, and they do that by protecting them from what they don't perceive until they can empower them to be all they were created to be.

The Kingdom Pyramid

As believers, we should all agree that the ultimate standard for who we are called to become is found in the life and example of the Word of God—Jesus Christ. And the model He demonstrated reflects what I would describe as a *Kingdom Pyramid.*

The church is not supposed to be a sub-culture, we're supposed to be a counterculture.[xiii] We aren't supposed to reflect corporate culture; we are supposed to model *Kingdom culture.* Godly systems often stand in direct contrast to secular ones. As Scripture reminds us, *His ways are not our ways, and His thoughts are not our thoughts* (Isaiah 55:8-9). The *Kingdom*

Pyramid reflects this truth—it is the opposite of the secular *Power Pyramid.*

Visually, the *Kingdom Pyramid* is flipped upside down and is the reciprocal of the *Power Pyramid.* Jesus modeled this *Kingdom Pyramid* form of leadership by positioning Himself at the lowest point rather than the highest. He demonstrated that true greatness comes through humility—His followers didn't serve Him by washing His feet; instead, He washed theirs. When a sacrifice was required, He took it upon Himself. In the *Kingdom Pyramid,* the leader carries the weight of the entire organization, not to elevate themselves but to protect and uplift those who are not yet strong enough to stand on their own. Everything Jesus did was to empower others to step into the purpose God had designed for them long before they were born.

Leadership, even in the traditional sense, is an essential calling. However, from a kingdom perspective, a key aspect of leadership is empowering others to become who God created them to be. Spiritual leaders, when leading from a Godly perspective, become *king-makers* by faithfully stewarding and empowering the gifts and callings of those they are leading through their developmental stages. What an honor!

True leadership is expressed from a *Kingdom Pyramid* perspective by fulfilling our personal calling while prioritizing the well-being, growth, and empowerment of those we lead. It doesn't diminish our responsibility as leaders; rather, it expands it to include the stewardship of others' potential as a core leadership priority.

Jesus modeled exactly what Paul reiterated in Ephesians 4:12-16 when he explained that a leader's place in the body of Christ is to equip the saints to do what God has called them to do.

Ephesians 4:12-13, 16 (TPT – emphasis by author)
*11 And he has appointed some with grace to be apostles, and some with grace to be prophets, and some with grace to be evangelists, and some with grace to be pastors, and some with grace to be teachers. 12 **And their calling is to nurture and prepare all the holy believers to do their own works of ministry**, and as they do this they will enlarge and build up the body of Christ. 13 These grace ministries will function until we all attain oneness into the faith, until we all experience the fullness of what it means to know the Son of God, and finally we become one into a perfect man with the full dimensions of spiritual maturity and fully developed into the abundance of Christ... 16 For his "body" has been formed in his image and is closely joined together and constantly connected as one. And every member has been given divine gifts to contribute to the growth of all; and as these gifts operate effectively throughout the whole body, we are built up and made perfect in love.*

Under the previous system, under the old covenant, men were limited in their abilities to know God, walk with God, and operate in power. They were limited by a human experience, but Christ empowered them to live beyond the confines of a physical existence. He taught them how to walk by faith and then, in the true nature of a father, did everything necessary to make sure that the ceiling of his time on this earth was the floor for future generations so that they could do even *greater things than He did because He was going to the Father* (John 14:12-14) and *sending the Holy Spirit who would be with them always and would never leave or forsake them.* (John 14:16)

The upside-down *Kingdom Pyramid* is a picture of Godly leadership. A child gleans from his father's wisdom and, when necessary, sits on his daddy's shoulders to protect them from whatever might bite them on the ground—empowering them to be future leaders led by His Spirit. It kind of reminds you of Jesus, doesn't it?

Effective and Affective Leadership

Paul writes about leadership as a Kingdom concept of co-laboring and says:

2 Corinthians 1:24
But I don't want to imply that, as leaders, we coerce you or somehow want to rule over your faith. Instead, we are your partners who are called to increase your joy.

I love that last line from The Passion Translation; *instead, we are your partners who are called to increase your joy.* It emphasizes an aspect of leadership that prioritizes emotional intelligence. Leadership is supposed to also involve the emotional well-being of those we are leading. Kingdom leadership involves the balance of *effective* and *affective* leadership.

Many leaders view leadership primarily as a matter of *effectiveness*—achieving goals and delivering results. However, there is another crucial aspect that sounds similar but is fundamentally different: *affective* leadership. This refers to a leader who prioritizes relationships, understands emotions, and fosters a positive, supportive environment for their team. I firmly believe that a Godly, Kingdom leader cannot be truly *effective* without also being intentionally *affective.* The most impactful leaders blend both approaches—driving success while also valuing the emotions, growth, calling, and well-being of the people they lead.

As we've explored in this chapter, the Kingdom Leadership Model stands in stark contrast to the corporate power structures that have crept into the church, often unconsciously, yet with damaging effect. It challenges not only the effectiveness of those models but the very spirit in which they operate.

Kingdom leadership isn't about titles, authority, or climbing to the top—it's about humbling ourselves, protecting those we lead, and empowering them to become everything God has created them to be. It flips the pyramid, placing the weight of leadership not on those below but squarely on the shoulders of those called to serve.

In the next chapter, we will take a deeper look at what Scripture specifically outlines regarding leadership. We'll examine not just examples but biblical directives that shape the foundation of godly leadership—leadership that not only transforms organizations but also nurtures healing, growth, and lasting impact within the body of Christ.

For Christian leaders to lead according to a Kingdom standard, they must first recognize what that standard is and clearly define what it looks like in practice.

Both Christian and secular leadership mentors and authors have provided us with powerful blueprints for success. These detailed, well-structured plans can inspire vision and renew purpose when we see them laid out on paper or observe them succeeding in another team or church. However, no matter how intricate or architecturally sound a blueprint may be, the entire structure will eventually collapse if built on an unstable or flawed foundation. Doing everything right on the wrong foundation will always lead to failure in the long run.

The Bible commands us to **seek FIRST the Kingdom of God**—His way of doing things—because there is a divine order that must be followed.

Following the Instructions

If you're anything like me, assembling furniture or toys has taught you some hard lessons. My tendency to process information quickly often leads me to skim over the instructions, assuming I know what to do, only to realize later that I missed crucial steps. More times than I'd like to admit, I've jumped ahead, thinking I had everything figured out, only to be required to backtrack and redo my work. The frustration, wasted time, and unnecessary effort all stemmed from failing to follow the instructions in their proper order in the first place. As the saying goes, *the right thing at the wrong time is still the wrong thing*—and in my repetitive experience, skipping the instructions only makes the process longer and more difficult.

This is why putting God's way first is so essential. Other leadership blueprints may be valuable, but they must be built *on top of* the foundation of His instructions—God's Word—not in place of it. When leaders fail to follow the proper sequence, they end up having to undo mistakes and fix what was *"built"* incorrectly.

The Bible provides clear guidance on what a Kingdom leadership foundation should look like, yet many Christian leaders attempt to implement someone else's leadership model before establishing the crucial biblical foundation. God's Word **must** be the bedrock of leadership, yet many will read countless books, highlight notes, and take in all the latest strategies—only to skim over the next section of this chapter detailing what the Word of God specifically says because they assume they already know the scripture. While others will read that last statement and immediately assume, *"I already have implemented a biblical foundation for my leadership structure."* These are actually the mentalities that were discussed in the previous chapter when we spoke about *"cognitive dissonance"* that a pastoral staff and volunteer team may wish their leader didn't misunderstand. But if they truly understood it, if they truly KNEW it, they would have already put it into practice.

I've heard this saying for years: ***You don't have to tell me what you believe or value—your actions show me.*** In other words, our behavior reflects our belief systems. Unfortunately, many who claim to be leaders reveal through their actions that they do not actually *know* or adhere to the biblical leadership principles they profess to follow.

I've been guilty of this myself, and it wasn't until I stopped *reading the Word* and started letting the Word *READ ME* on the topic of leadership that I actually began to see my own faults and failures as a Kingdom leader.

Reading Scripture as the Standard for Kingdom Leaders

Leadership is a privilege. Your influence may affect the trajectories of people's entire careers and, often, their lives![xiv] Recognizing that every Christian will at some point lead people in some capacity, we all at this point should be weighing the question, *what does God's Word say about how a Godly leader should lead?*

In this next section, I encourage you not just to read the Word but to allow the Word to examine your heart and READ YOU as I share various scriptures on Godly leadership. The bible presents the standard for what we should be as a leader and what we should expect from our leadership.

Throughout this book, I have intentionally chosen to reference ***The Passion Translation (TPT)*** for many of these passages. This newer translation presents often well-known scriptures in a fresh and unfamiliar way, making it less tempting to skim past them and instead inviting deeper reflection and meditation.

Personally, incorporating this translation into my own studies has helped me slow down and reconsider truths I've read hundreds—if not thousands—

of times. I encourage you to approach each scripture with intention, viewing it as direct instruction from God to you as a leader.

Leaders Refuse a Double Standard

Proverbs 20:10 (The Passion Translation)
10 Mark it down: God hates it when you demonstrate a double standard—one for "them" and one for "you."

Proverbs 11:1-2 (TPT – Emphasis by the author)
*1 Dishonest business practice is something that Yahweh truly hates. But it pleases him when we apply the right standards of measurement. 2 When you act with presumption, convinced that you're right, don't be surprised if you fall flat on your face! But **humility leads to wisdom**.*

Leaders Control Their Emotions

Proverbs 16:31-32 (TPT)
*31 Old age with wisdom will crown you with dignity and honor, for it takes a lifetime of righteousness to acquire it. 32 Do you want to be a mighty warrior? It's better to **be known as one who is patient** and slow to anger. Do you want to conquer a city? **Rule over your temper** before you attempt to rule a city.*

Leaders Keep Their Word and Do What They Say

Proverbs 12:22 (TPT – Emphasis by the author)
*22 Live in the truth and **keep your promises**, and the Lord will keep delighting in you, but he detests a liar.*

Leaders Guide, Protect, And Serve

1 Peter 5:1-3 (AMPC – Emphasis by the author)
*1 **Warn** and counsel the elders among you (the pastors and spiritual guides of the church) as a fellow elder and as an eyewitness [called to testify] of the sufferings of Christ, as well as a sharer in the glory (the honor and splendor) that is to be revealed (disclosed, unfolded):*
*2 **Tend** (nurture, guard, guide, and fold) the flock of God that is [your responsibility], not by coercion or constraint, but willingly; not dishonorably motivated by the advantages and profits [belonging to the office], but eagerly and cheerfully;*
*3 **Not domineering** [as arrogant, dictatorial, and overbearing persons] over those in your charge, but **being examples** (patterns and models of Christian living) to the flock (the congregation).*

Leaders Refuse to Be Corrupted by the World's Values

James 1:27 (TPT)

*27 True spirituality that is pure in the eyes of our Father God is to make a difference in the lives of the orphans, and widows in their troubles, and to refuse to be corrupted **by the world's values.***

On this subject, I encourage you to ask yourself, *what does the world value that spiritual leaders prioritize or are enticed by?*

Leaders Are Quick to Listen, Slow to Speak, and Sensitive to Be Led by the Foundation of God's Word

James 1:19-22 ((TPT – Emphasis by the author)
*19 My dearest brothers and sisters, take this to heart: Be quick to listen, but slow to speak. And be slow to become angry, 20 for human **anger is never a legitimate tool to promote God's righteous purpose.** 21 So this is why we abandon everything morally impure and all forms of wicked conduct. Instead, with a sensitive spirit we absorb God's Word, which has been implanted within our nature, for the Word of Life has power to continually deliver us.*
*22 **Don't just listen to the Word of Truth and not respond to it,** for that is the essence of self-deception. So always let his Word become like poetry written and fulfilled by your life!*

Leaders Are Responsible for Souls and Will Give Account for How They Lead

Hebrews 13:17 (TPT – Emphasis by the author)
*17 Obey your spiritual leaders and recognize their authority, for they keep watch over your soul without resting since **they will have to give an account** to God for their work. So it will benefit you when you make their work a pleasure and not a heavy burden.*

Leaders Live Above Reproach, Are Trustworthy, Even–tempered, And True to Their Word.

Titus 1:6-9 (TPT – Emphasis by the author)
*6 Each of them must be above reproach, devoted solely to his wife, whose children are believers and not rebellious or out of control. 7 The overseer, since he serves God's household, must be someone of blameless character **and not be opinionated or short-tempered.** He must not be a drunkard or violent or greedy. 8 Instead, he should be one who is **known for his hospitality** and a lover of goodness. He should be recognized as one who is **fair-minded**, pure-hearted, and **self-controlled.** 9 He must have a firm grasp of the trustworthy message that he has been taught. This will enable him to both encourage others with healthy teachings and provide convincing answers to those who oppose his message.*

1 Timothy 3:8,10 (TPT – Emphasis by the author)
*8 And in the same way the deacons must be those who are pure **and true to their word**, not addicted to wine, or with greedy eyes on the contributions. 10 And each of them **must be found trustworthy** according to these standards before they are given the responsibility to minister as servant-leaders without blame.*

Leaders Have Character Consistent with Godliness - Integrity

Titus 2:1-8 (TPT – Emphasis by the author)
1 Your duty is to teach them to embrace a lifestyle that is consistent with sound doctrine. 2 Lead the male elders into disciplined lives full of dignity and self-control. Urge them to have a solid faith, generous love, and patient endurance.
3 Likewise with the female elders, lead them into lives free from gossip and drunkenness and to be teachers of beautiful things. 4 This will enable them to teach the younger women to love their husbands, to love their children, 5 and to be self-controlled and pure, taking care of their household and being devoted to their husbands. By doing these things the word of God will not be discredited.
*6 Likewise, guide the younger men into living disciplined lives for Christ. 7 Above all, set yourself apart as a model of a life nobly lived. With dignity, **demonstrate integrity in all that you teach**. 8 Bring a clear, wholesome message that cannot be condemned, and then your critics will be embarrassed, with nothing bad to say about us.*

1 Timothy 3:1-7 (TPT – Emphasis by the author)
*1 If any of you aspires to be an overseer in the church; you have set your heart toward a noble ambition, for the word is true! 2 Yet an elder needs to be one who is without blame before others. He should be one whose heart is for his wife alone and not another woman. He should be recognized as one who is sensible, and well-behaved, and **living a disciplined life**. He should be a "spiritual shepherd" who has the gift of teaching, and is **known for his hospitality.***
*3 He **cannot be a drunkard, or someone who lashes out at others, or argumentative**, or someone who simply craves more money, but instead, **recognized by his gentleness.***
4 His heart should be set on guiding his household with wisdom and dignity; bringing up his children to worship with devotion and purity. 5 For if he's unable to properly lead his own household well, how could he properly lead God's household?
6 He should not be a new disciple who would be vulnerable to living in the clouds of conceit and fall into pride, making him easy prey for Satan. 7 He should be respected by those who are unbelievers, having a

beautiful testimony among them so that he will not fall into the traps of Satan and be disgraced.

Proverbs 25:26,28 (TPT – Emphasis by the author)
*26 When a lover of God gives in and compromises with wickedness, it can be compared to contaminating a stream with sewage or polluting a fountain. 28 If you live **without restraint** and are unable to **control your temper**, you're as helpless as a city with broken-down defenses, open to attack.*

Leaders Must Not Be Disgraced – Live at Peace – Not Argumentative

2 Timothy 2:21-26 (TPT – Emphasis by the author)
*21 But you, Timothy, must not see your life and ministry this way. Your life and ministry **must not be disgraced**, for you are to be a pure container of Christ and dedicated to the honorable purposes of your Master, prepared for every good work that he gives you to do.*
*22 Run as fast as you can from all the ambitions and lusts of youth; and chase after all that is pure. Whatever builds up your faith and deepens your love must become your holy pursuit. And **live in peace with all those who worship our Lord Jesus** with pure hearts.*
*23 Stay away from all the foolish arguments of the immature, for these disputes will only generate more conflict. 24 For a true servant of our Lord Jesus **will not be argumentative but gentle toward all** and skilled in helping others see the truth, having great patience toward the immature. 25 Then **with meekness** you'll be able to **carefully enlighten** those who argue with you so they can see God's gracious gift of repentance and be brought to the truth. 26 This will cause them to rediscover themselves and escape from the snare of Satan who caught them in his trap so that they would carry out his purposes.*

Proverbs 29: 1,4,11 (TPT – Emphasis by the author)
*1 Stubborn people who repeatedly refuse to accept correction will suddenly be broken and never recover. 4 A godly leader who values justice is a great strength and example to the people. But the one who sells his influence for money tears down what is right. 11 You can recognize fools by the way they give full vent to their rage and let their words fly! But **the wise bite their tongues** and hold back all they could say.*

Leaders Do Not Compromise Truth but Instruct with Wisdom and Patience

2 Timothy 4:2 (TPT – Emphasis by the author)
2 proclaim the Word of God and stand upon it no matter what! Rise to

*the occasion and preach when it is convenient and when it is not. Preach in the full expression of the Holy Spirit —with **wisdom and patience** as you instruct and teach the people.*

1 Timothy 4:12 (TPT – Emphasis by the author)
*12 And don't be intimidated by those who are older than you; simply be the example they need to see by being faithful and true in all that you do. Speak the truth and live a life of purity and **authentic love** as you remain strong in your faith.*

Leaders Live What They Preach

1 Timothy 4:16 (TPT – Emphasis by the author)
*16 Give careful attention to your spiritual life and every cherished truth you teach, for **living what you preach** will release salvation inside you and to all those who listen to you.*

Leaders Don't Use People for Personal Gain

1 Thessalonians 2:3-11 (TPT – Emphasis by the author)
*3 Our coming alongside you to encourage you was not out of some delusion, or **impure motive**, or an intention to mislead you, 4 but we have been approved by God to be those who preach the gospel. So our motivation to preach is **not pleasing people but pleasing God**, who thoroughly examines our hearts. 5 God is our witness that when we came to encourage you, we never once used cunning compliments as a pretext for greed, 6 **nor did we crave the praises of men**, whether you or others. 7 Even though we could have imposed upon you our demands as apostles of Christ, instead **we showed you kindness** and were **gentle** among you. We cared for you in the same way a nursing mother cares for her own children. 8 With a mother's love and affectionate attachment to you, we were very happy to share with you not only the gospel of God but also our lives—**because you had become so dear to us.***
*9 Beloved brothers and sisters, surely you remember how hard we labored among you. We worked night and day so **that we would not become a burden to you** while we preached the wonderful gospel of God. 10 With God as our witness you saw how we lived among you—in holiness, in godly relationships, and without fault. 11 And you know how affectionately we treated each one of you, **like a loving father cares for his own children.***

This passage from 1 Thessalonians reminds me to lead with a heart like that of a loving parent—marked by kindness and gentleness. Leadership isn't meant to be harsh or authoritarian, but rather a compassionate stewardship of the hearts entrusted to our care.

Leaders Walk in Unity – Putting Others Above Themselves (I'm not saying it's easy, I'm saying it's right!)

Philippians 2:2-5 (TPT – Emphasis by the author)
2 So I'm asking you, my friends, that you be joined together in perfect unity—with one heart, one passion, and united in one love. Walk together with one harmonious purpose and you will fill my heart with unbounded joy.
*3 Be free from pride-filled opinions, for they will only harm your cherished unity. Don't allow self-promotion to hide in your hearts, but **in authentic humility put others first and view others as more important than yourselves**. 4 Abandon **every display of selfishness**. Possess a greater concern **for what matters to others** instead of your own interests. 5 And consider the example that Jesus, the Anointed One, has set before us. Let his mindset become your motivation.*

Leaders Do Not Posture Themselves Above Those They Lead

Ephesians 3:7-8 (TPT – Emphasis by the author)
*7-8 I have been made a messenger of this wonderful news by the gift of grace that works through me. Even though **I am the least significant of all his holy believers**, this grace-gift was imparted when the manifestation of his power came upon me. Grace alone empowers me so that I can boldly preach this wonderful message to non-Jewish people, sharing with them the unfading, inexhaustible riches of Christ, which are beyond comprehension.*

Leaders Recognize That They Are a Part of Something Bigger Than Themselves

Ephesians 4:1-4 (TPT – Emphasis by the author)
*1 As a prisoner of the Lord, I plead with you to walk holy, in a way that is suitable to your high rank, given to you in your divine calling. 2 With tender **humility** and quiet **patience**, always demonstrate **gentleness** and generous **love** toward one another, especially toward those who may try your patience. 3 Be faithful to guard the sweet **harmony** of the Holy Spirit among you in the bonds of **peace**, 4 being one body and one spirit, as you were all called into the same glorious hope of divine destiny.*

Leaders Nurture and Prepare Others to Lead

Ephesians 4:12 (TPT – Emphasis by the author)
*12 And their calling is to **nurture and prepare all the holy believers to do their own works of ministry**, and as they do this, they will enlarge and build up the body of Christ.*

Leaders Oppose Hypocrisy and Disorder by Holding Others Accountable (Including Themselves)

Galatians 2:11-14 (TPT – Emphasis by the author)

11 When Peter visited Antioch, he caused the believers to stumble over his behavior, so I confronted him to his face. 12 He enjoyed eating with the gentile believers who didn't keep the Jewish customs—up until the time Jacob's Jewish friends arrived from Jerusalem. When he saw them, he withdrew from his gentile friends—fearing how it would look to them if he ate with gentile believers.

13 And so, because of Peter's hypocrisy, many other Jewish believers followed suit, refusing to eat with gentile believers. Even Barnabas was led astray by their hypocritical behavior!

*14 So **when I realized they were acting inconsistently** with the revelation of the gospel, **I confronted Peter** in front of everyone: "You were born a Jew, but you've chosen to disregard Jewish regulations and live like a gentile. Why then do you force gentiles to conform to these same rules?"*

Leaders Understand That No Matter How Gifted You Are, If You Lead Outside of Love You Are Failing

1 Corinthians 13:1-12 (TPT – Emphasis by the author)

*1I If I were to speak with eloquence in earth's many languages, and in the heavenly tongues of angels, yet I **didn't express myself with love**, my words would be reduced to the hollow sound of **nothing more than a clanging cymbal.***

*2 And if I were to have the gift of prophecy with a profound understanding of God's hidden secrets, and if I possessed unending supernatural knowledge, and if I had the greatest gift of faith that could move mountains, **but have never learned to love, then I am nothing.***

*3 And if I were to be so generous as to give away everything I owned to feed the poor and to offer my body to be burned as a martyr, **without the pure motive of love, I would gain nothing** of value.*

*4 Love is large and incredibly patient. Love is **gentle** and consistently **kind** to all. It **refuses to be jealous** when blessing comes to someone else. Love **does not brag** about one's achievements nor **inflate its own** importance. 5 Love does not traffic in **shame and disrespect**, nor **selfishly seek its own honor.** Love is **not easily irritated** or **quick to take offense.** 6 Love joyfully **celebrates honesty** and finds **no delight** in what is wrong. 7 **Love is a safe place of shelter**, for it never stops believing the best for others. Love never takes failure as defeat, for it never gives up.*

*8 **Love never stops loving.** It extends beyond the gift of prophecy, which eventually fades away. It is more enduring than tongues, which will one day fall silent. Love remains long after words of knowledge are forgotten. 9 Our present knowledge and our prophecies are but* *partial, 10 but when love's perfection arrives, the partial will fade away. 11 When I was a child, I spoke about childish matters, for I saw things like a child and reasoned like a child. But the day came when I matured, and I set aside my childish ways.*

*12 For now we see but a faint reflection of riddles and mysteries as though reflected in a mirror, but one day we will see face-to-face. My understanding is incomplete now, but one day I will understand everything, just as everything about me has been fully understood. 13 Until then, there are three things that remain: faith, hope, and love—yet **love surpasses them all**. So **above all else**, let love be the beautiful prize for which you run.*

Romans 12: The Biblical Outline for Godly Leadership

Romans 12:1-21 (TPT – Emphasis by the author)

*1 Beloved friends, what should be our proper response to God's marvelous mercies? To surrender yourselves to God to be his sacred, living sacrifices. And live in holiness, experiencing all that delights his heart. For this becomes your genuine expression of worship. 2 **Stop imitating the ideals and opinions of the culture around you**, but be inwardly transformed by the Holy Spirit through a total reformation of how you think. This will empower you to discern God's will as you live a beautiful life, satisfying and perfect in his eyes. 3 God has given me grace to speak a warning about pride. I would ask each of you to **be emptied of self-promotion** and not create a false image of your importance. Instead, honestly assess your worth by using your God-given faith as the standard of measurement, and then you will see your true value with an appropriate self-esteem. 4 In the human body there are many parts and organs, each with a unique function. 5 And so it is in the body of Christ. For though we are many, we've all been mingled into one body in Christ. This means that we are all vitally joined to one another, with **each contributing to the others**. 6 God's marvelous grace imparts to each one of us varying gifts. So if God has given you the grace-gift of prophecy, activate your gift by using the proportion of faith you have to prophesy. 7 If your grace-gift is serving, then thrive in serving others well. If you have the grace-gift of teaching, then be actively teaching and training others. 8 If you have the grace-gift of encouragement, then use it often to encourage others. If you have the grace-gift of giving to meet the needs of others, then may you prosper in your generosity without any fanfare. If you have the gift of leadership, be passionate about your leadership. And if you have the gift of showing compassion, then flourish in your cheerful display of compassion. 9 Let the inner movement of your heart **always be to love one another**, and never play the role of an actor wearing a mask. Despise evil and embrace everything that is good and* *virtuous. 10 Be devoted to **tenderly loving your fellow believers** as members of one family. **Try to outdo yourselves in respect and honor of one another**. 11 Be enthusiastic to serve the Lord, keeping your passion toward him boiling hot! Radiate with the glow of the Holy Spirit and let him fill you with excitement as you serve him. 12 Let this hope burst forth within you, releasing a continual joy. Don't give up in a time of trouble, but commune with God at all times. 13 **Take a constant interest in the needs of God's beloved people and respond by helping them**. And eagerly welcome people as guests into your home. 14 Speak blessing, not cursing, over those who reject and persecute you. 15 Celebrate with those who celebrate, and weep with those who grieve. 16 Live happily together in a spirit of harmony, and **be as mindful of another's worth as you are your own**. Don't live with a lofty mind-set, **thinking you are too important to serve others**, but be willing to do menial tasks and identify with those who are humble minded. Don't be smug or even think for a moment that you know it all. 17 Never hold a grudge or try to get even, but plan your life around the noblest way to benefit others. 18 **Do your best to live as everybody's friend**. 19 Beloved, don't be obsessed with taking revenge, but leave that to God's righteous justice. For the Scriptures say: "Vengeance is mine, and I will repay," says the Lord. 20 And: If your enemy is hungry, buy him lunch! Win him over with kindness. For your surprising generosity will awaken his conscience, and God will reward you with favor. 21 Never let evil defeat you, but defeat evil with good.*

Romans chapter 12 is both powerful and deeply challenging, especially for those in leadership. I want to take a moment to highlight just a few verses that I believe speak directly to the heart of what God expects from us as leaders.

In verse 8, *we are told to lead with passion.* Leadership isn't just a position—it's a calling that should stir something deep within us. We're not meant to approach it passively, but with zeal and conviction.

Verses 9 and 10 call us to *love our fellow believers sincerely and strive to outdo one another in showing honor and respect.* Imagine the culture we could create if this became our daily practice—leading not by dominance, but through honor.

Verse 13 encourages us to *stay continually aware of the needs of God's people and respond with action.* It's important to recognize that as a church or organization grows, it can stretch beyond our capacity to do this personally. That's why it becomes essential for leaders to empower others to carry out this care—just as Jesus nurtured the twelve and equipped them to minister to the multitudes. Even as we delegate, we must stay engaged with and attentive to the needs of our team.

Verse 14 might be one of the toughest: *bless those who persecute you—don't curse them*. This is where leadership gets real. Emotions can cloud judgment, especially when betrayal or rejection comes from people we once stood shoulder-to-shoulder with. Yet Paul's instruction is clear: don't respond in kind. Lead with grace, even when it's hard.

Verse 16 urges us to *value others as highly as we value ourselves*. It challenges us to lay down pride and embrace humility—to never see ourselves as above serving others, no matter how simple or unseen the task. What if we all led with that mindset?

I recently came across a quote that ties it all together:

"Don't do what's beneficial only for yourself. Some people always seek personal gain in every situation. Go out of your way to care about others' well-being. Help them reach their goals and arrive at their destination—and in doing so, you'll reach yours too. By helping others, you help yourself." [xv]

That's Kingdom leadership in action.

The standard is high, and it should be. Leadership in the Kingdom of God isn't casual. It carries weight, it carries accountability, and it carries influence that affects real people and real outcomes.

But here's something we have to remember.

Sometimes you can give your absolute best and still come up short.

You can pray. You can prepare. You can lead with integrity. You can love people well. You can do everything you know to do, and still not see the outcome you hoped for.

That's the part we don't always talk about.

Because somewhere along the way, many of us were taught that if we just lead well enough, structure things tightly enough, pray long enough, or preach clearly enough, the results will always just follow.

But leadership is not mechanical. It's spiritual. People are fighting a real enemy and we are there to help them navigate that fight if they will let us.

And there are moments when the only thing that balances the scales is the miracle-working hand of God.

The leadership standard is ours to pursue, but the outcome can also be influenced by their response and God's response.

If we confuse the standard with the outcome, we can either become prideful when things succeed or crushed when they don't.

Kingdom leadership requires excellence, but it also requires submission and dependence.

A Leader Loves and Values Others the Same Way They Love and Value

Themselves

Romans 13:8-10 (TPT – Emphasis by the author)
*8 Don't owe anything to anyone, except your outstanding debt to continually love one another, **for the one who learns to love has fulfilled every requirement of the law**. 9 For the commandments, "Do not commit adultery, do not murder, do not steal, do not covet," and every other commandment can be summed up in these words: **"Love and value others the same way you love and value yourself."** 10 Love makes it impossible to harm another, so love fulfills all that the law requires.*

Leaders Live Honorably and Don't Just Expect Honor

Romans 13:13-14 (TPT – Emphasis by the author)
*13 We must **live honorably**, surrounded by the light of this new day, not in the darkness of drunkenness and debauchery, not in promiscuity and sensuality, not being argumentative or jealous of others.*
*14 Instead fully immerse yourselves into the Lord Jesus, the Anointed One, and don't waste even a moment's thought on your former identity to awaken its **selfish** desires.*

Leaders Don't Live for Themselves

Romans 15:1-2 (TPT – Emphasis by the author)
*1 Now, those who are mature in their faith can easily be recognized, for they **don't live to please themselves** but have learned to **patiently embrace others** in their immaturity. 2 Our goal must be to **empower** others to do what is right and good for them, and to bring them into spiritual maturity.*

Leaders Serve Others: We have no greater example of Godly leadership than how Jesus served His disciples

John 13:14-17 (TPT – Emphasis by the author)
*14-15 So if I'm your teacher and lord and have just washed your dirty feet, then **you should follow the example that I've set for you and wash one another's dirty feet**. Now do for each other what I have just done for you. 16 I speak to you timeless truth: a servant is not superior to his master, and an apostle is never greater than the one who sent him. 17 So now put into practice what I have done for you, and you will experience a life of happiness enriched with untold blessings!"*

One of the most powerful leadership standards I see in John 13 is when Jesus—God in the flesh—demonstrates His expectations for how we are to lead by humbly washing His disciples' feet. What's especially striking is that He even washed the feet of Judas, fully aware that he would betray Him. Then, in verse 17, Jesus tells His disciples that if they will follow His example and put this into practice, it will become the catalyst for true happiness and abundant blessing in their lives.

Leaders Who Love Jesus, Do What He Says, and Models

John 14: 21, 23 & 24 (AMPC – Emphasis by the author)
*21 The person **who has My commands and keeps them** is the one who [really] loves Me; and whoever [really] loves Me will be loved by My Father, and I [too] will love him and will show (reveal, manifest) Myself to him. [I will let Myself be clearly seen by him and make Myself real to him.] 23 Jesus answered, If a person [really] loves Me, **he will keep My word [obey My teaching]**; and My Father will love him, and We will come to him and make Our home (abode, special dwelling place) with him. 24 Anyone who does not [really] love Me does not observe and obey My teaching. And the teaching which you hear and heed is not Mine, but [comes] from the Father Who sent Me.*

In all of John 14 and 15, Jesus goes into significant detail regarding the importance of doing what He has instructed us to do and, subsequently, how doing so will be the catalyst for overcoming the enemy in our lives as we stay connected to Him and *His way of doing and being.*

If you will take notice, many of the scriptures listed in this chapter on leadership reiterated over and over again the importance of walking in love, humility, patience, peace, gentleness, kindness, controlled emotions, empowering others, preferring the needs of others above your own. This is the foundational Kingdom standard for leadership from God's perspective.

It's no surprise that many of the most significant PTCD (*Post-Traumatic Church Disorder*) issues I've encountered among Christians stem from leaders failing to align with a Kingdom standard for leadership. Countless leaders dedicate hours to reading, highlighting, and even teaching their teams from the latest trending Christian leadership books, yet they often neglect to implement even the most basic principles that Jesus clearly demonstrated and commanded regarding one of the most crucial aspects of their calling—Godly leadership.

God's Word is the ultimate source of truth, and when it comes to leadership, it is the key to both life and success. Imagine the profound impact we could have if we led those entrusted to us with His Word as our foundational standard and guiding principle.

God's Word is the Irreplaceable Standard!

Recognizing that God's Word serves as the unquestionable guide for how believers should live, it is abundantly clear in Scripture what is expected of leaders in stewarding those entrusted to their care.

We are building a spiritual kingdom, leading others on a God-ordained mission to overcome a very real enemy. Like all Kingdom principles, God's standard for successful leadership is fundamentally different from the world's. While there are many well-structured blueprints that incorporate wise references and biblical parallels for establishing a workable model paralleling a corporate leadership framework, without first implementing foundational biblical principles, even the most well-organized structures will fail to withstand the relentless attacks of the enemy.

Kingdom leaders must lead from a Kingdom perspective. As Ephesians 6:12 reminds us, *our battle is not against flesh and blood but against principalities, powers, rulers of darkness, and spiritual wickedness in high places.* We cannot fight these forces with physical strength or worldly wisdom alone. While practical leadership strategies and organizational structures can enhance progress, they must remain secondary to the Kingdom principles God has established in His Word.

Attempting to lead spiritually using a carnal standard—without first aligning with God's design—ultimately undermines the very calling He has placed on our lives.

As we've seen, the Word of God isn't just a guide—it's the blueprint, the foundation, and the immovable standard by which all Kingdom leadership must be measured. But even when we know what Scripture says, there is a subtle yet dangerous tactic the enemy often uses to pull us out of alignment: *discontentment.* When our hearts begin to chase affirmation, influence, or personal ambition more than obedience to God's Word, we become vulnerable to deception. In the next chapter, we'll explore how Satan strategically leverages unmet expectations, internal insecurities, and the allure of worldly success to corrupt our calling—and how recognizing these traps is key to remaining grounded in biblical truth. The Word is our anchor, but discernment is our defense. Let's step into this next chapter with eyes wide open.

Chapter Seven

Discontentment Deception

everal years ago, Matt Redman wrote a worship song titled *"The Heart of Worship"* that took the Western church by storm. For a season, it became an interdenominational *anthem* that you could hear sung no matter what church you attended.

I'm comin' back to the heart of worship
And it's all about You
It's all about You, Jesus
I'm sorry, Lord, for the thing I've made it
When it's all about You
It's all about You, Jesus

Hands would raise around the room; tears would flow down the sincere cheeks of those who realized they had made this Kingdom of God and worship experience about themselves and lost sight of the *King* it was supposed to be all about… But *when the music faded,* and the emotional catalyst was removed, many who wholeheartedly acknowledged at the moment what *it was all about* refocused their priorities and paradigms back onto their true belief systems. While we can all acknowledge that our primary focus as a believer *should* be on loving God with our whole heart and living a lifestyle of worship to Him, it is still undeniable that we live out our belief systems, and when we look into the mirror of what our life is reflecting, for most of us, it's often still, *all about us.*

For decades, many in the church have been conditioned toward *consumerism,* fostering a mindset centered on self-gratification and convenience—*How does this make me feel? What do I like? What do I want?* Messages like *"Your Way Right Away"* have transcended fast food and ingrained within the church a perspective that prioritizes personal preference, instant satisfaction, and ego-driven decision-making. Many believers now approach life and church like a trip to the hardware store, expecting to find everything they want, and those expectations are often rooted in self-indulgence. This mentality aligns with the idea that if something feels good, you should do it—a sentiment echoed in Anton LaVey's (writer of the Satanic bible) philosophy: *Do as thou wilt.*

However, society's guidance stands in direct opposition to God's truth. The world teaches that contentment and feelings should determine your direction, but Scripture reminds us that *we walk by faith, not by sight.* Culture encourages us to *trust our gut* and chase what feels right, but the Bible calls us to seek first God's Kingdom—His way of doing and being—so that everything else falls into place. Society says, *if someone wrongs you, get even,* while Jesus commands us to *turn the other cheek.* The world promotes *accumulation and self-interest,* but God's Word teaches *give, and it will be given back to you abundantly.*

The principles of God's Kingdom and those of the world are completely different. As believers, we must intentionally renew our minds to align with His truth—even when it challenges our emotions and contradicts what feels comfortable.

It is human nature to prioritize self and to find discontentment in what we perceive is lacking. And that mentality actually goes back to the very first human beings to ever live. Think about it, Adam and Eve walked with God in the cool of the day. They lived in paradise. They didn't have to contend with sickness, disease, lack, the wages of sin, they didn't even have an overbearing mother-in-law that tried to control them and tell them how to live their lives and raise their kids. Yet, they were still deceived into becoming discontent with *perfection.*

Snake: Eve, you've got everything, but is that really enough? If you would just eat the fruit from that ONE tree He has restricted you from, you could be LIKE GOD!

I personally believe that the Garden of Eden was meant to be a temporary season for Adam and Eve, during which God would eventually equip them with the knowledge of good and evil—but in *His timing* and with the wisdom needed to handle it responsibly. Instead, they sought a shortcut to gain what God intended for them prematurely. As the saying goes, *the right thing at the wrong time is still the wrong thing.*

Even though steak is delicious, giving it to a baby before they have teeth could be deadly. Timing matters, and nowhere is that truer than in the *Kingdom of God.* Adam and Eve were in a season of learning and growth, but they allowed discontentment to take root when the enemy deceived them into prioritizing their desires over God's instruction.

Similarly, many people short-circuit their own success by growing impatient and discontent with the process that God is taking them through. They get ahead of God, stepping outside His will and plan by reaching for things prematurely—things that He has temporarily withheld for their growth and development. They see their peers advancing, their friends being honored, or the church down the street filling up on Sundays. Instead of trusting Christ to build them—and their ministry—as He promised, they let insecurity take over and attempt to force growth on their own terms, and *jealousy and insecurity become the assassins of honor.*[xvi]

One of the Ten Commandments instructs, *"Thou shalt not covet."* Another way to understand *covet* is to use the word *"compare."* How often do we fall into the enemy's trap when he sows seeds of discontentment and comparison and draws our attention to what we *don't* have instead of God as our provider? He convinces us that unless we take control back from God, we'll never get ahead—playing right into his discontentment deception.

Keep Your Eye On The Ball

Using a sports analogy, you can often predict the winner before the game even starts by watching how the teams interact on the field. If one team is focused, running drills, and practicing their strategy, while the other is standing on the sidelines, watching them, it becomes obvious who is actually going to lead in the game. The lesson here is that many people spend too much time trying to mimic others, believing they're *"studying the competition"* or *"learning from them."* But true success doesn't come from imitating what someone else does well—it comes from maximizing who you are and what you bring to the table.

If you show up as the best version of yourself, it doesn't matter what others are doing—they aren't your competition. Your only real competition is the version of you that falls short of your potential. This is especially relevant for insecure leaders who spend more time trying to mirror others than developing their own strengths. The paradox is that as long as they're fixated on someone else's game plan, they'll never fully step into their own. While imitation may be among the greatest forms of flattery, it will never make you the best version of yourself. *A life shaped by human approval will always fall short of Heaven's purpose.*[xvii]

Romans 6:11 in The Passion Translation says, *"...you must no longer give sin an opportunity to rule over your life..."* In the context of leadership, one of the most subtle yet destructive sins is comparison. It often becomes a gateway to other forms of ungodly validation, distorting motives and fueling insecurity.

An organization can only be as healthy as its leader.[xviii] When a leader becomes discontent and begins looking for validation in numbers, quotas, or the approval of people, they slowly lose sight of the only validation that truly matters—God's approval. And when that shift happens, their leadership model starts revolving around whatever gives them a sense of worth, even if that thing isn't godly. Comparison creeps in. Metrics become identity. And without realizing it, they stop building the Kingdom and start building castles. Whatever they're chasing to feel significant eventually becomes an idol. So, to the leaders, I challenge you with this perspective: *the primary question is not what you are accomplishing; it's who you are becoming.*[xix] If you are not becoming more loving, wise, humble, compassionate, forgiving, and holy then you may be receiving validation from something other than God.

When you give in to comparison, it quickly becomes a slippery slope that seeps into other areas of life. That same spirit of comparison can lead you to justify sin by making excuses— *"Well, he does that, and God still uses him."* It distorts conviction and compromises integrity.

Don't allow the enemy to shift your focus from God to your environment through the deception of comparison. *The devil cannot make hell beautiful, so often he makes beautiful the roads that lead us there.*[xx] To put it another way, many times Satan will use comparison and ungodly validation to convince us that we are on the right track when in fact, God would have us pursuing His will in a very different direction.

A Shift in Commitment

Almost nothing worth having comes without a fight. A common misunderstanding is that pain is always negative, but that's not entirely true. A great example of this is physical fitness—losing weight and building muscle. Though the process can be uncomfortable, the pain serves a purpose. It indicates that the body is shedding unhealthy fat and developing stronger, healthier muscles.

In the same way, growth in other areas of life requires effort and sacrifice. Healthy relationships take intentional work, achieving goals requires discipline, and following the Holy Spirit's guidance demands obedience. God's way isn't always easy—at times, it's uncomfortable or even painful. Sometimes, we must lay aside our own desires for a season and battle through our own discontentment, but it is always worth it. As Scripture says, *God is not mocked; whatever a man sows, that he will also reap.*[xxi] When you sow into God's Kingdom and follow His way, a Godly harvest is guaranteed.

The enemy understands this truth, which is why he will do everything possible to distract you from God and His ways, shifting your focus from Him to the deception of discontentment. Just as he deceived Adam and Eve, his goal is to derail the destiny God has planned for you. And just like in the Garden, he rarely reveals his true intentions or the full cost of what he is tempting you with.

When Satan tempted Adam and Eve, he didn't say, *I want to be your master!* —they would have never fallen for that. It would have been too obvious. Instead, his strategy wasn't to pull them from God to *evil* but from God to *self*. He convinced them to prioritize their own desires over God's instruction to them, and the consequence of that sin was separation and death—his goal all along.

Satan's tactics haven't changed. His most effective strategy remains the same: to get you to shift your focus from God to yourself. The moment your will replaces God's will as your priority, sin follows. The devil doesn't care how he gets you—only that he gets you! He knows that if you are serving yourself, you are not serving God… and that means, in time, he wins.

I'd like to leave you with a closing thought for this chapter from God's Word.

Galatians 6:9 (TPT – emphasis by the author)
*7 God will never be mocked! For what you plant will always be the very thing you harvest. 8 The harvest you reap reveals the seed that you planted. If you plant the corrupt seeds of self-life into this natural realm, you can expect a harvest of corruption. If you plant the good seeds of Spirit-life you will reap beautiful fruits that grow from the everlasting life of the Spirit. 9 **And don't allow yourselves to be weary in planting good seeds, for the season of reaping the wonderful harvest you've planted is coming!** 10 Take advantage of every opportunity to be a blessing to others, especially to our brothers and sisters in the family of faith!*

As we've unpacked the subtle but powerful danger of discontentment, it becomes clear how easily the enemy can distort our view—shifting our focus from God's purpose to our own ambition. When we become distracted by comparison and self-gratification, we risk exchanging God's process for a shortcut that leads to brokenness. But as you've read, God's way—though sometimes uncomfortable—is always the most fruitful. In the next chapter, we'll examine one of the enemy's most effective tools for derailing purpose: *elevating charisma and gifting over character and integrity*. It's a sobering truth—especially in leadership—that who you are matters more than what you can do. Let's explore why character must be the foundation of Kingdom leadership, and how to spot the red flags when it's not.

Chapter Eight
Charisma Vs. Character

In a world that often values charisma over character and applauds talent before testing integrity, the church has not remained untouched by this cultural drift. We've seen leaders promoted for their stage presence rather than their spiritual maturity, and many have suffered *Post-Traumatic Church Disorder* consequences of following someone who was gifted—but not grounded. It's undeniable that celebrity culture has had its impact on the church. As we move forward in this chapter, we will explore this tension as we challenge the standards by which we define leadership and consider what Scripture truly prioritizes: popularity vs. purity, showmanship vs. servant-heartedness, and we examine the difference between *charisma* that draws a crowd and *character* that actually builds the Kingdom.

For most of my adult life, I've had the opportunity to be around people who are considered *celebrities*. One day, while heading to lunch with a friend who is a well-known rock musician, my 10-year-old son was visibly excited. He loved this artist's music but had never met him before, and I could see how much he was emotionally invested in the moment.

Before we walked in, I looked my son, Rocky, in the eyes and said, *"In your life, you're going to have plenty of opportunities to meet famous people, and I want you to remember this: Just because someone is well-known doesn't make them special. They're just people with cool jobs. You can admire their talent and the hard work it took to reach that level, but never put them on a pedestal as if they're better than you or anyone else—because they're not."*

I then added, *"And if you ever find yourself in a position where others see you as a celebrity, never treat anyone as if they are less than you because of your status. Treat the makeup artist, wardrobe crew, and every behind-the-scenes worker with the same respect as the director or lead actor. Everyone has value—both in this world and in God's eyes."*

In the Western church, influenced by the corporate Power Pyramid leadership model, charisma and talent are often valued more than character and anointing. One of the biggest reasons for this is the failure to distinguish between emotional influence and the true movement of the Holy Spirit.

As a young man and a naturally charismatic speaker, I used to joke that once I had the audience emotionally engaged in my preaching, I could shout *"PEANUT BUTTER AND JELLY,"* and at least half the crowd would still cheer me on—without even realizing what I had said.

It's not that emotion and charisma in the pulpit are inherently bad—I personally enjoy listening to an emphatic preacher. However, when charisma is mistaken for anointing and emotionalism is prioritized over character, the consequences can be devastatingly compounding.

Celebrity Worship

As humans, we have a tendency to place others on pedestals, especially those who are gifted, make us feel good, or have achieved a level of success beyond our own. This often leads to elevating people to an unhealthy status in our eyes.

Even outside the church, society naturally categorizes individuals into elite groups based on their exceptional abilities. We admire top athletes, talented musicians, renowned writers, famous actors, incredible singers, stunningly beautiful individuals, highly skilled professionals, and the exceptionally wealthy… the list goes on. We often view them with greater admiration and treat them with higher regard, as if they are *elite* simply because they can do things we may not be able to do ourselves.

It's no different in the church when we prioritize charisma and ability over character and integrity. It's such a slippery slope when we pedestal the good-looking, trendy, smooth-talking orator and affirm them with the title of *"Leader"* because they appear to be an exceptional package—without having developed the character necessary to sustain true leadership. Subsequently, their inability to navigate this ungodly model for advancement often leads to personal failure or damage to the church. To be fair, this approach has been modeled and repeated for generations, so it's no surprise that it continues. However, when churches hire and promote based on this standard, the consequences can be severe.

I've heard it said: *"What you did to get there, you'll have to do to stay there."* If performance is the deciding factor in someone's promotion to leadership, the unspoken message is that performance is the top priority. The problem with this standard is that, from a Godly leadership perspective, performance was never meant to be the prerequisite.

Celebrity culture in the church poisons the gospel, trading truth for applause and substance for showmanship. It breeds shallow, teaching, performance-based, righteousness, and crowds that cheer for you one moment and crucify you the next.[xxii]

2 Cor 10:10 (TPT)
For I can imagine some of you saying, "His letters are authoritative and stern, but when he's with us he's not that impressive and he's a poor speaker."

I found 2 Corinthians 10:10 to be a very interesting scripture in light of this topic. When I have envisioned Paul, the writer of two-thirds of the New Testament, who was highly educated, dramatically called by God after being knocked off his horse, blinded during a personal visitation from Jesus, and impressively anointed with a miraculous ministry of wisdom and power, I never considered that the people of his day would have been critical of his public speaking abilities. Yet, here we see in the bible that, like Jeremiah and Moses, this was the case.

2 Corinthians 10:10 (footnote)
Greece was known as a land of eloquent speakers. Orators were professionally trained to address crowds. It seems some people were judging Paul by comparing his speaking gift to the eloquent speeches of others. Yet Paul was a brilliant teacher, not a trained orator. True leadership is much more than our speaking ability. Our influence is not limited to a rousing sermon, but we will affect the lives of many if we walk in purity, led by the Holy Spirit.

Then, in 2 Corinthians chapters 11 and 12, Paul explains how there are *"deceitful ministers"* (11:13) who place themselves on pedestals at the people's expense.

2 Corinthians 11:13 (TPT)
For they are not true apostles but deceitful ministers who masquerade as "special apostles" of the Anointed One.

Paul is trying to protect the church from these leaders who are *eloquent in speech* but arrogant and forcefully controlling while deceiving and manipulating people into a false gospel that *edifies and promotes the leader.* As you read further, in stark contrast, he then turns the focus to his own leadership example and how he feels an extreme weight and concern for the church's welfare. Not ruling over but restoring those who have been deceived by sin, not burdening the church but building them at the sacrifice of his own pain. As you read on into chapter 12, it is interesting to note how

Paul even shares a miraculous experience where he was taken to heaven and shown things he was not even permitted to speak about. Where this would have been a bragging point that an insecure, ungodly, or self-promoting leader would have used to prove his *elite* status, the experience further deepened Paul's humility. Paul realized that *the character of spiritual revelation was to exalt Christ, not people. It is a paradox that the greater our understanding of God, the less we truly know and the more humble we become. Paul refused to be exalted in the eyes of others. This is the nature of true apostolic ministry.*[xxiii]

I find it noteworthy that much of what the church understands about Godly leadership was presented to us through Paul. He penned and modeled this (sometimes in stark contrast to what is displayed or esteemed in the 21st-century church) as one anointed to be among the greatest influencers of the Kingdom of God in all of history.

Throughout Scripture, it seems that God consistently chose individuals who, by human standards, would have been otherwise viewed as *unqualified* or *underperforming*—Moses, Gideon, Jeremiah, David, and even the disciples, just to name a few. When charisma and performance become the criteria for advancement, it often results in leaders who are more focused on outperforming others to advance themselves rather than serving and empowering those they lead. This translates to an ego-driven and dangerous cycle where leaders feel validated based on how well they perform rather than how well they love and care for the people they are called to lead, creating an endless and unhealthy leadership Catch-22.

When a leader is elevated to a pedestal—or begins to view themselves as elite because of their performance—they often start prioritizing relationships with others they perceive to be on the same level. This mindset fosters an unhealthy separation between them and the very people they're called to lead. Rather than being present among their flock, they retreat to green rooms with peers, distancing themselves from the ones they were entrusted to serve.

It should be self-evident that a true shepherd smells like sheep. Real leadership requires proximity, presence, and genuine connection with those they are leading. And as Paul demonstrated in his writings, leadership does not come from a place of exclusivity or viewing oneself as superior to those that they are leading but in serving them with humility.

Leaders today are paving the path for what leadership tomorrow will look like. When a leader leads from an unhealthy and ungodly pedestaled position of superiority or exclusivity, they replicate those leadership values in the next generation of leaders. In like fashion, the leader who models biblical and true *Kingdom* leadership principles, equips and empowers the next generation of leaders with healthy paradigms and secure leadership foundations to build upon.

Don't Pedestal Actual *"Celebrities"*

As a side-note for leaders, I'd like to address another thought on the flip side of *"celebrity culture"* in the church. Years ago, I was at a conference where the guest speaker was one of the most *"famous"* pastors in the United States. His opening line was, *"You all realize there is a huge difference between being famous and being preacher famous, don't you?"*

He was unquestionably the most well-known speaker in the room, yet what he was communicating was important. There is a marked difference between being genuinely famous and being something more akin to a "TikTok influencer" or a big fish in a little pond. The heart behind his statement was essentially this: *No matter how well known you may be, don't put yourself on a pedestal, and when interacting with actual celebrities, recognize that you are not operating in the same reality they are.*

I believe that distinction matters. And in this Leadership Edition of PTCD, I want to address an issue that may not be as relevant to those outside of ministry leadership, but is very important for those within it: how we, as leaders, handle *actual celebrities* when we are in a position to influence them, disciple them, mentor them, pastor them, or simply walk alongside them spiritually.

Have you ever stopped to consider what it would be like to be a celebrity who is either a Christian or someone sincerely searching for God in a culture that constantly places them on pedestals and idolizes them for their talent, influence, and fame? Furthermore, have you considered what *Post-Traumatic Church Disorder* might look like through the lens of their experiences?

If they were genuinely seeking God, healing, or mentorship, what reasons might they have for avoiding church? What experiences might make them hesitant to trust pastors or spiritual leaders? What kinds of wounds might they carry from constantly questioning whether people value them for who they are or simply for what they represent?

I've had the opportunity to observe, participate in, and at times fail at properly balancing the responsibility that comes with influencing celebrities. Between living and pastoring in Nashville, along with having a fairly significant online presence, especially during the early years of social networking, I've had the privilege of ministering to several world-famous musicians I grew up listening to, as well as some of their family members. More than once, I've looked over my shoulder during a church service and seen a rock star or country music artist sitting quietly in the row behind me. I've had dinner with some of them. I've been in their homes. In some cases, I didn't even realize they were believers until I recognized them in one of our services and we eventually got to know each other.

What I have learned is that many people who live constantly in the public eye become understandably guarded because nearly everywhere they go, they encounter people looking for ways to benefit from proximity to them. Sometimes it is people trying to gain something through association. Sometimes it is people pursuing relationship because of what they do instead of who they are. And sometimes it is people placing unrealistic expectations on them that are neither fair nor healthy.

I have heard stories from celebrities who stopped attending certain churches because they felt like they had become the poster child for a pastor's ministry rather than a person being genuinely cared for. In other words, *"Look at this picture of me with so-and-so, who now attends my church."* What should have felt like spiritual covering instead left them feeling exposed and exploited.

From what I have seen, many people who live in the public eye often feel exposed and have very few environments where they can genuinely feel covered, protected, and safe when they are out in public with their families. The church should never be one of the places where they feel exposed. It should be one of the places where they feel safest. As leaders, we can be intentional about helping make that true. This is not about putting celebrities on a pedestal. It is about recognizing that their calling and level of visibility often make them, and their families, more vulnerable and targeted than most people in our congregations. When we lead with that awareness, we are better positioned to protect them, pastor them well, and help them genuinely connect, grow, and mature in Christ.

It goes without saying that part of both the blessing and burden of being famous is that people recognize you almost everywhere you go. We cannot always control how the public responds to those they perceive as influential, talented, or important. But as leaders, we can influence how we respond, how our teams respond, and how we help our congregations interact with them in healthy and honoring ways.

I have stood beside celebrities in church environments when someone recognized them from a previous service and immediately handed them a demo CD, hoping proximity to influence might create an opportunity for themselves. I have also heard stories of production teams repeatedly placing celebrities and their families on camera during worship services, only for them to quietly leave after realizing they were being spotlighted throughout the service instead of simply being allowed to worship.

I have even had one celebrity musician tell me that he absolutely did not want to be involved in worship because music was already what he did every day for a living. What he really wanted was the opportunity to quietly serve God in another capacity, maybe with the children's ministry or the host team.

It would have been easy to assume that because he was a talented musician, his natural desire would be to stand on stage with the worship team and share his gift with the church. But in reality, his heart was simply to serve in ways that did not place him on another pedestal or draw more attention to himself.

All of these scenarios help us better understand the lens through which celebrities may experience church life and why their experiences are often far different from what most leaders might assume. But they also reveal something important: with intentionality, wisdom, and integrity, pastors and spiritual leaders have a unique opportunity to help create environments where people who often struggle to trust, connect, or feel safe can genuinely encounter God, grow spiritually, and find meaningful connection within the local church.

First, as leaders, we need to understand that influence in any capacity is a responsibility, not a privilege. Not everyone will be entrusted with a voice into the lives of those who are *famous* or *highly influential*, but for those who are, it is critical to recognize that **you must move beyond the temptation to buy into celebrity culture yourself**.

Before they are celebrities, they are children of God who need pastors and leaders in their lives. As a leader, you must guard your heart against seeing them as a way to elevate your ego, your ministry, or your reputation. Your responsibility is not to benefit *from* them, but to be a blessing *to* them. **They need a pastor. You do not need a celebrity.**

They need to know that you care about them because of who they are, not because of what they can do for your ministry, your reputation, or your platform. They need to see that you value them as people, as families, and as fellow believers, not as celebrities. They need to know they can trust you with their lives, their struggles, and the people they love most.

And honestly, from what I have seen and experienced, many celebrities carry their own version of PTCD because leaders mishandled the responsibility of influencing them spiritually. But the pastors and leaders who steward that responsibility with humility, integrity, wisdom, and genuine love often gain a significant voice into an industry where very few people feel safe enough to truly trust spiritual leadership.

I dropped that ball once without meaning to.

For a season, I was *"pastoring"* a man who had been one of my favorite rock stars when I was growing up. He was looking for a pastor and reached out to me when my *"TattooPreacher"* ministry was in its prime. He needed a pastor, and one with tattoos and piercings seemed to resonate with where he was in life.

Amazingly, God gave me quite a bit of influence with him. The Lord would speak to me prophetically about things in his life. At one point, he reached out to a mutual friend and said, *"It's freaky. Aaron reaches out to me at the exact moments I need to hear from God and says exactly what I need to hear."*

He invited me into his home. He showed me what he was working on in the studio. He introduced me to his mother. We were beginning to develop a real friendship.

And then I made a mistake.

His mother was fighting a very serious health battle. Around that time, our church had a guest speaker with a strong reputation for praying for people and seeing miraculous healings. I took that guest speaker to my favorite restaurant, and over dinner I shared with him about my *rock star* friend and his mother. My heart was to try to set something up for him to pray with her.

But it was a crowded Friday night at a very popular steakhouse in Nashville, and I failed to be mindful of my surroundings.

I said my friend's name loudly enough that I believe someone overheard me sharing his and his mother's private business, someone who also knew exactly who he was. At the time, I didn't think much of it. But afterward, I remembered there had been another very *"rock star-looking"* guy with long hair sitting not far from our table. At one point, I noticed him looking at me with what seemed like disgust. I didn't understand it then, but later it began to make sense.

After that night, my friend never returned my calls.

I even called him the very next day to try to set up a meeting for him with the evangelist who was visiting our church. But after a few weeks of him avoiding my calls, it became painfully clear that something had shifted.

The only conclusion I could come to was that my conversation had been overheard, word had gotten back to him, and I had violated a trust. I opened my mouth when I should have protected him. And in doing so, I burned a bridge of influence that God had given me.

I saw him in public one time after that, and he barely acknowledged me.

I was left to piece it together on my own, but I am fairly certain that someone who knew him overheard what I said, passed it along, and made it clear that I had failed to protect him in an environment where I should have.

As a rule of thumb, I would recommend that you allow them to set the parameters for your friendship. Just because they invite you into their home to eat dinner with their wife and kids does not mean they are comfortable with you posting pictures on your social networks with them. There is wisdom in remembering that Scripture warns us not to assume the seat of honor or exalt ourselves in the presence of kings. In other words, do not *presume upon access.* Let trust, honor, and relationship unfold at the pace they are willing to give it. Let them post the pic on their social networks and then you repost it. Let them say, *"this is my pastor or friend"* before you mistakenly define the parameters of the relationship with assumption.

There are a lot of ways trust can be broken in situations like this. Celebrities can easily feel used or exposed by leaders they trusted when their names are dropped in environments that leave them feeling vulnerable instead of protected.

My own indiscretion cost me influence and a relationship with someone

I genuinely cared about.

Celebrity Does Not Equal Leader

Another very important issue that I believe every Christian leader should be mindful of, and one I have seen backfire in ways that caused significant damage to a celebrity's spiritual growth, is when pastors take newly *converted* celebrities and quickly platform them with leadership influence.

It is not wise to give a new believer a significant voice of spiritual influence simply because they already had a significant public voice as a celebrity.

1 Timothy 3:6 makes this very clear. In Paul's qualifications for overseers, he says a leader must not be a novice, or a new convert, lest being lifted up with pride he fall into condemnation. In other words, Scripture warns us not to elevate young believers too quickly. Why? Because platform before maturity can become spiritually dangerous... even detrimental. When someone is given influence before their character and foundation are ready to support it, the pressure and attention can set them up for pride, confusion, and failure.

I could point to several examples where Christian leaders were instrumental in a celebrity coming to faith and then, almost immediately, positioned them as the newest and most exciting face of Christianity. But leaders have to realize that everything is still so *new to them*. They are often barely able to define what they believe or explain why they believe it, and when platformed too quickly, suddenly they are thrust into a whole new arena of pressure, influence, and expectation that they do not yet understand how to carry.

And that is unfair to them.

It is unfair because when they fail, and especially early on they likely will, they can feel as though they have let God, their leaders, and the people they were prematurely positioned to influence down. There is a pressure that comes with the spotlight, a pressure to be more than they yet understand how to carry. And when they fail to meet the *group-think* expectations of other believers, harsh judgment often follows.

I can tell you from personal experience as a lifelong Christian who has not always met the *appearance-based* expectations that many so-called *Christians* have had for me, that I have had some horribly hateful things said about me and deeply unfair judgments made against me. And the harshest of those accusations have absolutely come from people who were supposed to be my *brothers and sisters in Christ.*

In recent years, I watched this same kind of *"celebrity exaltation"* happen again with a world-famous tattoo artist. I am paraphrasing what I understood her to say, but when I read about her experience, she communicated that some of the most hateful and judgmental treatment she had received in her very young journey as a Christian had come from people who claimed to represent Christ.

When that happens, the danger is great for a new believer to confuse the difference between how God feels about them and how people who misrepresent Him are treating them. That confusion can create distance between them and the very people who should be helping disciple and strengthen them. And if they become bitter toward the church because of how they are treated, that bitterness can also distort how they process God and His love for them.

During the writing of this book, a very popular music artist who has openly acknowledged a deeply checkered past, including prison, and whose wife has had an equally difficult history, came to a new understanding of who he is in Christ and publicly professed his faith in Jesus. He even released a song with a very well-known worship artist. And in traditional Christian fashion, I watched leaders far too quickly pedestal him as the newest and greatest representative of the Kingdom.

Don't get me wrong, I think it is a great thing when people, including celebrities, publicly profess Jesus, and I believe the church should rejoice with them in their newfound faith. **But there is a difference between public profession and pedestaled influence.**

With this man, I saw an enormous amount of pressure being placed on him to become the latest and greatest face of Christianity. And when I saw that happening, I literally said to myself, *"Goodness, they are setting him up for failure."*

Fast forward just a few months, and a very close friend of mine sent me a video about him made by some self-appointed Christian judge declaring, *"insert celebrity name here is not a real Christian, and this is why..."* The video then proceeded, point by point, to dismantle the message of grace as it applied to this man and his wife. They criticized his language, his Nashville-themed nightclub and its décor, his wife, and her clothing choices.

My friend asked me, *"What do you think about this?"*

I pointed out that there were so many unknown variables that neither I nor this guy who made the video could possibly know. When was the theme of the bar decided? Is it solely owned by him, or are there investors involved who designed and approved the branding, imagery, and contracts attached to his name? And even if every part of it was recently decided personally by him, it goes without saying that he is still a very young believer. Instruction on becoming a godly man should come from the pastors, leaders, and mentors in his life when his choices do not reflect Jesus.

I reminded my friend that Paul wrote 1 and 2 Corinthians to a church full of people who had spent their entire lives immersed in pagan worship and ungodly practice. It took a *"Paul"* to confront and correct what would have otherwise seemed *normal* to them because it had been part of their culture, upbringing, and way of life. They were doing CRAZY things in the church even after coming to know Jesus, and *pastor Paul* addressed it. As Scripture says, how will they know without a teacher?

While a man is spiritually transformed when he is saved, it often takes considerable time, discipleship, and leadership input before his life begins to reflect the Christ who has saved him, especially if he spent years living in ways that were completely contrary to the truth before coming to know Jesus. Salvation is instantaneous, sanctification usually takes time and discipleship.

My point to my friend was simple. God, in His love, kindness, and faithfulness, drew this man to Himself and began a good work in him. And it is God who will be faithful to complete that work. But more often than not, that is a process. It takes time. And it is worked out over a lifetime of successes, plateaus, failures, and growth as a person becomes the man or woman God created them to be.

I share these thoughts because I've either been directly involved in, or close enough to observe, situations where I have seen leaders both succeed and fail in ministering to this demographic. That is why I believe it is important to challenge leaders to be mindful of the process God has people in when He gives you influence in the lives of influencers. **Do not rush them, and do not rush the process God has them in.** Lead that relationship with wisdom and discernment.

Jesus said in Matthew 11, *"Come unto me, all you who are weary and heavy laden, and I will give you rest."* The key word there is rest. Yet far too often, the church has become known for placing heavy yokes on people, pressuring them to quickly become *"like us,"* and then either exalting them or condemning them based on how well they measure up. That creates a no-win situation where people feel they must either put on a front or risk being alienated. But 2 Corinthians tells us that we are ambassadors of reconciliation, pleading with people, *"Come back to God."* That should be the heart of every leader and every believer in how we walk with and lead those who are new in the faith.

Remember, the key components of godly leadership are to **protect and empower** people. And when it comes to celebrities, because of their level of influence and the unique temptations and pressures that surround them, it takes a great deal of intentionality, trustworthiness, and integrity to lead them where God wants to take them while protecting their hearts and empowering the *calling* He has placed on their lives. Do not let your need for influence hinder their spiritual progress. And do not let your ego turn someone else's journey into your opportunity. Be cautious not to use the people God has called you to love.

It can be just as damaging to place *celebrity* in leadership before they are ready as it is to place *charisma* in leadership before character has been fully developed.

Charismatic Advancement and Its Impact on Staff Culture

When advancement, promotion, and favoritism are based primarily on charisma or public performance, it fosters an unhealthy staff culture where team leaders compete to outshine one another rather than focusing on serving, protecting, and empowering those they are called to lead.

This creates a spirit of comparison and competition, breeding strife within the team and undermining Godly principles of love, stewardship, and collaboration. Instead of embracing their unique roles as co-laborers in the body of Christ, leaders in this unhealthy staff culture become more focused on personal recognition and often lose sight of fulfilling their true calling.

As discussed in the previous chapter on the *deception of discontentment*, one of the Ten Commandments states, *"Thou shalt not covet,"* which, at its core, can be understood as *"Thou shalt not compare."* Yet, when a staff culture prioritizes performance over anointing and character, it inevitably makes comparison and competition the standard for promotion.

When this happens, the culture of leadership shifts from *pure* to *pride*. Those with true God-given leadership anointing—who refuse to engage in political maneuvering, flattery, or the pursuit of elite status—often bow out, seeking environments where they are valued for their heart to love and serve people, rather than their ability to perform for them.

I recently read, *"The best Teams are made up of a bunch of nobodies who love everybody and serve anybody and don't care about becoming somebody."*[xxiv] *When ministry becomes performance, then the sanctuary becomes a theatre, the congregation becomes an audience, worship becomes entertainment, and man's applause and approval become the measure of success.*[xxv] When you reward *performance* you produce *entertainers*—not generals. Performers aren't equipped for battle, but generals are! We are called to war, not the Grammys or the Oscars!

Why We Do What We Do

While taking classes to learn to be a more professional speaker, or dressing in the latest trendy style, or carrying yourself with the most confident projection of personality, or studying to present the most thought-provoking content, or learning *how to win friends and influence people* can significantly up your influence as a leader, if all of those things are not built on the foundation of genuinely loving God, loving people, and serving those you are leading from the Godly leadership standard of protecting and empowering people, it's not *God's Kingdom* you are building, it's *Pride's*. Leadership from a Kingdom perspective should always be focused on filling your leadership lane by protecting, equipping, and empowering those you are called to lead.

Pedestals are Unhealthy for Everyone

Within the church, there's often a delicate balance between honoring our leaders and placing them on an unhealthy pedestal that was never meant for them. And when I say *"unhealthy pedestal,"* I'm not just referring to the impact on the followers—it can be just as damaging to the leader.

The enemy is always looking for ways to twist what God intended for our good. Qualities like being able to speak or convey thought exceptionally, being good-looking, a naturally magnetic personality may very well be God-given gifts designed to equip someone for their calling. But when a leader is elevated solely because of those gifts—without doing his part to develop the character to steward them well—those same strengths can become their greatest weakness. What God meant to be *tools* can quickly become *traps* when they're used to define the man instead of support the mission.

When leaders are elevated for their charisma or giftings before their character is fully formed, the risk of failure increases significantly. There's a quote that says, *"If you don't heal what hurt you, you'll bleed on people who didn't cut you"*—and nowhere is that more true than in leadership. Take insecurity, for instance. An insecure leader will often default to a secular, corporate-style *Power Pyramid* model of leadership, where positioning themselves above others helps mask their inner instability and reinforces their need for validation. This mindset makes it nearly impossible to lead from a *Kingdom* perspective, which flips the Power Pyramid upside-down and places the leader in a posture of service and empowerment. Insecurity can't handle that kind of humility. To the insecure leader, leadership is a competition, and when others excel or shine, it feels like a threat to their leadership position instead of a victory for it.

But what if they had a mentor—someone who could speak directly to that insecurity and help shape their character before they were ever thrust into leadership? What if, through that guidance, they learned to recognize and rise above the limitations of such a significant leadership hurdle? Not only could they have become healthier leaders themselves, but they might also have been equipped to raise up a new generation of healthy leaders—including those facing the very same insecurity they once overcame.

The issue arises when individuals are elevated to leadership too soon—while still operating from a place of brokenness—and begin to interpret promotion or outward success, driven by charisma and performance, as validation. When character strongholds remain unaddressed, these early successes can falsely appear as God's approval or indifference toward their undeveloped integrity. As a result, those celebrated for their charisma before cultivating godly character often justify their sin or distorted thinking by reasoning, *"I must be doing fine—God is clearly blessing me with influence and growth."*

Don't be misled by this illusion. People can be incredibly fickle and often lack discernment. They're drawn to *"celebrity"* and feel validated by associating with something—or someone—they perceive as greater than themselves. As a result, if you're more charismatic, better looking, or more culturally relevant than they are, you'll naturally attract followers who don't possess those same qualities. But don't confuse attraction with leadership— being appealing isn't the same as being equipped to lead.

It is absolutely possible to be called by God and do what He has called you to do THE WRONG WAY. In a similar fashion, you can also step out and do it at the WRONG TIME before you are ready. The Bible tells us in Romans 11:29 that God calls people *without repentance*; in other words, when He places a calling in you, He doesn't take it away. And furthermore, he's not removing the gifts (resources) that He put in you to accomplish that calling.

One essential truth every called and charismatic leader must grasp is this: while God may have gifted you with tools and talents, the greater responsibility lies with you. There's one thing God will not do for you— develop your character and integrity. That part is yours to pursue. Stewarding the gifts He placed within you requires intentional growth, maturity, and accountability. And thanks to free will, the decision to develop into the kind of leader who can carry those gifts well is 100% yours to make.

If you believe God has called you to lead others, then you must invest just as much—if not more—intentional effort into developing integrity, godly character, and love as you do into honing your gifts and talents. Neglecting this inner foundation leaves a wide-open door for the enemy to destroy your influence down the road—and tragically, he'll use *you* to do it.

Integrity, Trust, and Unnecessary Offense

A person's character is ultimately defined by whether or not they exercise integrity, and one of the greatest contributing factors I have experienced as the source of PTCD (*Post-Traumatic Church Disorder*) in people's lives is when a leader does not embody integrity. Many leaders would quickly summarize integrity as a *moral compass* where sin is not a dominant force in their lives, but *integrity is* actually much more than that and should be understood before one assumes to operate in it. So many unnecessary (but justifiable) offenses could be avoided if leaders were simply intentional to walk with integrity.

Integrity, at its foundation, is about living with honesty and unwavering moral conviction. It means choosing to do what is right—even when it's hard, inconvenient, or unseen—and being someone others can trust and depend on.

Here's a more detailed breakdown:
- Honesty and Truthfulness:
  - Integrity is fundamentally about being truthful and honest in your actions and words.
- Strong Moral Principles:
  - It involves adhering to a strong and unwavering code of ethics and values.
- Consistency:
  - Integrity means acting in accordance with your values, even when it's challenging or unpopular. Doing what you say you will do.
- Trustworthiness:
  - A person with integrity is someone you can rely on and trust, as they are known for being honest and ethical. Honoring your word.
- Incorruptibility:
  - Individuals with integrity are not easily swayed or influenced by external pressures, and they remain true to their moral compass.
- Doing the Right Thing:
  - Integrity is about consistently choosing to do what is right, even when it's not the easiest or most convenient option.

As has been stated in earlier chapters, you don't have to tell people what you believe; your actions show them because you live out your values and belief systems. If you truly value people and believe that they are important, you will display that by responding to them in ways that show them that they are valued. On the flip side of that coin, if you actually see yourself as more important than others, you will also display that in your responses.

Matthew 5:37a (AMPC)
37 Let your Yes be simply Yes, and your No be simply No;

Leaders should do what they say they will do. People are watching.

What You Tolerate, You Authorize to Exist

A few weeks ago, I had breakfast with a friend who travels as an evangelist, and our conversation turned to the topic of integrity—specifically the importance of keeping your word and following through on commitments. I shared with him that one of the most common integrity issues I've observed among Christian leaders, particularly pastors, is how they handle other people's time—whether they honor it or take it for granted.

Time is the most valuable asset any of us possess. We can't create more of it, and once it's gone, it's gone for good. That's why giving someone your time is one of the greatest gifts you can offer—because it's truly irreplaceable. So when you make an appointment and promise to be there, integrity keeps that promise. If you genuinely value people, you'll honor their time by showing up when you said you would.

As I shared with my friend, people of strong character honor their commitments. Yet, in my experience, pastors often have a reputation for running late. While occasional delays are understandable, chronic tardiness reveals a deeper issue—one that ultimately reflects a lack of integrity.

I'm not suggesting that a pastor who is consistently late lacks *all* integrity. However, failing to prioritize other people's time is undeniably an integrity issue—whether it's intentional or simply an overlooked area that needs attention.

The cause may be poor time management, inadequate planning, lack of margin, an inability to say no, or even maybe it's simply inconvenient for them to show up on time. However, failing to honor commitments and respect others' time, regardless of the reason, sends a clear message: *their time and priorities are not as important as yours*. Over time, this inconsistency affects how people perceive your reliability and trustworthiness, ultimately becoming a reflection of your integrity as a leader.

After I shared those thoughts with him, he said, *"I never really considered that before."* My response to him was, *"That is the problem; most don't consider it."*

Most of us have had our leaders respond to us in such a way that when we do it to others, we don't even consider it a poor reflection of our leadership or integrity. We are just "cutting the ends off the ham like grandma did." But that doesn't excuse the lack of integrity at the root of the actions.

I went on to explain to him that I believe the weakest forms of leadership in churches today often model one or more of these characteristics:

- An inability to balance their calendar (always late)
- A failure to honor commitments
- Leading from a place of insecurity
- Leading from a place of micromanagement or control
- Responding as divas who place themselves on pedestals, view themselves as elite, and expect honor from others before demonstrating honor themselves.

When leaders adopt these patterns, they undermine their leadership foundation, diminish their ministry's effectiveness, and drive away strong leaders—often the very ones God may have sent to serve alongside them, but who value character and integrity over charisma and won't serve weak leadership long-term.

Integrity Impacts Influence

To help drive home this point about integrity, honoring your word, and honoring others, I want to share a story that would almost be funny—if it weren't true. To this day, whenever it crosses my mind, I still shake my head and laugh in disbelief that it actually happened to me. I feel safe telling it because I'm 100% certain the person involved will never read this book—and aside from my wife, no one else knows who he is.

A pastor friend of mine once called and invited me to be his guest at an event in a major city. The event included a nice dinner followed by a concert. It sounded like a great time, and I thought it would be nice to catch up with him, so I agreed to make the drive and meet up with him.

Now, after being in ministry for a long time, I understand how unpredictable pastoral schedules can be. Emergencies happen—but more often than not, SO DOES POOR CALENDAR MANAGEMENT. (That lack of planning is actually the cause of many of the offenses people experience with church leaders.) Wanting to be proactive, I called him the day before to confirm our plans. He assured me everything was still on.

So, I drove to his city, arrived early, and called him about 30 to 45 minutes before our scheduled meeting to finalize the details. I was taken aback by how flippantly he responded when he said, *"Hey Aaron, I'm sorry man—I ran into [insert celebrity's name here], and I gave him your ticket to the event...but go grab some dinner somewhere in the city on me and I'll send you the money to reimburse you..."*

I absolutely COULD NOT BELIEVE the lack of consideration or integrity that I was experiencing at that moment. I just laughed, thinking, *"You have got to be kidding me! There is no way this just happened! Who does that to people?!"*

There was no heads-up. No courtesy call. No recognition of the time I had set aside, the distance I'd traveled, or the family time I gave up to be there. The plans changed—not because something *urgent* came up—but because a *more convenient, ego-boosting* opportunity presented itself, and he chose that over honoring our plans.

Let me be clear to any future leaders reading this: DON'T EVER DO THAT TO PEOPLE! It is horrible leadership!

Integrity honors commitments. It values others and respects their time. What this pastor did was incredibly inconsiderate and dishonoring. Whether he realized it or not, his actions sent a loud and clear message about how much—or how little—he valued me, and how highly he viewed himself in comparison.

While I still have a hard time believing he responded to me that way—and I'd definitely be hesitant to prioritize time with him again—I'm not angry anymore. I was upset in the moment, but I've moved past it. I'm sharing this story now simply to offer a clear, real-world example of how some leaders treat people—and why that kind of response is not acceptable. If it happened to me, there are (or will likely be) parallels in your experiences.

It's up to you to lead with integrity. Strong people will not follow weak leadership long-term. They may extend a season of grace, assessing whether their gifts can help balance what is lacking in an organization and if those resources will be valued and utilized. That season of grace may even be extended by the leading of the Holy Spirit, who had a reason for sending them there in the first place. However, if there is no intentional effort to embrace growth, change, or exemplify integrity, they will eventually move on—leaving the organization to miss out on the very gift in them that God had sent to strengthen it.

Most leaders go their entire careers believing they are good leaders, never fully recognizing the traits in their leadership style that may be sabotaging their effectiveness and placing a ceiling on their progress.

The reality is, most people don't confront leaders with hard truths. They communicate approval or disapproval through loyalty—or by leaving. When people reach the point where they can no longer tolerate the issues within an organization, they often *quit* rather than have the uncomfortable conversation.

As a result, leaders often explain turnover as a flaw in those who left rather than pausing to consider whether something in their own leadership contributed to the departure. It's far easier to label people as disloyal, uncommitted, immature, or quitters than to examine whether we created an environment where they no longer felt compelled to cast their vote of confidence with their presence.

But the truth remains: the buck stops at the top. The success or failure of any organization rests primarily on the leader and the habits that shape their leadership.

No one is a perfect leader. Even as I write this, I'm aware that I likely carry traits that limit me from leading to my fullest potential.

But if you're willing to look at yourself honestly in the mirror of this text and ask, "How much of this applies to me?" you may discover the very breakthrough that takes you to your next level of leadership.

And if you've felt *plateaued*, you may finally understand why.

You may be Solomon in wisdom, or David in praise, or Abraham in faith, or Joshua in war, but if you're not Joseph in discipline, you'll end up like Samson in destruction.[xxvi]

Whether you are leading a family, a class, a team, or a church, remember that YOU are the leader. What you tolerate in your own life, you ultimately authorize to exist within your organization.

If you want people to trust you, you must model trustworthiness. You must demonstrate time management if you expect volunteers to be on time for Sunday service. If you want people to uphold strong moral standards, you must lead with consistency. If honesty and integrity matter to you, you must embody them yourself. If you expect people to do what is right, you must show them what it looks like—even when it's inconvenient. This includes something as simple as keeping your word and showing up on time for the commitments you make. Charisma can't take you there; only character can.

In a world that constantly affirms performance over purity and elevates style over substance, it's critical that we—as Kingdom leaders—return to the foundation of what truly matters: character, integrity, and servant-hearted leadership. The damage caused by elevating charisma over character is real, and it has left countless individuals wounded and disillusioned. But there is hope for a different kind of leadership—one that refuses to compromise values for applause or anointing for affirmation. It starts with us. It starts with the daily decision to walk in humility, to honor others, to live with conviction, and to lead with purpose. You may have the gifting, the platform, and the influence—but if you don't also have integrity, the weight of your calling has the capacity to crush you. So let this be the moment you draw a line in the sand. From this day forward, choose to build your leadership on the foundation of character, not just charisma. You're the leader, so lead with integrity.

Chapter Nine
Trauma Lenses

Anyone who has ever experienced trauma understands that there are moments in life when a single experience can fracture the lens through which they've always viewed the world. For many, trauma doesn't just wound—it redefines. Whether it comes through betrayal, abuse, or disillusionment, these moments can shift our spiritual and emotional vision in ways that are often long-lasting. In this chapter, we will explore how trauma—particularly when it happens within trusted institutions like the church—alters our perception of leadership, faith, and even God Himself. Through personal narrative and parallel experiences, we'll uncover how deeply these distortions run, why they matter, and how healing begins with first acknowledging the cracks in the lens.

As we explained in previous chapters, leadership often plays a key role in whether or not people have a positive or negative church experience. Healthy leaders can create an environment within their organization for their team and congregants to grow and flourish, while unhealthy leaders have the capacity to be the catalyst for the PTCD (*Post-Traumatic Church Disorder*) that people experience.

To help illustrate how trauma can reshape even a strong believer's spiritual perspective, I want to share a personal story that isn't about *"church"* but reveals how traumatic experiences altered the way I viewed the world.

After just three years as a police officer, I was honored as *"Officer of the Year,"* which led to a promotion to the S.W.A.T. team and a position as a detective sergeant in the Criminal Investigations Division. On my very first day as a detective, my Lieutenant called me into his office and said, *"Aaron, this job is going to change you."* He liked me and respected my ministry background but understood how limited my exposure had been to the *"darker side"* of human nature.

At the time, I all but dismissed his warning. From my perspective, it was a secular viewpoint from someone who didn't really understand a believer's mental and spiritual capacity in this field. What I heard when he said this was, *"You're weaker than you know…"* but what he was actually saying had nothing to do with strength or weakness, and I understand now he was simply warning me that, *"You can't experience the things you will experience and it not impact you…"* and he was right. I was convinced that my faith gave me an advantage the Lieutenant couldn't relate to. I thought I would be the exception to his rule.

Looking back, I now realize how naïve I was. I didn't know what I didn't know. What shattered my worldview the most wasn't just the criminals I was commissioned to protect my community from but the realization that corruption also existed on my own side of the law—within government leaders, attorneys, judges, and even fellow officers. It was this discovery— the betrayal of those I expected to uphold justice—that disillusioned me the most. My Lieutenant understood this reality through years of experience, but I had yet to learn it firsthand. He was a good man who served for the right reasons, and he knew that what I was about to witness would change my entire perception of justice.

I've come to describe this experience as *"seeing behind Oz's curtain,"* referencing *The Wizard of Oz*, when Dorothy and her friends discover that the all-powerful wizard was just an ordinary man behind a curtain, flipping switches and speaking into a microphone.

When the clear distinction between good guys and bad guys became blurred, it deeply impacted my ability to trust those in positions of power. It forced me to question everything, making me wonder whether I ever truly knew who the good and bad guys were. And just as my Lieutenant had warned me on that first day—that perspective changed me.

The impact proved to be long-lasting when, even years after retiring, my eight-year-old son Rocky asked me one day while driving down the highway, *"Daddy, why don't you trust people…?"* I'm not sure what I projected or what he heard me say that brought him to that conclusion, but it troubled me to admit to myself that this was what he perceived about his father—and he was right.

I'll admit that, in the beginning, my perspectives and distrust were fueled by pessimism. However, I've long since moved past that. It's no longer about being pessimistic—it's about having a clearer understanding of what reality actually is. My perspective has shifted, and I've had to learn how to navigate and function within this new, *informed* reality.

The Parallel

If you've experienced PTCD (*Post-Traumatic Church Disorder*), you'll instantly recognize the parallels in my detective story. The moment when rose-colored glasses are shattered is a universal human experience. At some point, everyone encounters pain or trauma that alters how they see the world (if not permanently, at least temporarily.)

However, the impact can be even deeper when this happens in a spiritual context. Churches and spiritual leaders are supposed to be *"safe places"*— the *"good guys"* you can trust. When that trust is broken, it has the capacity to create a profound crisis in how you perceive faith, leadership, community, and sometimes even God.

God's Word reminds us in Matthew 11:28: *"Come to me, all who are weary and burdened, and I will give you rest."* Similarly, 1 Peter 5:7 instructs us to *"Cast all your cares upon the Lord, for He cares for you."*

But when trauma and deep-seated wounds occur within the church, it can feel as though the very place you once turned to for peace, rest, and safety has been tainted—leaving you disoriented and unsure of where to find safety or refuge.

When someone's home is burglarized, the violation runs deeper than just the loss of possessions—it shatters their sense of safety and trust in what was once their *secure* place. The same is true, and often even more devastating, when the trauma comes from within the church—from God's people, spiritual leaders, or those who were supposed to represent Him.

Before becoming a police officer, I expected bad people to do bad things. But when I saw wrongdoings committed by those I considered the *"good guys"*—even individuals I previously respected—the disillusionment was profound. The same applies to spiritual leadership.

Imagine being taught all your life to call the police for help, only to have them show up and be the very ones to harm you. The betrayal and violation of that moment could completely distort your perception of law enforcement as a whole.

Likewise, when we turn to spiritual leaders for guidance, protection, and Godly wisdom, only to experience hurt or betrayal at their hands, it can deeply impact our trust in the entire institution of spiritual leadership— making it difficult to separate God from the failures of those who were meant to represent Him.

I've heard people use the analogy of a restaurant when talking about PTCD events and say, *"If you had a bad experience at a restaurant, you wouldn't quit going to restaurants altogether, would you?!"* The problem with that analogy, like the guy who said, *"When life deals you lemons, make lemonade,"* it's not taking into consideration the totality of the circumstances or the depth of pain that may have been experienced. When someone is deeply wounded in church, they aren't being wounded or having their trust betrayed by food; they have been traumatized by people who, many times, are even closer to them than family – that kind of pain cannot be trivialized.

When I was around 8 or 9 years old, my pastor was caught in a sexual affair. Even forty years later, I still know people from that church who quit attending and have never returned. The pain and betrayal they felt cut so deeply that some never recovered.

While we all understand that placing leaders on pedestals is unhealthy and that no one's failure should have the power to dictate the course of our lives, that doesn't erase the reality of the damage caused. My pastor's choices and actions deeply wounded people, leading to devastating consequences.

We know it's not wise to give individuals that much influence over us, nor is it healthy for them to hold such power. However, in a fallen world, outside of ideal circumstances, the disillusionment and pain caused by a leader who *"should have been better"* but wasn't are very real.

Even Jesus reminds us in Luke 12:48 that to whom much is given, much is required. Whether you're a parent, teacher, employer, or pastor, those who lead in the Kingdom of God are entrusted with the hearts and growth of God's children. That kind of responsibility calls for a deeper level of care and intentionality—because the weight of influence carried by spiritual leaders is no small thing.

At this stage in my life and healing journey, I find myself in a different place of wholeness and perspective regarding PTCD (*Post-Traumatic Church Disorder*) than I once was. As I outlined this chapter and reflected on the many instances of failed spiritual leadership I've personally witnessed, I was shocked by how much I had forgotten. It wasn't just one experience—it was many.

Looking back, I can recall countless examples of leaders misrepresenting God through their actions—fornication, adultery, child abuse, broken promises, financial dishonesty, blatant lying, manipulation, insecurity, arrogance, double standards, abuse of authority, betrayal of trust, selfish ambition, and even intentionally harming others for personal gain. When I say I could go on and on, I don't mean that figuratively. And that's just events from my story—what about yours?

In every one of *my* situations, many others were affected—people who shared in the hurt and fallout caused by leaders who were supposed to represent God but failed to do so.

If you've been one of those leaders and are feeling convicted or condemned by what has been written so far, please know this—later chapters will explore grace, redemption, reconciliation, and how to process these failures through a Godly lens. However, before healing can begin for those who have been deeply wounded, it is necessary to acknowledge the reality of these events—they have happened, they do happen, and they absolutely create real obstacles for those who are left spiritually wounded and disillusioned.

Though trauma can distort our perception and cause deep spiritual disorientation, it doesn't have to define the rest of our story. Yes, pain alters the lens through which we see—but we are not powerless. At some point, we are each faced with a decision: will we continue to live defined by what was done to us, or will we choose to rise, reclaim our vision, and walk in the wholeness God still offers? In the next chapter, we'll begin to explore what it looks like to shift from being a victim of *church hurt* to becoming a victor in spite of it—not by ignoring the wounds, but by refusing to let them have the final say.

Trauma has a way of leaving us stuck between what happened to us and who we believe we still are because of it. It can feel like the pain handed to us by others is now the story we're forced to carry—but what if it isn't? What if the defining line between staying wounded and stepping into healing begins not with what was done to us but with how we choose to respond?

Those who have suffered trauma at the hands of others often describe a profound sense of helplessness. It can feel like being trapped in limbo—where you have no control over what happened to you, yet you're the one left picking up the broken pieces of a painful experience, uncertain how to heal or move forward.

In this space, disillusionment can set in quickly. Much like the biblical story of Terah we shared in a previous chapter, settling in Haran, there's a strong temptation to give up on the journey when those who were supposed to love and protect you let you down. It becomes easy to adopt an *"If you can't beat them, join them"* mentality—settling for less than what God intended rather than pressing forward into healing and restoration.

Receiving Dishonor

"Honor creates identity shifts and opens new spheres of authority. The enemy also knows that dishonor restricts the identity and authority we will need to fulfill God's amazing plan for our lives that will help so many others. He can't cancel the plans of heaven, so he creates events specifically intended to dishonor us." – Dale Mast[xxvii]

It was a sunny summer Nashville morning as I sat by my pool, reflecting on a passage of scripture I had just read. I was in the process of developing the content for this book, and as I meditated, my mind naturally drifted to how I had processed my own experiences with PTCD (*Post-Traumatic Church Disorder*). I wasn't feeling sorry for myself, but because I knew I would one day write about this subject, I was revisiting the sequence of events that had compounded over time and led to where, in one particular event, things ultimately ended badly.

A thought came to mind: *The Bible says that God is not mocked and that we will reap what we sow… yet, in my circumstances, when I had done my best to sow seeds of honor, the harvest I received felt nothing like the reward of those seeds.* I also reflected on the early warning signs I had once dismissed—small attitudes and subtle reactions from leaders I had trusted, who would later fall or fail. At the time, those details had seemed insignificant, but in hindsight, they were not. In criminal investigations, we call these *"tells"*—verbal or nonverbal cues that reveal deeper inclinations. In this case, the *tells* were something of a foreshadowing of things to come, and I couldn't help but wonder: *Had I discerned those tells more clearly, could I have avoided some of the challenges that came with those relationships?*

As I sat with these thoughts, God, knowing exactly what was on my heart, spoke to me: *"Aaron, you have received much dishonor."* In the moment, I was a bit surprised because I wasn't really expecting to hear anything from God, but feeling validated in my reflections, I immediately responded, *"Yes, Sir, I have."*

But then, His next words stopped me in my tracks: *"I don't think you heard me correctly. I didn't say you have 'experienced' much dishonor—I said you have 'received' much dishonor."*

I was left speechless. The Holy Spirit had just shifted my entire perspective in a moment.

There's an old saying: *"You can't always choose what happens to you, but you can choose how you respond."* In that moment, I knew God was confronting me—not about the dishonor I had experienced, but about my response to it.

Allow me to use a rather graphic but effective analogy: Imagine someone approaches you and says, *"Hold out your hands; I have a gift for you."* When you extend your hands in expectation, they suddenly reveal a fistful of fresh, mushy dog poop, and attempt to place it in your hand.

Would you accept it? Of course not!

Why? Because the very thought is disgusting—no one willingly takes hold of something so filthy. And if, by some chance, they caught you off guard and got even a little of it on you, you'd immediately do whatever was necessary to wash it off because until you do, it will contaminate everything you touch.

God revealed something powerful to me in that moment—I hadn't just *experienced* dishonor; I had *received* it. And because I held onto it, it was affecting everything I touched. It was time to let it go and wash my hands of it.

I made the statement earlier: *"The guy who said, 'When life gives you lemons, make lemonade,' has never been dealt a rotten lemon."* I still stand by this, especially when people judge another's trauma through the lens of their own experience—or, more often, their inexperience.

However, there is another side to that coin; we also have a responsibility to recognize that there is a fine line between acknowledging trauma and adopting a victim identity because of it.

Purpose can't be revealed when your identity is trauma.

Before you get upset with that statement, understand—I'm no stranger to trauma. One of the most severe experiences of my life happened when, while trying to help two men, they turned on me and tried to kill me.

That attack cost me my career, a business I built, a year in therapy, countless hours of physical rehabilitation, a brutal battle with post-traumatic stress and panic attacks, and ultimately, over a million dollars in lost wages. I paid a lot for the knowledge I have on this subject, and while my experiences may be different from yours, I'm not speaking from a theoretical position—I've lived through the physical, emotional, and financial consequences of trauma. And I've learned how to move forward without embracing a *victim's* mindset.

That doesn't mean I never struggled with feeling like a victim—in my lowest moments, it felt sometimes impossible not to see myself that way. But over time, I realized that holding onto that identity from my past was impacting my present and future. So, I made the choice to let it go—to wash my hands of it—and move forward.

We live in a society that actively encourages adopting a *victim identity*.
- Were you abused? You're a victim!
- Picked last in gym class? Victim!
- Passed over for a promotion? Victim!
- Have a learning disability? Victim!
- Too fat? Victim!
- Too skinny? Victim!
- Too white? Victim!
- Too black? Victim!
- Make too little money? Victim!
- Make too much? Victim!
- Wrongfully judged? Victim!
- Labeled unfairly? Victim!
- Not as talented? Victim!
- Not as privileged? Victim!

- People were mean to you? Victim!
- People don't agree with you? Victim!

According to today's woke culture, everyone is encouraged to see themselves as *victims.* But *wokeness breeds weakness,* and once that mindset takes root—once it is validated and affirmed by the voices around you—it becomes a stronghold in your heart and mind, one that shapes your future actions, choices, and identity.

It almost seems like those who have bought into this narrative are competing to prove who is the most victimized or oppressed and it's unprofitable for growth or advancement in life.

As a kid, I remember sitting with a group of friends when one of them would share a bad experience. Without fail, someone else would chime in, trying to one-up their suffering: *"You think that's bad? Listen to what happened to me!"*

The difference now is that we're doing it as adults, and it's being adopted as part of our identity. Pain doesn't need to be compared or measured to be valid. We don't need to justify our trauma by proving it was worse than someone else's. And we certainly don't need to wear it like a badge of dishonor influencing our view of self or a *label of limitation* for what we can become.

Good God, that mentality is the antithesis of who Christ died for you to be!

1 Corinthians 7:23 (TPT)
23 Since a great price was paid for your redemption, stop having the mindset of a slave.

In the Old Testament, when the Israelites were freed after 400 years of slavery in Egypt, it didn't take long before they began complaining and acting like captives—despite no longer being in chains. This reveals a powerful truth: you can take the slave out of Egypt, but it's much harder to take Egypt out of the slave.

They had yet to see themselves as the free children of God that they truly were—instead, they still thought and responded like the oppressed. And as long as you see yourself as a victim, you will continue to live and act as one.

I've often said, *"You don't have to tell me what you believe—your actions will show me."* Because it's undeniable: we live out what we believe.

Henry Ford was quoted as saying it this way, *"Whether you believe you can or you believe you can't, you're right."*

This concept is not just theory—it's scientific. Psychology even has a term for it: *self-fulfilling prophecy.* In simple terms, this means your beliefs shape your actions, ultimately creating the outcomes you expect.

Every enemy—whether physical or spiritual—understands this. They know that people who believe they are powerless are much easier to manipulate and control. If I were your enemy, I would take the path of least resistance: convincing you that you've already lost and are a victim. Because once you believe it, you'll start acting like one—and my work would be nearly complete.

You have a choice: You can be a victim, or you can be a victor—You can be pitiful or powerful—but you cannot be both.

This is why the way you see yourself, the identity you adopt, and the words you speak about who you believe yourself to be are so important.

Be Careful: Victim Language Can Destroy Your Potential

The Bible instructs us on several occasions regarding the words that we speak.

Job 22:28 (AMPC)
28 You shall also decide and decree a thing, and it shall be established for you; and the light [of God's favor] shall shine upon your ways.

Mark 11:23 (TPT)
23 Listen to the truth I speak to you: Whoever says to this mountain with great faith and does not doubt, 'Mountain, be lifted up and thrown into the midst of the sea,' and believes that what he says will happen, it will be done.

Proverbs 11:23-24 (TPT)
23 So above all, guard the affections of your heart, for they affect all that you are. Pay attention to the welfare of your innermost being, for from there flows the wellspring of life. 24 Avoid dishonest speech and pretentious words. Be free from using perverse words no matter what!

Luke 6:45 (TPT – Emphasis by author)
*45 People are known in this same way. Out of the virtue stored in their hearts, good and upright people will produce good fruit. Likewise, out of the evil hidden in their hearts, evil ones will produce what is evil. <u>For the overflow of what has been stored in your heart will be seen by your fruit and **will be heard in your words.**</u>*

Proverbs 18:21 (AMPC)
21 Death and life are in the power of the tongue, and they who indulge in it shall eat the fruit of it [for death or life].

The way you speak to yourself and others shapes your reality. Victim language—statements like *"It's not my fault," "I can't do anything about it,"* or *"Why does this always happen to me?"*—can subtly sabotage your growth and keep you stuck.

- Why Victim Language is Dangerous
    - **It Reinforces Helplessness:** It convinces you that external, ungodly factors control your life, leaving no room for personal responsibility, action, or power.
    - **It Kills Growth:** If you blame circumstances, you miss opportunities to learn, adapt, and improve.
    - **It Invites Negativity:** It attracts similar energy and people who reinforce a mindset of defeat.[xxviii]

You have the power to choose whether you will be the victim or the hero in your own story, and it begins with who or what you allow to define you.

Consider David—just before he defeated Goliath, his older brother Eliab belittled and disrespected him. Now, imagine if David had internalized that dishonor, allowed it to define him, and walked away instead of stepping into his destiny. The course of his entire life and the future of a nation would have been impacted.

This is a powerful reminder that opportunities to quit often come at the same moment as opportunities to rise. The choice in how you respond to those opportunities is yours.

How You See You Matters

The pit I believe many people fall into as a result of their traumatic experiences is that they accept the labels that are often associated with the pain. Do you believe that you are permanently broken? Do you accept that you are an irreparable victim? If so, then you have likely adopted a mode of operation that is consistent with the victim mentality that we are discussing. As long as you see yourself primarily through the eyes of weakness and victimization, you will respond as a *victim.*

A few years ago a close friend asked me why I hated weakness in myself so much and strived so hard toward the warrior image I projected. He asked me if I was a mamma's boy when I was a child and then asked me if I had been molested.

As he confronted me, I wanted to run. I wanted to lash out. I was so angry with his questions! Every part of me wanted to change the subject. But I knew he was right. I did hate weakness, especially in myself. And I answered him honestly, saying, *"Yes, I was molested, and I was a mamma's boy. I cried easily as a child. If another kid got yelled at in my presence by a teacher at school or their own parent, I would get nervous and get emotional. I was soft-natured."*

My friend followed up his questions with another series of questions. *"Aaron, do you believe originally that God created you as that sweet-natured child who was in touch with his feelings, felt compassion, and felt emotion?"*

I had to agree that, as weak as I perceived it to be, God had likely created me that way. His next question floored me. *"Aaron, then who do you think God would be more likely to use, the you HE created or the you that YOU have created?"*

My friend elaborated further, *"Aaron, you are the sum total of who God created you to be and your life's experiences. But as long as you fight the softness that God created you to possess so you could feel compassion and empathy, you will never be the complete leader you were created to be...Aaron, you are created to be the Mamma's Boy Warrior. Like King David, the harp player/giant slayer, or Jesus himself, who was moved with compassion by the needs of people, unless you embrace that mamma's boy, you'll never really find a place of fulfillment in your life's pursuits!"*

I had adopted a label of victimization. Because I was soft-natured and I cried easily, because the other kids made fun of me for crying, and because I was ashamed of the molestation (particularly my participation in it; I wondered if maybe I could have influenced the outcome or changed it), I adopted a self-image of being weak, even broken, in comparison to others who I thought had it more together than I did. Then, because I refused to continue to be weak, I did everything I could to become some distorted version of *strong* that I adopted along the way. I so deeply hated being the kid that the other children laughed at for crying that I spent most of my life suppressing emotion, doing that which I feared until I wasn't afraid anymore, and destroying the image of weakness in myself by lifting weights, getting strong, projecting an image of toughness, and not allowing people to walk on me.

As a result, strongholds of pride, self-assurance, self-reliance, and arrogance (all rooted in fear) set in to compensate for what I believed was *wrong* with me. The truth was, I was just a kid who had experienced hurt and carried that pain into my adulthood.

The pain was real, but the label I adopted was not![xxix]

What Does God's Word Say?

We have the opportunity to embrace labels from infinite sources telling us who we are and what we can do, but my encouragement is for you to allow God and His word to define you, not your enemy or your experiences.

So, what does God's Word say?

Romans 8:33-39 (TPT)

33 Who then would dare to accuse those whom God has chosen in love to be his? God himself is the judge who has issued his final verdict over them—"Not guilty!"

34 Who then is left to condemn us? Certainly not Jesus, the Anointed One! For he gave his life for us, and even more than that, he has conquered death and is now risen, exalted, and enthroned by God at his right hand. So how could he possibly condemn us since he is continually praying for our triumph?

35 Who could ever divorce us from the endless love of God's Anointed One? Absolutely no one! For nothing in the universe has the power to diminish his love toward us. Troubles, pressures, and problems are unable to come between us and heaven's love. What about persecutions, deprivations, dangers, and death threats? No, for they are all impotent to hinder omnipotent love, 36 even though it is written: All day long we face death threats for your sake, God. We are considered to be nothing more than sheep to be slaughtered!

37 Yet even in the midst of all these things, we triumph over them all, for God has made us to be more than conquerors, and his demonstrated love is our glorious victory over everything!

38 So now I live with the confidence that there is nothing in the universe with the power to separate us from God's love. I'm convinced that his love will triumph over death, life's troubles, fallen angels, or dark rulers in the heavens. There is nothing in our present or future circumstances that can weaken his love. 39 There is no power above us or beneath us— no power that could ever be found in the universe that can distance us from God's passionate love, which is lavished upon us through our Lord Jesus, the Anointed One!

Romans 8 declares who you truly are in Christ: You are not guilty. You are not condemned. You are loved. You are triumphant. You are more than a conqueror. You are victorious over everything! No matter what has happened in your past, God says you are NOT a victim!

Think about this—you have survived 100% of your worst days, and you're still standing. There are very few things in life with a 100% success rate, but this is one of them! Every scheme the enemy has used to steal from you, break you, or destroy you has failed.

You are still here! You are a victor—just like God says you are!

Choosing to walk as a victor rather than a victim doesn't just change your personal story—it strengthens the greater story God is writing through you as a part of His body. When individuals begin to see themselves the way God sees them—healed, whole, and empowered—it becomes the foundation for something far more powerful than just personal breakthroughs. It becomes the starting point for collective restoration. Because when victors come together—refusing to be divided by offense, fear, or past wounds—the Body of Christ becomes an unstoppable force. In the next chapter, we'll explore how healing is multiplied when unity is prioritized and why the Church is always strongest when it stands together.

Chapter Eleven
The Strength Of The Wolf

P TCD isn't just the byproduct of bad church experiences—it's the result of a *strategic assault* on believers designed to wound deeply enough to drive them into isolation. Like any effective strategy of war, the enemy knows that if he can't destroy you directly, he can at least try to convince you to walk away from your assignment, abandon your community, and disconnect from the very body that was designed to bring you strength. This chapter pulls back the curtain on one of hell's most calculated tactics: emasculating the spiritual strength of those who were meant to lead and fight—by separating them from the pack, silencing their influence, and neutralizing their impact within the body of Christ.

As we have laid the groundwork up to this point, we understand *Post-Traumatic Church Disorder* is a real and complex issue. Like anything that has traumatically impacted our lives, there are propensities to allow those events to set ceilings for our progress and for the sake of healing and wholeness for all who are reading this book; I'm not content to fail in confronting and shattering those ceilings. I don't excuse the unhealthy actions projected toward us by unhealthy leaders, but each of us needs to be reminded that God is bigger than our trauma, and as we discussed in the last chapter, *"victim"* is not a label He has given us.

Why Am I Here?

Know thy enemy and know yourself; in a hundred battles, you will never be defeated
Sun Tzu - The Art of War

Have you ever felt certain that God led you to do something, only to find yourself feeling as lost as last year's Easter egg in the middle of it? Maybe you believed God directed you to a specific church, but you didn't fit in once you arrived. Or perhaps you followed His lead to take a job, yet once you got there, you struggled to see any real purpose in it.

If you've walked with God for any length of time, you've likely experienced this—or will at some point. Through the years, in moments of frustration, God has gently reminded me, *"Aaron, you're there because what you are wouldn't be there if you weren't."*

My dad has often said, *"It's not easy to remember that your original intent was to drain the swamp when you're up to your butt in alligators."* And he is right. The reality is that stepping into God's plan often reveals unexpected challenges. But the good news is that as children of God, we are never alone. We have His presence, His guidance, and His promises to sustain us—even when following His direction feels overwhelming or unclear.

Resolve In Spite of Rejection

Years ago, a friend invited me to attend a pastor's conference, where many of the attendees were leaders of some of the largest churches in the country. At the time, online ministry was booming, and as the online campus pastor for a ministry that was pioneering digital outreach, I was asked to speak at a breakout session.

The social dynamics of the conference were interesting. Most of the pastors already knew each other, and while I had met a few when they came to speak at our church, I definitely felt like an outsider. It was a bit like transferring to a new high school in your senior year, where everyone had long-established friendships. My wife and I left the conference that year feeling unsure that there was much benefit from attending.

Still, I'm not a quitter, and I genuinely wanted to build connections. So, despite the previous years' experience, we spent thousands of dollars on reservations and flights to attend again. It was even worse this time—not just distant, but blatant rejection.

At the end of the first day, one of the conference leaders took the microphone and emphasized the importance of *"connection."* He specifically said, *"If you're new here and don't know anyone, come talk to me—I'd love to connect with you."*

Later that evening, I decided to take him up on that offer. My wife was tired and went to rest, so I headed to the pool, where I saw a large group of pastors chatting and laughing. Then, I noticed the same *"come talk to me"* speaker sitting alone in the hot tub. Seeing an opportunity to introduce myself, I stepped in and said, *"I really appreciate what you said earlier about connection. My name is Aaron."*

I kid you not when I say it became the weirdest, most awkward interaction I had ever had. I'm not joking or exaggerating the details when I say, He looked at me like I was speaking a foreign language, then immediately stood up, got out of the hot tub, and walked around the pool to join the larger group of pastors on the opposite side—without acknowledging that I had spoken to him at all. I sat there alone and completely confused about what had just happened. That year, the conference ended with pretty much the same *feeling like an outsider* result as the previous year.

As a result, when it came time for the conference for the third year, I was determined to save my money and dignity by skipping it. But I felt God nudging me to go back. Frustrated, I argued, *"God, I don't want to go back. I'm not getting anything out of it."*

His response stopped me in my tracks: *"Aaron, how do you know I don't need you there—not for what you can get, but for what you can give?"*

That left me with no choice but to go.

That year, I attended with a new mindset. Instead of trying to connect with those already connected, I looked for the people who were alone—the ones like me in past years who clearly didn't know anyone. I made it my mission to ensure they didn't feel overlooked the way I had.

More than a decade later, some of the connections I made that year remain strong—proving that sometimes, God sends us places not for what we can receive but for what we can give.

The Body of Christ

It's easy to go through life focusing on what we can gain, often overlooking the greater purpose behind our God-given talents and gifts—which were designed not just for our benefit but for others in His Kingdom.

When we become believers, a spiritual transformation occurs, and we step into something far greater than ourselves. The Bible doesn't just describe this as a family—it's more profound than that. We become part of an army, a machine, or, as Romans 12 puts it, a BODY, where every member is essential to the overall function. Nothing and no one is insignificant in God's design.

Romans 12:4-8 (TPT)
4 In the human body there are many parts and organs, each with a unique function. 5 And so it is in the body of Christ. For though we are many, we've all been mingled into one body in Christ. This means that we are all vitally joined to one another, with each contributing to the others.
6 God's marvelous grace imparts to each one of us varying gifts. So if God has given you the grace-gift of prophecy, activate your gift by using the proportion of faith you have to prophesy. 7 If your grace-gift is serving, then thrive in serving others well. If you have the grace-gift of teaching, then be actively teaching and training others. 8 If you have the grace-gift of encouragement, then use it often to encourage others. If you

have the grace-gift of giving to meet the needs of others, then may you prosper in your generosity without any fanfare. If you have the gift of leadership, be passionate about your leadership. And if you have the gift of showing compassion, then flourish in your cheerful display of compassion.

When we embrace our gifts, uniqueness, and calling without elevating our own importance above others, we begin to operate as God intended—working together, complementing one another, and striving toward a shared Kingdom purpose. Just like a football team moves toward the end zone, we are all called to advance God's mission together.

The saying *"Teamwork makes the dream work"* is especially true in the Kingdom of God and the Body of Christ. The hand cannot function without the arm, the arm depends on the torso, and even the seemingly insignificant baby toe plays a vital role in balance. Beyond what is visible, internal organs like the heart, lungs, and liver are essential for life, and even on a microscopic level, the body relies on blood cells to carry oxygen. Every part, no matter how seen or unseen, plays a critical role—just as every believer has a purpose in God's greater plan.

There is no scenario in which individual parts of the body of Christ function independently from the rest of the whole. We are all vitally interconnected for the overall health and life of the body. This single analogy is one of the most essential lessons for any believer or Christian leader to understand and embrace.

I used to say, "If you will take care of me, I will take care of you. "Now I say, I will take care of me for you, if you will take care of you for me."
— Jim Rohn[xxx]

None of us are more or less essential in the body of Christ and our enemy knows it! I believe this is why he works so hard to deceive us into pridefully overvaluing (or insecurely undervaluing) ourselves or others in an attempt to cripple the body by separating essential parts from their God-ordained function within the body. You don't *just have a gift* from God; your life *is a gift* from God. There is something inside of you that the world and the church need, and that gift is only present when you are present.

By Devious Design

Even though God is greater than our trauma and capable of healing even the deepest, most painful wounds, many who experience PTCD and suffer emotional wounds caused by someone in the church choose to distance themselves due to the offense they've endured. While it may seem like this separation is just a way to protect themselves from pain, frustration, or grief, the reality is that this very isolation was the enemy's intended outcome when he attacked them in the first place. The ultimate strategy behind the attack was not just to wound them—but to disconnect them from the Body of Christ altogether. They unintentionally fall into the enemy's trap by withdrawing from their church community.

Although the enemy's tactics aren't overly complex or unpredictable, he is calculated and strategic. Fortunately, Scripture gives us clear insight into his methods and reveals who he is and how he attacks. By recognizing these patterns, we can better guard our hearts, minds, and spirits, ensuring that we don't become blindsided when spiritual warfare arises.

In Genesis 3, we see Satan use deception and lies to lead Eve into sin. 1 Peter 5:8-9 warns that *the devil prowls like a roaring lion, seeking someone to devour.* John 8:44 describes him as *a murderer and the father of lies, devoid of truth.* 1 Corinthians 11:14 reveals that he disguises himself as *an angel of light, twisting things to appear good.* John 10:10 portrays him as *a thief whose mission is to steal, kill, and destroy.* In Revelation 12, we see that he is *the accuser of God's children,* and in Matthew 4:1-11, when he tempts Jesus, he even *manipulates Scripture* in an attempt to lead Him into sin at His weakest moment.

When we see that this is how Satan has operated throughout history, we can expect his attacks to come in similar forms today—lies, deception, accusations, scripture manipulation, and making evil appear good—all in an effort to steal, destroy, or derail God's plan for our lives. Recognizing these tactics allows us to be better prepared and equipped to resist his schemes and stay aligned with God's will.

Identifying the Pattern

Since I started writing this book, I've encountered many individuals who have been deeply wounded by experiences within the church. Just days ago, I overheard a woman in a restaurant say, *"The most hateful people I've ever met have been in church."* She wasn't even talking to me; I just heard her saying it to someone else.

In a conversation with a fellow pastor, he shared how he and his wife had served in multiple major ministries before founding their own thriving church. Though they have found healing, the pain of past experiences made it incredibly difficult for a few years for his wife to trust and open up to those they now lead. Another pastor, still recovering from his time working in a nationally recognized ministry, admitted that while he loves God and people, he struggles with the deep frustration and disappointment he feels toward the dysfunctional leadership models he has observed in many churches.

These conversations—along with my own experiences and a number of other discussions over the years—have fueled my conviction that this book is necessary in this season of church history. The body of Christ is under a real and targeted attack, one that has triggered a traumatic response in many people's perception of the church.

I am convinced that PTCD is more than just a pattern of disappointment; it is a strategic attack from the enemy designed to infiltrate the church and prevent us from walking in our full authority as the victorious Bride of Christ that God intended. Until we recognize and address it, this stronghold will continue to hinder the church as an institution from being what God has called her to be.

We are spiritual beings housed in physical bodies—what I like to call *"earth suits"*—temporarily navigating life in a physical world. Because our daily experiences are primarily filtered through our five physical senses, it's easy to become disconnected from the reality that Scripture makes abundantly clear: there is an unseen spiritual realm that significantly influences the physical world we perceive and experience.

Ephesians 6:12 (AMPC)
12 For we are not wrestling with flesh and blood [contending only with physical opponents], but against the despotisms, against the powers, against [the master spirits who are] the world rulers of this present darkness, against the spirit forces of wickedness in the heavenly (supernatural) sphere.

Beneath the pain, dysfunction, pride, arrogance, narcissism, insecurity, and cruelty we encounter from others, there is a spiritual force at work—a puppet master pulling the strings. As much as we may want to, we cannot fight spiritual battles by physical force.

Though the conflict may feel deeply personal—carried out through people and situations that leave lasting wounds—the real battle isn't against flesh and blood. At its core, it's spiritual. I've often heard it said that "Satan's greatest power lies in his ability to deceive," and this couldn't be more true when it comes to PTCD. Many have been deceived into interpreting spiritual attacks as purely physical issues—or worse, attributing them to God Himself. This confusion not only clouds our perception but also allows the true enemy to operate undetected.

Division Deception

The most powerful aspect of deception is that those who are deceived rarely realize it. When the enemy misleads believers, he often uses pain and disappointment to make them accept and justify a reality that is contrary to God's truth. He then distorts scripture to help them rationalize their experiences, subtly rewriting their theology to accommodate their tragedy.

Phrases like *"This must just be God's will," "God won't give me more than I can handle,"* or *"Everything happens for a reason"* can become justifications for their pain.

From this mindset, when life becomes overwhelming, and they've already convinced themselves that God was behind their suffering, bitterness can take root. They begin to blame God for their trauma, distancing themselves not only from His people but sometimes from Him altogether—feeling as though He let them down.

When we reach a point of rationale where *God was responsible* for the pain that we experienced, what started as a subtle deception can lead to a complete disconnect from what we previously understood as *faith*. This has always been the enemy's strategy: to weaponize pain, turning it into a wedge that separates believers from their Source, knowing that once that person blamed God for their pain, it would ensure that they distanced themselves from the only real place that healing and strength would be found.

The Hunt: Divide and Conquer

1 Peter 5:8 describes the devil *as a roaring lion,* constantly *seeking someone to devour.* If you've ever watched lions hunt, you'll notice they rarely charge straight into a herd to attack randomly. Instead, they create chaos—circling their prey, stirring up fear, and waiting for an opportunity. Eventually, one animal—whether weaker, younger, or simply disoriented—becomes separated from the herd. That's when the lion strikes.

This tactic is known in military strategy as *divide and conquer.* There is strength in numbers, but a divided enemy is far easier to defeat.

In the context of PTCD, I believe the enemy effectively uses this same strategy to isolate believers from the very thing God designed to sustain them—the rest of the body of Christ.

First, we lose sight of the real battle. Instead of recognizing the attack as spiritual, we get caught up in the physical elements—the people, the circumstances, or the offense. The enemy's goal is to make us believe the battle is against a person or situation rather than against him. When our focus shifts away from the true spiritual fight, we lose the power to overcome because he knows you can't fight *spiritual* beings by *physical* means.

Next, as we become emotionally invested in the perceived *physical* conflict, the enemy stirs more chaos—fueling our emotions, clouding our judgment, and influencing our responses.

Finally, in an effort to escape the turmoil, many choose to withdraw from the very place or people they associate with their pain—in the case of PTCD, *the church.* But in doing so, they unknowingly separate themselves from the strength of the *herd.* And just like the lone prey in a lion's hunt, isolation leaves them vulnerable to his endgame attack.

The enemy understands the power of unity and will attempt to plant thoughts that justify division, leading us away from the strength of the rest of the body when we are vulnerable to his attacks. At times, separating ourselves may even feel like a wise choice, but it is crucial that we seek God's direction rather than reacting to spiritual battles with purely physical responses. As 2 Corinthians 10:5 reminds us, we must take every thought captive and make it obedient to Christ, ensuring that our actions align with His truth rather than the enemy's deception.

2 Corinthians 10:3-6 (TPT)
3-4 For although we live in the natural realm, we don't wage a military campaign employing human weapons, using manipulation to achieve our aims. Instead, our spiritual weapons are energized with divine power to effectively dismantle the defenses behind which people hide. 5 We can demolish every deceptive fantasy that opposes God and break through every arrogant attitude that is raised up in defiance of the true knowledge of God. We capture, like prisoners of war, every thought and insist that it bow in obedience to the Anointed One. 6 Since we are armed with such dynamic weaponry, we stand ready to punish any trace of rebellion, as soon as you choose complete obedience.

The Strength of the Pack

In *The Jungle Book*, Rudyard Kipling writes, *"The strength of the pack is the wolf, and the strength of the wolf is the pack."* This highlights a powerful truth—while the pack relies on the individual strength of each wolf, the individual wolf is strongest when supported by the pack. The same principle applies to the body of Christ.

Hebrews 10 urges us to *"not forsake gathering with fellow believers,"* and I firmly believe that *the strength of the pack* is why. Each of us contributes to the strength of the collective body, just as the body strengthens and supports us. When we stand together, we are unshakable, but when we are divided, we become vulnerable.

Mark 3:24-25 (TPT)
24 No kingdom can endure if it is divided against itself, 25 and a fragmented household will not be able to stand, for it is divided.

When the enemy succeeds in deceiving us into viewing fellow believers as the source of our struggles—rather than recognizing the real adversary operating behind the scenes—it breeds division within the body of Christ. Then, instead of working together in unity, members who should function as healthy parts of the body turn against each other, ultimately leading to self-destruction.

Once you recognize the attack that is truly happening, you can't ignore it—but until that moment of awareness, defending against it is nearly impossible.

Years ago, I worked with young adults preparing for their GED, many of whom had little prior adult influence or guidance and none of which had ever played chess. Most were familiar with checkers, but while both games use the same board, I would teach them that chess demands a completely different level of strategic thinking, using the same three to five opening moves to quickly demonstrate this contrast by repeatedly placing them in checkmate. They remained vulnerable to the same attack until they learned to recognize the pattern. However, once they identified the strategy, a switch flipped in their minds—they adapted, learned to defend against it, and changed their approach.

The same principle applies to spiritual battles we face in the body of Christ. Until we clearly see the satanic strategy, we often go through life unaware of the spiritual forces influencing the physical struggles we face. We remain confused and frustrated without recognizing the enemy's strategy, repeatedly falling into the same traps. But once we identify the pattern—once we see it for what it is and realize our battles are spiritual rather than merely physical—everything changes. The moment you understand the attack, you gain the ability to counter it, adjust your defense, and fight back more effectively.

Rotten Separation

As we continue uncovering the satanic strategies behind PTCD, we'll keep building on this revelation in the chapters ahead. But before we close this one, I want to revisit a powerful biblical image—God's reference to us as His body. Scripture teaches that believers are members of the body of Christ, and it's important to recognize this truth: when a part of the human body is severed from the rest, it doesn't thrive—it rots.

The enemy's strategy is division. If he can isolate you, he can limit you. He doesn't need to destroy you—he just needs to disconnect you. Satan will do everything in his power to distract you from your calling, and in my experience, he will use any attack necessary to keep you from continuing to be fruitful where God has placed you. When becoming frustrated with their church or relationships, I've heard people (even leaders) say, *"Go where you're celebrated, not where you're tolerated."* But that mindset is entirely unbiblical.

As believers, we're called to follow the leading of the Holy Spirit, obey His voice, and remain faithful to the assignments He's given—until He clearly releases us. If He says to leave, then by all means, leave. But there are times when God intentionally places us in uncomfortable environments, not to harm us but to grow us, or help grow others. In those moments, our obedience becomes critical. Sometimes our presence isn't just about what we're meant to receive—it's about what we've been sent to impart.

When you feel weary, disoriented, or discouraged, remember that anything truly valuable in life often comes with a fight—including relationships. You were never meant to do this alone, and neither were they. Healing is multiplied when unity is prioritized, and that's exactly how God designed it, so don't be deceived into division when your power is rooted in unity.

*"The strength of the pack is the wolf, and the strength
of the wolf is the pack."*

There are no lone wolves in the Kingdom of God. If the enemy had the power to destroy you outright, he would have already done so. Instead, he works to gain your consent—convincing you to see your situation as pitiful instead of powerful, leading you to separate from the very body that is there to provide you with strength. Stay connected, stand firm, and recognize the strategy behind the attack.

If the enemy's strategy is to isolate and disarm us, then heaven's strategy is to unite and empower us. There is power in what God never designed you to do alone—not in life, not in healing, and certainly not in leadership. And while the previous chapters have focused on identifying the spiritual warfare surrounding PTCD, the next chapter will turn the corner toward restoration—starting with those entrusted to lead. Because the health of the body begins with the heart of the shepherd, and leadership that reflects the nature of Christ will always prioritize those being led. If we want to break the cycle of dysfunction in the Church, it starts with redefining what it means to lead from a posture of service, humility, and intentional care.

Leadership is not about title or position—it's about responsibility, sacrifice, and putting others first. In a culture where leadership is often confused with control or recognition, Kingdom leadership looks radically different. True spiritual authority doesn't elevate itself; it stoops to serve. This chapter explores what it means to lead like Christ—through humility, protection, and selflessness. Because at the end of the day, the leaders who leave the greatest legacy aren't the ones who demand honor—they're the ones who earn it.

Have you ever worked for a leader who only stepped in to do the hard work when they knew someone important was watching? A leader who usually left the heavy lifting to others but suddenly got their hands dirty when cameras were rolling, or their boss was present? It's frustrating and disheartening to work under someone who prioritizes their own comfort, recognition, or jockeys for position while allowing their team to carry the weight.

Nothing breeds resentment toward a leader more than when they put themselves first at the expense of their team. But the opposite is also true—nothing builds stronger loyalty than a leader who genuinely invests in their people. A leader who prioritizes their team's success, growth, and well-being—even at personal cost—earns deep respect and commitment.

If you want to earn the trust and loyalty of those you lead, they need to know that you genuinely care about them and would never ask them to do something you wouldn't be willing to do yourself—alongside them if necessary. In the book, *Leaders Eat Last*, Simon Sinek highlights how one of the most powerful examples of leadership is when a leader prioritizes the well-being of their team. When everyone is hungry, a great leader ensures their team is fed before taking their own portion. This simple act displays a powerful message: leadership is about service, sacrifice, and putting others first. Because they have seen him prioritize them, they will follow him.

"The leadership lesson nobody teaches: Leaders eat last, take credit last, and get paid last in start-ups. But they take responsibility first, make decisions first, accept blame first, and face danger first. Leadership isn't about being in charge; it's about taking care of those in your charge. It's not about power; it's about service. Most people want the title. Few want the weight."[xxxi]

True leaders inspire loyalty not through position or power but through selflessness. People will go above and beyond for a leader they know would take a hit for them. As the saying goes, *"Leaders are not responsible for the results; they are responsible for the people who produce the results."* When you take care of your people, they take care of you—and success follows naturally as a byproduct of intentional and effective leadership.

It's easy to follow a leader when nothing is on the line. It's much harder when following requires risk. In the most dangerous moments of my career, I learned something that leadership books can't fully explain: you will follow the leader who stands with you when it costs something. And I had the privilege of serving under one of those leaders.

My First Encounter with Lt. Jim Brady

One of the greatest leaders I've ever known was Lieutenant Jim Brady. He was my S.W.A.T. team leader and later my boss when I became a criminal investigator. Jim was thirty years older than me—to the day—and quite literally half my size. He was tough as nails and, until I got to know him, one of the most intimidating people I had ever met. But over time, I came to see that behind his tough exterior was a leader who embodied integrity, loyalty, and an unwavering commitment to his team.

Our first personal encounter didn't go as I would have hoped. As a rookie police officer, I was at the gun range, qualifying to carry my pistol for the first time. Jim was the range master that day, overseeing about twenty-five officers. I had heard stories about how tough he was, and from what I had seen of him walking around the department, I had no doubt they were true.

I was positioned in the middle of the range at target 12 or 13, surrounded by other officers. We began shooting at the two-yard line, then moved back to the five-yard line. Everything was fine. Jim called out, *"Two to the chest, one to the head,"* and we all fired. Then, *"Two center mass,"* and we shot again. At that short distance, I was hitting my marks perfectly.

But somewhere between the seven and fifteen-yard line, I took my focus off of my target and started shooting the target of the guy next to me. Maybe it was nerves. Maybe I just got distracted. I'm really not sure what happened, but by the time we reached the end of qualifying at the twenty-five-yard line, my target barely had any hits, while my neighbor's target was riddled with extra holes. To anyone looking, it appeared that I had missed nearly every shot. I was mortified.

When Jim walked up and saw my target, he looked at it in utter disbelief. Then, in his thick Tennessee accent, he yelled out, emphasizing every word as if it were its own sentence: *"WHAT. IN. THE. H***. HAPPENED. HERE?! Were you trying to shoot his feet off?!"* I tried to explain, and Kyle, the poor guy next to me, had to explain why his target looked like it had been through a war zone. Jim shook his head in frustration and walked away. And to add to my embarrassment, I had to requalify—alone, in front of everyone.

For years after that, I kept my distance from Jim, intimidated and convinced that he thought I was an idiot. But three years later, Jim became my boss after I was awarded the honor of *"Officer of the Year"* with a promotion to S.W.A.T. and the Criminal Investigations Division (CID).

Learning Leadership from a Giant

It didn't take long for me to realize that Jim wasn't just a great officer—he was an exceptional leader. He had high standards, but they were never unfair or unrealistic. He didn't demand anything from us that he wasn't willing to do himself. He led from the trenches, and if we made mistakes, he had our backs. Sure, he'd give us an earful later, but we never doubted that he was fighting for us.

One day, on a S.W.A.T. call, I was the #1 guy, meaning I was to be the first through the door when we breached the house. Jim was right behind me as the #2. As we approached, about five feet from the front porch, the armed, barricaded suspect we were there to apprehend suddenly bolted out the door, charging straight at us. Without hesitation, Jim shoved me out of the way and tackled the guy with the force of an NFL linebacker. It wasn't by-the-book protocol, but in that moment, Jim's instinct as a leader was to protect me, putting himself in harm's way.

Another time, Jim and I heatedly argued over a case. I had called him for advice because I was in a situation where handling it incorrectly could open me up to a lawsuit. I didn't know that Jim was also working the case from a different location, surrounded by people who made it impossible for him to safely explain the full situation. His answer infuriated me when I questioned his directive, and he replied, *"Because I said so."*

Later that day, when I returned to the office, Jim was waiting for me in the hallway outside of our offices. *"Spider, we need to talk,"* he said (my nickname on the S.W.A.T. team was Spider). Still furious, I replied, *"No sir, we do not need to talk right now. Let's talk tomorrow."* But Jim wasn't backing down. *"We need to talk now,"* he insisted.

I tried to walk into my office, but he followed me in, blocking the door, and then said more authoritatively, *"SPIDER, WE NEED TO TALK!"*

All my frustration, anger, and resentment boiled over at that moment. I lost it. I stepped into his personal space, towering over him, and screamed at the top of my lungs, unleashing a string of curse words that would've made a sailor blush. I accused him of putting me in a compromising position without explanation and of leaving me out to dry. I was so mad that I think I even made up new curse words.

Jim never flinched. He just stood there, unwavering, staring up at me dead in the eyes. When I finally ran out of words, he cocked his head slightly, squinted his eyes, and calmly but very directly asked, *"You done?"*

I braced myself for the inevitable *"Pack your stuff—you're fired"* response.

Instead, he said something that changed my perspective on leadership forever: *"Welcome to Criminal Investigations. Now let's talk."*

He sat down and explained everything—why he had to handle the phone call the way he did, why he couldn't give me details earlier, and most importantly, how he had actually been protecting me all along.

I felt like a fool. A hot-headed, immature rookie who had just been given the most important leadership lesson of his life. Jim had every right to put me in my place, to throw his rank around, to take my outburst personally. But he didn't. Because he remembered what it was like to be in my shoes— to feel uncertain, out of control, and not yet aware of what I didn't know. Instead of crushing me, he used the moment to teach me.

From that day forward, I never had to question Jim again. Lesson learned.

Honoring Jim was effortless because he was both honorable and honoring. He led with a sense of security, owning his mistakes while protecting us from ours. He never used his rank to assert superiority; in fact, it often felt like the opposite. As a true leader, he took responsibility for our missteps, shielding us when necessary. Jim understood that honor cannot be demanded—it must be earned. And because he treated us with respect and integrity, we naturally honored him in return. He simply reaped what he had sown.

There's a saying: *When I talk to managers, I get the feeling that they are important. When I talk to leaders, I get the feeling that I am important.*[xxxii] That is the essence of an honorable leader. True leadership isn't about self-importance; it's about lifting others. What we do for ourselves fades with time, but what we do for others leaves a lasting legacy.

A Leader Who Had My Back

Jim wasn't just my boss—he became a mentor, a leader I would have followed anywhere. From a physical standpoint, he was probably the smallest man in our department, but in terms of leadership, he was a giant.

On my last day in criminal investigations, a couple of guys tried to kill me. I ended up in the hospital, lying in a bed with a shattered nose, a top lip split nearly all the way through, swollen eyes, missing teeth, and blood all over my face. Jim stood over me with tears in his eyes.

"You need to listen to ol' dad," he said. *"Spider, you can't take those kinds of chances. All you would have had to do is ask, and I would have come with you."*

"Ol' dad." That's how he referred to himself with me and two other guys in our division that he was especially close to. And that's exactly who he was—a leader who treated me like a son, put himself in the line of fire to protect his men, and modeled leadership in a way that shaped me for the rest of my life.

Jim may not have intentionally led from a biblical perspective, but he embodied Kingdom leadership principles throughout the years I served under him. He protected me from mistakes I might have made due to inexperience, shared his wisdom and years of expertise, and empowered me to become the best officer I could be. To this day, I have nothing but love and respect for that man.

Most of those experiences happened more than 20 years ago, yet the leadership lessons I learned during the five years I worked with Jim remain with me. His impact on my life didn't end when I left law enforcement—it carried forward into every leadership role I've stepped into since.

A few years ago, Jim passed away, and I had the profound honor of officiating his funeral. It was a bittersweet moment, but I can honestly say I have never felt more privileged than to stand and honor one of the greatest leaders I've ever known.

Many leadership failures can be prevented by simply valuing and prioritizing the people you lead. When you invest in them, they will, in turn, invest in you. A leader who puts others first earns loyalty and respect—when leaders eat last, those they lead will never forget it.

Not everyone will be privileged to serve under a leader like Jim Brady before stepping into leadership themselves. That's why I encourage you to take notes along your journey. Observe the leaders around you—learn from their strengths, but also take note of their shortcomings and how they impact others. Then, when your time comes to lead, strive to be the leader you always wished you had.

You represent a kingdom much bigger than you—represent well.

Leadership that reflects the heart of God doesn't seek the spotlight—it seeks to serve. The legacy of leaders like Jim Brady reminds us that lasting influence isn't measured by titles held but by lives impacted. As we move forward, we'll dive deeper into what it truly means to lead with that kind of heart—one that prioritizes the needs of others, builds trust through humility, and sees leadership not as a right to be exercised but a responsibility to be stewarded. Because in the Kingdom, the greatest leaders are always the greatest servants.

If there's one thing that can complicate how we navigate our faith and theology, it's people. Every person we encounter carries their own history, wounds, filters, and assumptions—and when those collide with our own, it can feel like navigating an emotional minefield.

Relationships, especially in church communities, are messy because people are messy. And yet, God still calls us into community—not because it's easy, but because it's necessary. It can be very difficult to navigate human experiences with grace, truth, and emotional maturity in a world where offense is easily taken and often deeply rooted. Before we write people off, it's so important that we remember—they're in process, just like we are.

A study by Lifeway Research found that 37% of adults who stopped attending church cited *"disenchantment with pastor/church"* as a reason for their departure. Within this group, 17% mentioned that church members *"seemed hypocritical"* and *"were judgmental of others,"* and 12% felt that *"the church was run by a clique that discouraged involvement."*[xxxiii]

Additionally, research focusing on young adults (aged 23 to 30) revealed that 73% identified church – or pastor-related reasons for leaving, with one-third of these respondents perceiving churches as hypocritical or judgmental.[xxxiv]

I don't know that anything in life is more complicated than people. The second law of thermodynamics, paraphrased, states that without intentional effort, everything moves toward disorder—and this principle is perhaps most evident in human relationships.

Every individual brings their own personality, quirks, insecurities, emotional baggage, and free will into interactions with others. This results in a complex, often chaotic dynamic where maintaining order, balance, and peace—let alone personal sanity—can feel like an uphill battle.

I've often joked that leadership would be simple—if it weren't for people. We all come with our own opinions, strong convictions, and a desire to be right. And yet, despite our flaws, we're usually slow to admit just how much we don't know. You'd think we'd learn to listen more, but pride often gets in the way. Thank God for Jesus and the Holy Spirit—because without divine direction, none of us would stand a chance… that is, if we're even willing to listen and submit to Him in the first place.

Many people were raised in churches that upheld strict, legalistic standards—often with good intentions but ultimately fostering a sense of bondage. Painful experiences like these are not uncommon in a believer's journey. I say *"good intentions"* because I don't believe all leaders enforced these rules out of a desire for control, at least not maliciously. Instead, some were simply leading in the same way they had been led. If their pastor had been harsh, judgmental, or controlling, they often mirrored that approach, believing it to be the acceptable standard for leadership. While their leadership style was undeniably unhealthy, it doesn't necessarily mean they were *bad* people.

I will admit that it's difficult to understand how they could read the Bible and not recognize the unbiblical nature of their actions, but their perspective on life and Christianity may have been shaped by generations of distorted teaching and even abuse creating a lens of deception that influenced their leadership style.

Power Corrupts

There's an old saying: *"Power corrupts."* While it may not be a consistent and universal truth, there are certainly times, even within the church, when it sadly proves accurate. Sometimes, insecure and unequipped individuals are elevated to leadership positions without a true biblical foundation to support the weight of that role.

You may have encountered leaders who used manipulation as a tool to gain control—perhaps trying to pressure you into giving money, guilt you into overcommitting your time, or even attempting to isolate you from your family or other trusted voices of wisdom and support.

Maybe you've seen leaders enforce rigid standards for appearance or behavior that had more to do with tradition than Scripture. And when you didn't meet their expectations, you were cast aside, not with grace or compassion, but with judgment and rejection.

I remember receiving a phone call that emphasized this point from a woman I led to Christ. I had walked closely with her and her family for several years through some of the darkest moments of their lives. Spiritually, I had been like a father to her.

She started working for a business tied to a ministry, and her boss—someone she saw as a mentor—told her flatly one day that *she was now the sole spiritual authority in her life and that she shouldn't speak to me anymore about spiritual matters.* I can't tell you what the catalyst for this conversation was, but when my friend conveyed it to me, she was very taken aback. It was manipulative, controlling, cultish, and completely out of alignment with God's heart for leadership.

For those who may have experienced something similar, I will say this: When a leader tries to isolate you and exert unhealthy control over your life—especially under the guise of spiritual authority—it's usually a sign of deeper, ungodly motives. And when that control comes from someone you once trusted, the betrayal cuts deep. But let's be clear: manipulation, control, and shame-driven leadership do not reflect Jesus. They are the opposite of the servant-hearted leadership examples that God's Word calls us to walk in.

Cleanliness Is Not Godliness

I recently came across a video of an angry pastor delivering a Sunday morning sermon in which he publicly rebuked young men in the congregation for their haircuts. In his *"King James Bible-carrying, Independent Baptist church"* (his words), he insisted that a godly man's haircut should resemble a high-and-tight barbershop cut, not something that looked, in his words, *"like a liberal from a beauty salon."* As he ranted, many in the congregation loudly shouted *"Amen!"* in agreement.[xxxv]

In a similar video, a bald, clean-shaven pastor gripped the microphone and shouted that more bearded men were in the church than on the streets, declaring, *"Facial hair is not apostolic—no matter how you cut it!"* [xxxvi]

These were not a passionate plea against sin or a heartfelt call to repentance—they were a legalistic alienation rooted in personal or traditional preference rather than biblical truth. More importantly, they were not delivered with love but harshly with judgment, reinforcing the rigid, stereotypical expectations that many have of pastors and the church, which often repel people instead of drawing them in.

If, as the Bible states, God's kindness draws people to repentance, then it's unlikely that these pastor's approach would inspire much genuine repentance. I couldn't help but think that displays like this are likely a major reason why people often feel disconnected from 21st-century Christianity.

All a Work in Progress

No one is perfect. None of us has fully arrived, and ironically, those who believe they have often found themselves further from their true destination than those who recognize they still have a journey ahead.

No matter how polished we appear on the outside, no matter how clean the haircut or if they look like they had it styled *like a liberal from a beauty salon,* we all have flaws—myself included. Those closest to me, including my wife and the people I've led, could certainly attest to that. Because of this imperfection, even those who are supposed to represent godly leadership will, at times, make decisions that negatively impact others. Whether out of insecurity, pride, or unchecked emotions, people fail to submit fully to God's Kingdom—and when they do, others get hurt. This is most often the foundation from which we experience PTCD in our lives.

But here's the reality: this is everyone's story unless you live alone in the wilderness.

Even in our closest, most intimate relationships, disappointments are inevitable. I love my family more than anything on this earth, yet if you ask my son, Rocky, he could tell you the numbers of times I've responded wrongly or unhealthily toward him—times when I had to come back later to apologize and make things right.

We are all just people navigating a human experience, and one of the greatest tests of your character is how you handle those who mishandled you. This doesn't excuse bad behavior or mean we should tolerate being mistreated. However, as we engage in any social dynamic, we must remember that everyone we encounter is also trying to navigate life—just like us. No one will always meet our expectations, and no matter how much love exists in a relationship, at some point, we will inevitably let each other down in some capacity.

Minimizing People's Pain

Speaking of the human experience, I was recently driving and thinking about this Leadership Edition of *PTCD* when a memory surfaced—one that I believe the Lord gently brought back to my attention for leaders in this section of the book.

I remembered standing on a stage, leading prayer in front of our entire Sunday morning congregation. As a leader who is daily navigating *the human experience* myself, I understand the desire to inspire faith in others and how sometimes that desire can take on a kind of bravado—leader meets motivational speaker—where you want to stir courage and bold belief in the room.

I'm a fighter. I believe in the power of God. I believe in the authority we carry against the enemy as joint heirs with Christ. But because I'm wired for war, sometimes I also fail to recognize that others are wired differently.

During that prayer, I declared, *"We serve a big God, and at the name of Jesus every knee must bow!"* I still believe that statement is true, biblical and powerful.

But then I lifted my hands in the air and mockingly said, *"Oooo cancer!"* *"Oooo COVID-19!"* as if to taunt *the enemy.*

In my mind, I was mocking the enemy who I know is subject to the name of Jesus. What I failed to consider was that in that room were people who had recently lost family members to those very diseases. While I was attempting to inspire faith, I may have unintentionally minimized someone's pain.

Jesus stood at the tomb of Lazarus knowing full well He was about to raise him from the dead. Yet before He performed the miracle, the bible tells us He wept. He allowed Himself to feel the weight of the grief around Him. He entered into the pain of those He loved before He demonstrated His power. He was present with them a cared about what concerned them.

That moment has stayed with me.

Recently, I heard a pastor preach about a painful season he walked through in his twenties. The event he referenced had happened decades earlier. Since that time, he has experienced victory after victory and season after season of success. For years now, he has lived in a place of visible stability and momentum.

The truth he preached was sound. His theology was right. The analogy of his life experience was a solid parallel. But the tone felt distant.

His *"everything is going to work out—just hold on"* carried less emotional weight than it might have when the pain was fresh because he was far removed from that pain today. And I found myself wondering how someone currently living in that kind of hardship would feel—not just listening to his words, but sensing what was being communicated underneath them. The truth hadn't changed. But his proximity to the pain had. And even when words are accurate, delivery can unintentionally feel dismissive.

As leaders, we must be careful that those who are hurting never feel as though we are so far removed from their reality that we unintentionally communicate, *"Let them eat cake,"* while they feel like they're starving.

It's easy, when you've been riding high for a while, to forget how sharp the edge of hardship once felt. But remember: with those you are leading, perception determines reception. That doesn't mean we avoid hard truths. We certainly do not water down our testimony of victory so that people can somehow feel appeased in their pain. But it does mean that we are intentional to follow the leading of the Holy Spirit with wisdom, compassion, and love.

I've just seen it happen a lot in ministry where people who finally reach a place of success project the answer in a way that creates condemnation in those who aren't *"there"* yet. I think being aware of that leadership habit can help us to be careful not to minimize someone's season of pain simply because we are far enough removed from ours that it no longer hurts the same way. Ultimately, if people sense that you cannot relate to their pain, they will struggle to receive your message—no matter how true it is.

The old saying still holds: people don't care what you know until they know that you care.

And nowhere is that more evident than when you as a leader are willing to weep with them before you raise their brother from the dead.

Offense - The Bait of Satan

I read John Bevere's book *The Bait of Satan* several years ago. In it, Bevere highlights *"offense"* as one of the enemy's most effective and destructive weapons against believers.

Resisting offense can be incredibly challenging when someone deliberately tries to offend you. Yet, it's crucial to recognize that far more is at stake than just your own hurt feelings. Similar to fishing, the enemy strategically uses offense as bait, hoping you'll take it. Once you've taken the bait, you're hooked—allowing him considerable control over your movements and limiting how far you can go before he tries to reel you back in.

Scripture underscores this principle by warning that, *"where strife exists, every evil work is present."* As believers, we have the responsibility to decide how we will respond to Satan's bait of offense. Our choices in those moments profoundly impacts our spiritual health and the lives of everyone within our sphere of influence.

James 3:16-18 (AMPC)
16 For wherever there is jealousy (envy) and contention (rivalry and selfish ambition), there will also be confusion (unrest, disharmony, rebellion) and all sorts of evil and vile practices.
17 But the wisdom from above is first of all pure (undefiled); then it is peace-loving, courteous (considerate, gentle). [It is willing to] yield to reason, full of compassion and good fruits; it is wholehearted and straightforward, impartial and unfeigned (free from doubts, wavering, and insincerity).
18 And the harvest of righteousness (of conformity to God's will in thought and deed) is [the fruit of the seed] sown in peace by those who work for and make peace [in themselves and in others, that peace which means concord, agreement, and harmony between individuals, with undisturbedness, in a peaceful mind free from fears and agitating passions and moral conflicts].

S.W.A.T. Team

As explained in previous chapters, I served on the S.W.A.T. (Special Weapons And Tactics) team during my time in law enforcement. Our role required specialized training, advanced weaponry, and tactical precision to de-escalate or neutralize high-risk scenarios when situations escalated beyond routine police response.

I had a teammate with whom I never saw eye to eye. Our personalities clashed, leading to frequent tension and minimal conversation unless absolutely necessary. However, when duty called, none of that mattered. The moment we put on our bulletproof vests and tactical gear, our differences faded into the background. The mission—protecting our community—took precedence. No matter how much we disagreed personally, in the heat of a high-risk operation, I wouldn't have hesitated to take a bullet for him.

The mission far outweighed our personal differences. Both of us had taken an oath to serve and protect our community, and that commitment outweighed any personal conflicts. We didn't need to be friends to fulfill our duty. Both of us understood that lives could be hanging in the balance, and we simply needed to put aside our differences when it came time to do the job. No matter how frustrating our clashes were, they were insignificant compared to the greater purpose we were called to fulfill. And for those willing to recognize it, this example carries a profound spiritual parallel.

We are engaged in a daily battle where the lives—and even the eternal destinies—of those within our sphere of influence are at stake. Unfortunately, far too often, we allow our personal emotions to overshadow the greater mission at hand.

Consider a scenario where a father or mother takes offense at a church leader. Maybe the pastor said something they didn't agree with, or the worship leader didn't acknowledge their gift as musicians, or someone in leadership said something rude to them. Whatever the case, rather than addressing the issue in a healthy way, they choose to simply leave the church entirely, pulling their entire family out with them…In this scenario, I ask, *"At what cost?"*

What is the true cost to a family that walks away from church because of offense? For their children, it may mean the loss of regular biblical instruction, the absence of godly mentors, and missed opportunities to build friendships with peers who share their values. It could mean growing up without seeing faith lived out in community, making it harder to grasp the importance of spiritual connection later in life. For the parents, it might lead to isolation, the loss of meaningful friendships, or a drifting from the support system that once held them up in hard times. And what about the spiritual consequences—bitterness taking root, strife becoming normal, or trust in God being quietly replaced with cynicism and hurt? Even things like missed opportunities to serve, to grow in leadership, or to receive encouragement in moments of personal crisis are all part of what slowly slips away when a family disconnects from the body of Christ. The fallout of *offense* is rarely immediate, but its ripple effects can last for generations.

While there are certainly times when seeking a new church due to *leadership failures* may be necessary for spiritual growth, many make the mistake of abandoning church altogether when they experience degrees of disappointment or pain. This decision isn't just unhealthy—it's spiritually damaging for everyone involved.

While we are on this subject, I've also heard many people over the years say to me, *"I don't need to attend a church to be a Christian."* While it's true that going to church is not a prerequisite for going to heaven and reading your Bible or watching a sermon online can provide biblical instruction, neither can replace the personal connection, accountability, purpose, and fulfillment that come from being an active part of the body of Christ who is connected to the church not only for what they can receive but what God has them there to impart.

Scripture reminds us in 2 Corinthians 5:7 to walk by faith, not by sight. Sometimes, that means staying the course even when emotions tempt us to exit, and at times, faith calls us to remain steadfast, even when every part of us wants to turn or even RUN away.

In the Kingdom of God, we do what is right not because it is easy, not because it is comfortable, not because it is convenient, but because it is what God has instructed us to do.

James 2:18 (TPT)
18 But someone might object and say, "One person has faith and another person has works." Go ahead then and prove to me that you have faith without works and I will show you faith by my works as proof that I believe.

Convoluted Logic

The final takeaway from this chapter on people navigating the *human experience* is that you don't always know what you don't know. There is a concept called *Convoluted Logic,* where conclusions are reached based on seemingly logical reasoning—except that reasoning is unknowingly built on flawed or incomplete information.

In many cases, convoluted logic causes us to weave together multiple events from our personal experiences as though they are all interconnected. We may incorporate missing, unnecessary, or irrelevant details, creating a tangled web of context supporting our desired conclusion. However, when the missing pieces are revealed, we often realize that the narrative we constructed wasn't entirely true.

I recently reconnected with a friend I hadn't spoken to in a long time. He lives over a thousand miles away, so our interactions were rare. We had walked through some incredibly difficult seasons together, and for a time, he was one of the most influential and encouraging voices in my life.

As the years passed, our conversations became less frequent. The last time he reached out was on a particularly emotional day for me—the day I stepped down after two decades of ministry in the same church. After that day, I didn't hear from him. I tried reaching out a few times online but received little or no response. Naturally, I began forming my own assumptions about our relationship. In my mind, I had built an entire narrative that justified what I was feeling—I assumed I had been *"ghosted,"* that I no longer mattered to him, and I convinced myself I knew why.

Then, out of nowhere, I received a text. He was in town and wanted to meet. When we finally sat down together, tears streamed down my face as he shared what had happened in his life since our last conversation. The truth was heartbreaking—he hadn't *ghosted* me at all. He had suffered a mental breakdown and had spent the past year simply fighting to survive.

I had no idea. For a whole year, I had allowed assumptions to shape my reality, feeding into hurt and rejection. But the truth? I just didn't know what I didn't know. I was experiencing *convoluted logic.*

Every person's life (including church leadership) is layered with complexities we could never fully understand. Countless variables shape their actions, reactions, and interactions with the world. We are each a unique combination of who God created us to be and the experiences that have shaped us. The enemy thrives on exploiting the gap between our expectations and reality, stirring up confusion, disappointment, and emotional turmoil (often through convoluted logic).

The good news is, as believers, we are not left to navigate these challenges alone. God has given us His Word and the Holy Spirit to guide us through pain and uncertainty so that we are not consumed by them.

Jeremiah 33:3 instructs us to *call on God, and He will answer—revealing things we do not yet understand.* But notice, the verse doesn't say we will automatically have all the answers just because we are believers. It requires action on our part. We must actively seek God's guidance; when we do, we need to pay attention to what He reveals. Sometimes, those revelations are insights we may have been blind to before.

Each of us carries a unique combination of personal experiences, emotional wounds, and spiritual moments that influence the way we perceive people, the Church, and even God Himself. In the next chapter, we'll explore how these experiences shape the lenses through which we interpret life—and how those lenses directly affect how we relate to faith, leadership, and the community around us.

God has equipped us with His Word and His Spirit, but He has also given us free will. It is up to us to decide whether we will walk by faith or by sight.

Leadership in the church is rarely as clear-cut as it appears from the outside. Each role within the body—whether pastoral, staff, volunteer, or board member—carries its own set of expectations, pressures, and perspectives. And just like congregants, leaders are not immune to trauma. In fact, their position often places them at the epicenter of it. As we begin this next section, we'll examine the unique ways PTCD shows up within church leadership, and how each lens—shaped by personal experience and position—can either distort or deepen our understanding of the situations we've walked through. The goal isn't to defend dysfunction, but to expand perspective—because sometimes healing begins when we realize that others were hurting too, just in ways we didn't see.

Disillusionment is one of the enemy's most subtle and dangerous tactics. It clouds our judgment and influences our decisions—especially when we think we understand the full story. But the truth is, we often don't. In many cases, we only know a small piece of what's really going on, and if we knew the part we're missing, it might completely shift how we view the situation.

Consider the story of a woman arrested for stealing groceries. At face value, it's a crime—but learning she has children at home with empty stomachs adds layers of complexity. Or picture a woman caught prostituting herself, only to find out she's desperately trying to pay for life-saving medication for her child. While we may disagree with their choices, understanding the *why* behind their actions has the power to transform judgment into varying levels of understanding, if not compassion.

Through my journey as a husband, father, pastor, church member, detective, and even bystander, I've witnessed a consistent pattern—we often believe we know more than we actually do. But when all the facts finally came to light, it became clear that we were missing crucial information—

details that could have drastically altered how we judged the situation or chose to respond.

As a pastor, I've been the target of harsh judgment from people who only had access to a portion of the story—the part that could be shared. Many outside of pastoral leadership may not realize that there are legal and ethical constraints surrounding what can be disclosed. Like *"attorney-client privilege,"* pastors are often entrusted with confidential information that, by law and conscience, cannot be shared.

Maybe my background as a detective heightened my sensitivity to this, but there have been moments—even with my own wife—when I've chosen not to share certain details about people or situations in the church. Not because I didn't trust her but because I felt a deep responsibility to protect the reputations and privacy of those who confided in me. I've watched people interact with her, clearly assuming she knew what they had told me, but she didn't—because I kept their confidence.

There have also been situations where I sincerely sought God's guidance on how to handle delicate or volatile matters. I did what I believed He was leading me to do—yet, for some, I didn't act quickly enough, and for others, I was too direct or firm. The difficult part in all of it was knowing I was one of the only people who knew all the facts and understood the full picture. Meanwhile, many of those who judged my decisions only had fragments of the truth—fragments shared publicly by those who disagreed with me but who either couldn't or wouldn't disclose vital information that would have brought more balance to public perceptions.

One situation in particular has cost me more relationships and brought more criticism than anything else I've ever faced. In the midst of it, one of the very few people who actually knew the full story privately sent me a letter apologizing. They expressed sorrow for how I was being targeted by others who only knew fragments of what had really happened. This person acknowledged that with just a paragraph or two of explanation, I could set the record straight and vindicate myself from the judgment being projected upon me. But they also understood that I wouldn't—because doing so would hurt the hearts and legacy of people that I cared about, and I wasn't willing to tarnish their reputation in order to preserve mine.

In response to their letter, I simply said, *"The family is hurting, and if they need some place to direct their arrows, I'm a safe target—because I won't hold their arrows."* That's a reality of the pastoral leadership lens most people never see. Sometimes, you absorb the arrows in silence, not because you're guilty, but because protecting others is part of the call.

It still hurts to know I've been judged and distanced by people who never had the full picture. But that's part of the burden of leadership. When you lead from a Kingdom perspective, protecting and empowering others often comes at a personal cost. Sheep can run, hide, and bury their faces in the hay—but the shepherd may be bitten by the wolves he's guarding them from.

I'm sharing that example from a pastoral perspective, but the *pastoral lens* is really just one of many within church leadership. Most people's *Post-Traumatic Church Disorder* experiences are shaped by a blend of intersecting perspectives—whether personal, familial, relational, staff-related, congregational or from governing bodies like church boards. Each of these roles represents a unique part of church leadership, offering varying levels of access, responsibility, and insight. Because of that, they each influence how individuals interpret events, form judgments, and ultimately process their church experiences, and it's often much more complex than many would know or assume.

Scripture tells us that Christ is the head of the Church. That means He—and His Word—sets the standard for leadership and authority. The Church is His design, not ours. And the Bible clearly states that it's Jesus who builds His Church. As the body of Christ, we're not only part of this divine structure—we're also called His bride. That's a weighty title. So, when we interact with the Church, in whatever role we play, we would do well to remember who she belongs to. No matter what our position, we should approach her with reverence, humility, and care.

I've always admired how David responded to King Saul in Scripture. Even when Saul was actively trying to take David's life, David chose a higher path. He spared Saul, declaring, *"I will not lay a hand on the Lord's anointed."* David saw Saul through a different lens. Where others would have justified retaliation based on emotion or circumstance, David recognized the spiritual authority that God had established—and he chose to honor God by honoring Saul.

I believe that, in parallel, no matter what level you serve in the church, that same lens is vital for us today. We often see honoring leadership through the lens of honoring the honorable. But I would challenge you with an additional perspective; I believe that, like David in the case of Saul, honor and respect are, more importantly, a reflection of *your* character, not *theirs*.

In his outstanding discipleship workbook, *The Disciple's Blueprint*—which, in my opinion, should be in every pastor's library—Pastor Clint Thomas communicates the culture of honor in a way I've rarely heard expressed so clearly.

The Culture of Honor

In any healthy family or kingdom, there is a "Culture of Honor." Honor is the ability to recognize and value the "weight" or "glory" that God has placed on another person. It is seeing people not "according to the flesh," but according to their divine calling and spiritual future. (It is a common mistake, for those less mature, to view brothers and sisters "as they currently are" rather than who The Father is shaping them to be.)

In the Kingdom of God, honor is the "currency" that keeps the family functioning and the power flowing.

Honor is the spiritual "connective tissue" that allows the family to thrive. Without honor, we see our brothers and sisters through the lens of their mistakes or their past, which creates friction and division. But when a disciple chooses to honor others, they are essentially saying, "I choose to see the Father's investment in you." This recognition creates an atmosphere where people feel safe to grow, safe to fail, and safe to step into their unique roles.

True Kingdom honor is the ability to see the Gold in the midst of the dirt. It is a spiritual "eye" that allows you to speak to a brother or sister's Destiny even when may be currently struggling with their history. When you choose to honor a fellow disciple, you aren't ignoring their flaws; you are choosing to believe that the new creation inside them is more real than the old man they are shedding. This kind of honor is what creates the "soil" for growth. In this house, we don't wait for people to become perfect before we honor them; we honor them so that they have the strength to become who the Father says they are.

Furthermore, honor is the key that unlocks the grace on someone else's life for your benefit. When you honor a brother or sister for the gift they carry, you gain access to the blessing of that gift. In the Father's house, we don't tear each other down to climb higher; we lift each other up so the whole family ascends together. By cultivating this culture, we demonstrate to a broken world that we are not just a club or an organization—we are a family defined by the same selfless honor that the Father, Son, and Spirit have for one another.[xxxvii]

"Honor all people. Love the brotherhood. Fear God. Honor the king." (1 Peter 2:17, NKJV)

"Be kindly affectionate to one another with brotherly love, in honor giving preference to one another." (Romans 12:10, NKJV)

As believers, we are all part of the body of Christ, filled with His Spirit and marked by His anointing. That reality should change how we treat one another. When we understand what it means to carry His anointing, it adds weight and depth to the command to *"love the Lord with all our heart and to love our neighbor as ourselves."*

It's important to note that when David spared Saul, David had already been anointed as the next king of Israel. Technically, both men were anointed. But David never used his own anointing to elevate himself or diminish Saul's. Unlike the corporate *Power Pyramid* model that postures our anointing on a pedestal above everyone else, the *Kingdom Pyramid* flips that model upside down. True spiritual leadership places others first—protecting, covering, and lifting those we're called to serve.

David didn't act out of insecurity or offense. He saw Saul through a lens that was greater than his own. Not just as a threat or rival but as a man anointed by God. That kind of spiritual insight and maturity—choosing to honor the anointing in someone else even when it threatens your own future—only comes by yielding to the guidance of the Holy Spirit.

Honor is an anointed force that accelerates the kingdom of God and its activities on the earth. – Dale Mast[xxxviii]

As you continue reading the chapters ahead, I encourage you—like King David, who was known as a man after God's own heart—to consider viewing your PTCD experience through different lenses. While this shift in perspective may not erase the pain or alter the facts of what you've endured, it can open the door for greater understanding. As God reveals additional dimensions and perspectives, He may begin to heal places in your heart that have long felt missing or broken—offering clarity, restoration, and peace through insights you hadn't seen or experienced before—because the way we see is just as important as what we've seen.

Chapter Fourteen
Pastoral Lenses

Pastoral leadership is often romanticized from the outside—seen as a calling filled with purpose, vision, and spiritual influence. But for those who have carried the weight of it, the reality is far more complex. Beneath the sermons, smiles, and Sunday morning presence lies a leader deeply invested in the lives of others—often absorbing pain that most will never know. In this chapter, we take a deeper look through the lens of a pastor: the heartbreaks few talk about, the cost of staying emotionally open in the face of betrayal, and the unseen spiritual battles waged in silence. This isn't just about highlighting the pressures of ministry—it's about cultivating a greater understanding of what it means to lead God's people with compassion, conviction, and a heart that refuses to harden.

To offer a perspective that many outside pastoral ministry rarely see, I'd like to begin this chapter with a story. A few years ago, a college student reached out online to interview me for a paper on pastoral leadership. One question, in particular, stuck with me: *"What's one of the most difficult challenges you've faced as a pastor—something most people outside ministry might never consider?"*

They might have expected me to say something like officiating the funeral of a child, or praying with everything in me for someone's healing only to watch them pass. Maybe they assumed I'd mention sitting at a hospital bedside, comforting grieving families, guiding couples through infidelity and reconciliation, or walking with someone through the darkness of addiction—only to watch them relapse. Perhaps they thought it would be the quiet, gut-wrenching moments where you're expected to be strong and have answers, even when you feel there is nothing more you can do.

And let me be clear—all of those things are deeply difficult. Every pastor could name their own *"hardest thing,"* and each one would be valid. But

125

what I shared with that student didn't come from a singular moment of tragedy. In fact, it wasn't something most would even label as *"tragedy"* at all.

The truth is, if you're truly pastoring well, it means you deeply care for the people you're leading. Walking with families through their most painful moments—whether grief, tragedy, or loss—isn't just part of the job; it's a personal investment of your heart and love into their lives.

For me, the hardest part of pastoring hasn't been those moments of crisis themselves but what sometimes comes afterward when I've walked with families through their darkest days, been a steady presence through pain, and then—as healing begins—my presence becomes a reminder of their trauma. And in some cases, the final step in their healing journey is to create distance between their future and the person who reminds them of their past and pain – me.

I don't blame them—I understand why. But it hasn't made it any less painful for me. The most difficult part of ministry, in my experience, has been losing relationships that I poured the most love and heart into.

In my experience, when that happens again and again, it's a battle not to let your heart grow guarded. For me, there has sometimes been an internal struggle to remain open, desire to invest deeply in new relationships, and resist the temptation to protect yourself by staying at arm's length because, where the rubber meets the road, building relationships takes time and energy, and weighing the cost can at times, feel like a lot.

While I certainly don't live in a state of fearing that I'm going to get hurt or avoiding intimacy so that I don't set myself up for pain in the future, I'd be lying if I didn't admit that the idea of building new relationships after the loss of former relationships that I poured deeply into, has been an occasional difficult aspect of the call for me.

I've been intentional to say, *"in my experience,"* because this is not every pastor's perspective, it's mine. I'm not sharing this to suggest that every pastor's journey is the same, but rather to offer a glimpse into one pastoral perspective—highlighting an aspect that you may have never considered simply because you've never lived it yourself and possibly never will.

It's easy to make assumptions about someone else's experience when you haven't walked in their shoes. I can't count how many times I've heard people say how nice it must be to have a job where you only *work* for an hour on Sunday morning, an hour on Sunday night, and maybe an hour midweek. That perspective often comes from those who slip in and out of church services without building relationships or engaging beyond the surface, and those three visible hours are all they see of pastoral ministry.

But anyone who has actually carried the weight of the role—or walked closely with someone who has—knows better. There's a reason Forbes once listed pastoral ministry among the top five most stressful professions. The visible moments are only a fraction of the full picture, and the unseen aspects are where much of the real work, sacrifice, joy, and pain lies.[xxxix]

With that in mind, and as we move into what's ahead, I want to emphasize clearly that pastoring has been one of the greatest joys of my life. I have loved fulfilling that call of God, and it has been extremely rewarding for me. Additionally, I'm not attempting to foster a sense of victimization for any person or any role that we address in this book, including pastors. However, *PTCD: Addressing the Elephant in the Sanctuary* is about healing, restoration, and ultimately walking in victory after experiencing pain in your church experience, and I've met so many leaders and pastors who also war with the trauma they encountered because of their leadership roles in the church.

In the same way that doing what you've always done will get you what you've always gotten, we cannot expect different results without intentionally evaluating and recalibrating our leadership models. I hope to help you, the reader, gain access to perspectives you may not have encountered before—perspectives that might help you reframe or process your own PTCD experiences in a healthier, more complete way.

So, when I speak about the pastoral lens or the challenges of ministry, it's not to cast ministry in a negative light or create a narrative of suffering. It's to offer an additional layer of understanding that you might not otherwise have considered.

If The Enemy Can't Make You Bad, He'll Make You Busy.

Several years ago, I had a conversation with the pastor of a thriving *"megachurch.* As we talked, he proudly listed off the countless hours he was putting in each week and all the ministry initiatives they were undertaking with him at the helm. It was both impressive and, honestly, a little alarming.

As he spoke, I couldn't shake the growing concern I felt for his personal well-being and his family's relational health. He looked tired and from where I stood, it seemed impossible to keep up that pace, and it appeared to me like he was burning the candle at both ends. And while there are certainly seasons where pushing hard is necessary, it's a known fact that no one can sprint endlessly without collapsing. Without intentional balance, eventually, the wax runs out—and burnout becomes inevitable.

I gently voiced my concern about continuing at that pace, but he quickly shot back, *"I CAN DO ALL THINGS THROUGH CHRIST WHO GIVES ME STRENGTH!"* It was clear from his expression that he didn't appreciate my immediate response when I replied: *"Pastor, just because you can doesn't mean it's wise to try."*

I don't typically speak that directly or confrontationally with other pastors. But in that moment, I truly felt prompted by God to say it. Unfortunately, about a year later, he experienced a moral failure that cost him both his church and his family. While I'll never know the full story, I've wondered if the caution I felt for him regarding *"burning the candle at both ends"* played a part in what ultimately transpired.

There's a saying I've heard many times: *If the enemy can't make you bad, he'll try to make you busy.* And it's true—sometimes, we become so wrapped up in doing things for God that we miss what God is trying to do in us. Rest is not optional—it's part of God's divine design. Even in agriculture, God commanded the land to rest every seventh year so it could be restored. And since we were formed from the dust of the earth, I think there may be a *resting the soil* parallel to consider—if we don't allow ourselves to rest, our spiritual nutrients will eventually run dry.

Now, I absolutely believe God equips and strengthens us to carry out the assignments He gives. And when we walk in step with Him, it can be deeply fulfilling and full of joy. But that doesn't remove the need for wisdom and intentionality. There's a big difference between doing what *we think* God might want and actually obeying what He's *told* us to do.

In my own journey as a pastor, what I've wanted to do hasn't always aligned with what God was instructing me to do. There were times I was ready to quit when He whispered, *"Hold on just a little longer."* And other times I was eager to charge ahead into the fight, only for God to stop me and say, *"This battle is Mine—let Me handle it."*

When Scripture says, *"They that wait upon the Lord shall renew their strength,"* the word *wait* can mean different things depending on the context. Sometimes, *"wait"* refers to being still and patiently trusting God's timing. Other times, *"wait"* carries the image of actively serving—like a waiter attending to guests in a restaurant. In either case, God promises to provide strength, rest, and peace when we follow His lead. The key is discerning whether He's asking us to pause—or to move—with Him.

That being said, it's worth acknowledging that pastoral leadership carries a level of complexity, nuance, and pressure that most people outside of it may never fully understand. Studies and statistics confirm just how multifaceted this calling truly is.

- 75% of pastors report being "extremely stressed" or "highly stressed" (1)
- 90% work between 55 to 75 hours per week (2)
- 90% feel fatigued and worn out every week (1)
- 70% say they're grossly underpaid (2)
- 80% will not be in ministry ten years later and only a fraction make it a lifelong career (1).
  - On average, seminary trained pastors last only five years in church ministry (2)
- 100% of 1,050 Reformed and Evangelical pastors had a colleague

who had left the ministry because of burnout, church conflict, or moral failure (2)

- 91% have experienced some form of burnout in ministry and 18% say they are "fried to a crisp right now" (7)
- 70% of pastors say they have a lower self-esteem now than when they entered ministry (1)
- 70% constantly fight depression (2)
- 50% feel so discouraged that they would leave their ministry if they could, but can't find another job (2)
- 80% believe their pastoral ministry has negatively affected their families and 33% said it was an *outright hazard* (1)
- 80% of ministry spouses feel left out and unappreciated in their church (2)
- 77% feel they do not have a good marriage (2)
- 38% are divorced or divorcing (1)
- 50% admit to using pornography and 37% report inappropriate sexual behavior with someone in the church (1)
- 65% feel their family is in a glass house (2)
- 70% do not have someone they consider a close friend (1)
- 44% of pastors do not take a regular day off (5)
- 90% say they have not received adequate training to meet the demands of ministry (2)
- 85% have never taken a Sabbatical (6)[xl]

When you consider these statistics in light of the pain many have experienced and the unhealthy leadership patterns shaped by the dysfunctional corporate-style *Power Pyramid* leadership model that has crept into many church organizations, it becomes more understandable why some pastors—who began with sincere hearts to love God and shepherd His people—eventually find themselves disconnected and unable to relate to the very people they were called to lead.

It's not easy to faithfully seek God's direction and try to follow His lead, only to have a board member—driven by money, insecurity, or a need for control—use their position to undercut your leadership just because they can. But it happens.

It's not easy when three influential families in the church have conflicting ideas about the church's future and threaten to leave unless you align with their vision for how to lead. But it happens.

It's not easy when people—including the brand-new member you haven't even met yet—feel entitled to critique your leadership, spreading gossip and stirring division without knowing the whole story. But it happens.

It can be incredibly challenging to lead when it feels like certain individuals are constantly looking for a reason to be offended. But it happens.

It's not easy when staff members you trusted, who had hidden motives or personal ambitions, work behind the scenes to undermine your leadership, sometimes leading to outright mutiny and church splits. But it happens.

And when it happens over and over again, it becomes incredibly difficult not to take it personally—to not close your heart, become guarded, or even grow bitter.

But when that happens, something even more dangerous occurs: it creates a ceiling on your leadership potential. The only way to push past that ceiling is through intentionality, faith, and a fierce determination to obey God—regardless of fear, self-preservation, or the desire to never be hurt again.

You will only overcome what the enemy is trying to use to limit your future if you resist the temptation to self-protect and instead boldly follow the call of God—even through the fire.

When you grasp the fact that Jesus was crucified by the very ones He came to rescue, it shifts your perspective on scriptures like *"Take up your cross and follow Me"* and *"To whom much is given, much is required."* Leadership carries a higher cost—because with the call comes greater responsibility, and with that responsibility comes greater expectations.

Familiarity: An Unhealthy Pastoral Lens

An essential part of that *"greater responsibility"* connected to the calling of being a leader or pastor in a church is the intentional stewardship of relationships with those you lead. The only way to truly lead by example is through genuine proximity and connection. I include this section on *familiarity* in this chapter on *pastoral lenses* with future leaders in mind—those who will one day carry the weight of influence and need to understand the value of relational leadership, especially if they've not seen it properly modeled.

Recently, I had a conversation with a pastor friend who leads well with an upside-down *Kingdom Pyramid* leadership foundation—one rooted in protecting and empowering those he serves. As we discussed the topic of pastoral relationships with their staff, he shared a story about a time he was mentoring a younger pastor. During the discussion, the younger leader admitted that he intentionally avoided developing close relationships with his staff. His reasoning? He didn't want to foster a sense of *familiarity*.

(In this context, *familiarity* within church culture often refers to the idea that if people grow too comfortable with their leader, they may lose sight of the leader's role as *"the pastor"* —not so much from a *positional* but *power* perspective. This concept is frequently adopted and reinforced by leaders who confuse the role of a *shepherd* with that of a *ruler*—often stemming from their own insecurity, desire to protect themselves, or set themselves apart from those they lead. It allows for minimal emotional engagement between them and their team, but at a high cost: it fosters disconnection, often breeds resentment, and undermines influence and growth with those they are leading.)

The term *familiarity* has become increasingly common in church circles over the past few decades, particularly within the context of the *Power Pyramid*, the corporate-style leadership model we have discussed, where the man of God is placed at the top, and everyone else exists primarily to support his vision.

The young pastor in question likely adopted this language from another leader who operates with a similarly dismissive and exclusive leadership style—one where the *"king"* remains detached from the *"commoners,"* where their anointing entitles them to exaltation. It's an unhealthy model usually steeped in pride, self-importance, and spiritual elitism—quite frankly, it's repulsive in this context. However, in the next chapter, I will address another parallel aspect of *familiarity* as it pertains to properly showing honor for leadership that I believe is important for any subordinate leader.

The point in sharing this isn't to suggest that leaders shouldn't hold a position of authority that postures them to address, correct, or confront inappropriate behavior when a team member steps out of line. Leading people absolutely includes an aspect of necessary boundary setting, accountability, and authority. I once had a team member yell at me during a staff meeting I was leading—in front of everyone—after I asked him to take on a task that turned out to be more demanding than I initially understood that it would be. He responded out of frustration and acted out in a way that crossed a boundary. At that moment, I had to correct him and clarify that his behavior was unacceptable.

However, instead of letting that be the end of it, I met with him privately afterward to understand what triggered his frustration, clarify my expectations for how he responded in meetings, and to figure out how we could prevent similar situations in the future. I'm sure there was an element of *"familiarity"* in his initial response—he was more casual and reactive than he should have been with me—but rather than creating distance or shutting him out, I chose to lead by exploring the feelings behind his reaction. That decision led to a healthier relationship and stronger communication in the future.

Correcting his behavior didn't require rejection; it required leadership. The goal wasn't punishment but guidance—helping him understand how to respond more appropriately going forward.

While it's essential for any team to maintain a culture of honor and respect—and to offer clarity when those expectations aren't understood—responding to mistakes by creating an exclusive hierarchy rather than addressing and correcting the issue directly is a misstep in leadership.

Choosing a preemptive *"familiarity"* gap between you as a leader and your staff as a preventative measure, rather than offering relational correction on the rare occasion that someone reacts in a manner that is out of line, will cause more harm than good. It can foster disconnection and disunity between leaders and their teams, ultimately weakening trust and cohesion.

When I reflect on Jesus and how He related to His followers—including His disciples—it's clear that *"avoiding familiarity"* was the last thing on His leadership agenda. In fact, when His disciples tried to prevent the children from coming to Him, Jesus responded, *"Let the children come to me and do not hinder them, for the Kingdom of Heaven belongs to such as these."* In other words, in God's Kingdom, as the head of the church, Jesus modeled a leadership that is relational, approachable, loving, accessible, and touchable—even to those the world might consider the smallest and least.

During the conversation with my friend mentoring the younger leader, the young pastor was clearly seeking validation when commenting on his *"breeding familiarity"* leadership approach. However, he didn't receive the affirmation he was hoping for when he made the statement. My friend, a more seasoned leader, had witnessed firsthand the damage caused by the typical *Power Pyramid* leadership model in churches and had intentionally chosen a different path for his organization.

Rather than calling the young pastor out directly, my friend simply stated, *"I stay very connected to the lives and families of my staff. They are some of my closest friends…I'd rather spend time with them than anyone else. We're like family!"* I know his staff, and what he told the young leader was true. He leads relationally, and his team loves him for it. Hopefully, the younger pastor gained some insight from that discussion; if so, his team will certainly benefit from it.

Just because inviting people into close proximity carries the risk of them becoming more casual or *familiar* than wisdom or honor might suggest, don't let that potential keep you from leading relationally with approachability, authenticity, and love. Leaders need to resist the urge to mirror negativity—keep loving well. We are called to serve even those who mishandle us.

Today's pastors face the challenge of unifying people in a culture where division is accepted as normal.[xli]

Castle Builders -Vs- Kingdom Builders

Ultimately, every day in leadership presents an opportunity to lead from a Kingdom mindset—or drift from it.

Not every leader builds with the same motive. Some are building the Kingdom. Others are building their castle.

Castle builders tend to be territorial. They protect their platform. They guard influence. They measure success strictly by numbers and metrics.

They react defensively. They hold decision-making close. And deep down, they fear losing control.

Kingdom builders just look different.

They empower people in their gifts. They celebrate multiplication—even when it means releasing someone into their calling somewhere else. They measure success by obedience, not applause. They build people more than platforms. They share leadership. And they genuinely rejoice when those they lead succeed—even if it means being surpassed.

And when you layer all of this with the reality that every leader carries history, brokenness, and humanity, one thing becomes clear: we cannot navigate this high calling without the firm foundation of God's Word and the steady compass of His love.

The line between castle building and Kingdom building isn't drawn in boardrooms or staff meetings—it's drawn in the heart. And when that line begins to blur, what's at stake is far more than structure or success. It becomes a spiritual battle.

The Real Enemy

Scripture reminds us that we don't wrestle against flesh and blood, and we certainly have a very real enemy who is constantly at work. He attempts to derail destiny by sowing discord, strife, and division in relationships. He uses subtle tactics— *"the little foxes that spoil the vine"*—repeatedly until a leader is often deceived into embracing *self-preservation* over Spirit-led obedience.

Each hardship can feel like a calculated chess move, inching you closer to checkmate. But the moment a leader realizes the true nature of the battle is not against people but against spiritual forces—they can begin to fight back effectively. None of it is accidental. The enemy knows that if he can take out the leader, the sheep will scatter. That's why spiritual leaders are so often in his crosshairs.

Though the enemy is undeniably *beneath our feet*, and we can *declare with confidence that we can do all things through Christ who gives us strength*—believing that *every knee must bow* to the name of Jesus, that *all authority in Heaven and Earth has been given to us*, and that *we will do even greater things* because of our covenant with God through Christ—there remains a vital truth: we must walk in complete submission to Him and be empowered by His Spirit to carry out that calling.

It's not by our strength, anointing, talents, or even our position, but by His Spirit that we *live, move, and have our being*. That reality demands a willingness to be vulnerable—to be hurt, misunderstood, or let down—again and again if necessary. If we are truly going to lead God's way, we must embrace the call to deny ourselves, *take up our cross, and follow Him* wholeheartedly. This kind of leadership isn't just for influence here and now—eternity is on the line.

Pastoring is a sacred and costly calling—one that demands both strength and tenderness, conviction and compassion. It asks leaders to pour themselves out daily, often in silence, often without recognition, and often in the face of betrayal or heartbreak. Yet, it is through this very vulnerability that Kingdom leadership finds its power. When we choose to lead like Christ—close enough to be wounded, but strong enough to keep loving—we reflect the heart of the true Shepherd.

S erving on a church staff often places you in one of the most tension-filled spaces within ministry—called to lead, yet still under authority. It's a role full of opportunity and pressure, where vision must be carried out faithfully, even when it's not always your own, and where your gifts must often be held in tension with humility, timing, and submission. In this chapter, we'll explore what it means to steward that middle ground well—navigating leadership from beneath, honoring authority even when it's imperfect, and learning how to grow through the frustrations that so often come with it. Because whether you're called to remain in a supporting role or one day step into senior leadership, how you lead when you're not in charge reveals more about your future potential than any title ever will.

Leadership is a God-ordained institution—a sacred calling, in fact. I believe it's a high calling that should be approached with deep intentionality. Leaders are vital for casting vision, setting direction, establishing structure, and offering both empowerment and protection to those they lead. God entrusts leaders with His children's care, growth, and well-being—and that is no small task. It's a responsibility that goes far beyond personal preferences, desires, or the pursuit of self-fulfillment. That's why leadership carries such weight—because with greater influence comes greater responsibility.

In the next few chapters, I'll be focusing on *Post-Traumatic Church Disorder* from the perspective of staff and volunteers—both of which are subordinate leadership roles in the church. As the Roman Centurion stated in Matthew 8:9–11, you are *a man in authority and under authority* in those positions. Staff and volunteers often lead teams or departments yet still look to the senior leadership of the church for direction and guidance. This role is not just helpful—it's essential. Senior leaders simply can't do it all, and the contributions of staff and volunteer leaders are vital to the healthy function of the church body.

These roles create a unique tension for those called to lead. On the one hand, they're faithfully walking out their God-given calling to lead, develop, protect, and empower their teams—ideally while being supported and guided by a secure leader who is doing the same for them. On the other hand, because these individuals are gifted with leadership themselves, they're often tasked with carrying out the senior leader's vision while also having their own valuable insights and ideas about how things could—or should—be done. More often than not, these staff or volunteer leaders are the ones on the front lines, closest to the team, and fully aware of the dynamics within their specific area of responsibility. Yet they may find themselves executing plans that aren't always as effective as the approach they would choose if they were the ones making the final calls.

Staff Lenses

Those serving in subordinate staff roles today are present and future leaders of the Kingdom of God. You've been strategically placed in a position that requires both exercising authority and submitting to it—where you can grow not only in leadership but also in perspective. I've heard it said countless times: *"If serving is beneath you, then leadership is beyond you."*[xlii]

Leadership is never about *"me."* It's about *"we."* I've often said, *"Pay attention to the team member who never has a garbage bag in their hands."* That perspective applies at every level of leadership.

No one enjoys taking out the trash. But the person who consistently waits for someone else to handle the unpleasant or unnoticed responsibilities reveals something about their leadership posture. When someone avoids the hard, hidden, or thankless tasks, they're not operating as a team player— they're operating as a *"me"* player.

And that mindset, if left unchecked, will limit how far they can go individually—and how far the team can go collectively.

A critical component of developing as a leader is learning how to faithfully support and serve the vision of the leader God has placed over you during your season of growth. You will inevitably find yourself in situations where you don't see eye to eye with decisions being made—but it's in those moments of honor and, at times, submission that God shapes you into the kind of leader others will follow.

Sometimes, in ministry, boardrooms can start to feel more like battlegrounds when a pressing issue arises, and as a team, we come to the table with differing viewpoints from various leaders and department heads. But regardless of those differences, we have to leave that room united—with a clear strategy and game plan in hand.

You won't always agree with every decision made by your leader or the direction the "coach" chooses to take. Still, there are times when you're called to carry out a plan you wouldn't have chosen yourself. Conflict emerges when pride or the need to be right outweighs the greater mission— serving people well. When winning the argument becomes more important than loving and leading people, the ministry suffers.

Whenever I reflect on leadership, I'm reminded of King David in the Bible. Although he was anointed by the prophet Samuel to be the next king of Israel, that calling was known only to David and his family. God then placed him in King Saul's household, where he served under Saul's authority as a young man. It wasn't an *easy* assignment—but it was a *necessary* one. David was deeply devoted to God, a skilled leader in his own right, and spiritually mature beyond his years. He had the courage to face wild animals and giants that others feared. And while his gifts, relationship with God, and anointing surpassed those of King Saul, God still required him to humbly serve under Saul's leadership. Despite the challenges, David honored the process—and he honored Saul.

Familiarity

In the previous chapter, we explored the concept of familiarity, including the account of a young pastor who intentionally avoided forming close relationships with his staff. His reasoning stemmed from a fear that too much *familiarity* might disrupt the leadership hierarchy or undermine his ability to lead effectively.

But there's another side to that conversation—a responsibility that lies with staff and volunteer leaders. They must be careful not to let close proximity or *familiarity* lead them to overstep their position or role, posturing themselves outside of honor or prematurely attempting to step into a deeper level of leadership that, while they may be called and anointed, is not yet their time for. David's experience with Saul provides a powerful example. While David had already been anointed as the next king, Saul was still the reigning leader. David had to navigate that tension with great humility and restraint. Had he lost sight of God's timing or attempted to assume leadership before his appointed moment, it could have cost him everything—including his life and the lives of those closest to him.

I imagine it must have been conflicting for David—being anointed by God as the next king, yet still having to serve a king who, in moments of rage, would hurl spears at him and try to take his life without cause. It likely weighed heavily on him to know that God had rejected Saul, and yet his own path to the throne remained on hold. He had to carry the tension of knowing that when Saul trembled in fear before Goliath, David had the faith and courage to defeat the giant with nothing more than a sling and a stone. Surely there were moments when David looked at Saul occupying the throne and silently wrestled with the reality that it was the very seat God had chosen him to fill. And yet—he served. He honored. He submitted to the process God had put in place, a process that would ultimately shape him into the greatest leader Israel would ever know.

Years ago, I heard a pastor say something that has stuck with me ever since—something I believe David understood well: *"When you're truly ready to step into the destiny God has prepared for you, there won't be a devil in hell that can stop you—but it won't happen until you're ready. And if you try to force it ahead of God's timing, you risk short-circuiting the process."*

As a subordinate leader or even what I often refer to as an MIT (Minister In Training), it's not your senior leader's job to create relational boundaries to protect your heart from dishonor or over-familiarity—it's yours. This is a lens that most young leaders will not fully understand until they become senior leaders themselves (if not in the title, in age). You must be intentional in guarding that space between you and the leader you are serving because if you don't, you're the one who stands to lose the most. It becomes your test, your responsibility, and your moment of decision—to honor God by seeking God's guidance and respecting the process He's placed you in for your development. You are called and destined to become more than you are presently but the road to your destiny always involves a Divinely inspired process for your development.

A good leader will do their best to protect and empower you as you grow into your own calling, but not everyone has the luxury of being mentored by someone healthy. David certainly didn't. His mentor, King Saul, was mentally and spiritually unstable. Yet, despite Saul's instability and failures, God remained faithful to develop David into becoming everything He created him to be.

It's safe to assume that Saul caused David a great deal of pain—wounds and offenses that he had to process through. And for many developing leaders in God's Kingdom, your journey will likely include challenging, even deeply hurtful seasons, as God works through imperfect people to shape the character needed for your calling. The lenses and perspectives developed in those difficult seasons are vital for your future. They will provide perspectives that will make you so much better if you will process them from the right posture.

Now, let me be clear—I'm not suggesting you tolerate abuse or excuse leaders who misuse their authority. I'm not advocating blind submission to leadership that dishonors you or mistreats others. That is extremely unhealthy. What I am saying is this: don't be shocked if God uses flawed leaders and messy situations as tools to shape you into the kind of leader who gets it right. And while you're in the thick of it, it may not feel like growth—

but it is. God doesn't waste pain, and even in traumatic situations, He's too faithful to allow trauma to have the last word in your life.

The most important thing you can do is follow the guidance of the Holy Spirit. If your season of serving under a leader becomes challenging, but God tells you to stay and hold your position—then stay. Stay faithful until He releases you or clearly leads you elsewhere.

Over the years, I've served under some incredible leaders and a few difficult ones. In each season, God showed me when to remain, how to lead from my current position both *effectively* and *affectively*, and when it was time to move on. It wasn't always comfortable. It wasn't always easy. I've made hard choices and significant sacrifices because God asked me to. But through it all, He's been faithful. And looking back, I can say with certainty—each of those seasons shaped me into a stronger, wiser, and more compassionate leader. It seems counterintuitive to say, but it's absolutely true that, in my experiences, the most painful and negative encounters I have faced in ministry have molded the most positive leadership values into my character. I am undeniably a better person and leader, having experienced them.

If God has placed a leadership calling on your life, you can be sure the journey will come with its share of challenges. In my experience, each new level of growth brought with it fresh—and often compounded—obstacles. But every passing season becomes a training ground for what lies ahead, equipping you with the faith, mindset, and wisdom needed for the next step.

Reflecting on it all reminds me of learning math in school. You can't get to multiplication and division without first understanding addition and subtraction, and you won't make it to algebra without mastering all of those foundational skills. I remember having to take pre-algebra twice in middle school—it was tough for me to grasp abstract concepts. But once I got it, I was able to move forward into Algebra I, Algebra II, and eventually Pre-Calculus. Every level was a building block for the next.

Leadership development is much the same. Each season is a prerequisite for the one to come. Skipping ahead in the process isn't an option because God uses each stage to shape you. And while the path may not always get easier, your capacity to carry the weight of leadership increases as He prepares you to become who you were created to be.

Like progressing in math, there were seasons when I had to return to *"the professor"* for clarification after failing a test. At times, I even had to repeat *"the class"* altogether because I hadn't yet grasped what was necessary for that season to move forward. It was all simply part of the growth process in leadership development in the Kingdom of God.

People Before Programs and Processes

As a staff member, you're continually in a season of growth—being shaped and prepared for who you're becoming. Every moment is an opportunity to sharpen your leadership skills because true leaders never stop learning and developing their understanding. One of the perspectives that can be *learned* for those willing to look outside of the lens of their current perspective is that you don't always clearly see what you don't clearly see.

It's interesting how often leaders make statements like "W*e put people before processes or programs"* but then treat their staff and teams primarily like the facilitators of the processes or programs they desire to implement instead of valued individuals they claim to prioritize in that statement.

I once heard a story about a pastor who, during one of his staff leaders' birthday celebrations with family, called him and instructed him to leave the party and officiate a funeral that the senior pastor had previously agreed to— but decided last minute not to attend. While this situation may seem extreme, I've encountered countless similar stories where senior leaders viewed staff and volunteers more as functionaries in a machine than as the vital, God-ordained members of the body of Christ that they were called to lead. These kinds of experiences can become painful but formative lessons in a young leader's developmental journey.

As challenging as it may be, walking through a season under a leader who claims to prioritize people over programs but fails to treat you like a valued individual can shape you into a leader who leads with more empathy and true greatness. Why? Because you know firsthand what it feels like to be overlooked or mishandled by someone in authority and have the perspective for why it is important to lead differently.

Resentment and Entitlement

As we continue talking about putting people before process, consider a parallel from the corporate world and how it applies to Kingdom leadership.

When leaders require something from their team that they themselves would consider unacceptable, it creates tension. When a system benefits the organization at the expense of the individual, resentment and entitlement begin to take root.

In a corporate setting, it's easy for a company to justify decisions that protect the bottom line. Leadership can explain away added expectations, extra hours, or increased demands as "part of the job." But employees see through a different lens. They exchange their time, energy, and skill for compensation. When they feel that exchange is imbalanced or unfair, dysfunction begins.

For example, imagine a company expects an employee to take on additional responsibilities but decides not to compensate them for the added time or investment. In that moment, the employee is forced to interpret the decision through one of two lenses.

The first lens is **resentment.** *"I'm being taken advantage of."*

When that mindset sets in, commitment begins to erode. The employee may start doing the bare minimum. They may justify cutting corners or reclaiming time in subtle ways because, in their mind, the company already did the same to them. The cost to the organization becomes disengagement, reduced productivity, and eventually turnover.

The second lens is **entitlement.** *"I've done this favor for the company. Now they owe me."*

That mindset produces a different kind of dysfunction. It may show up as time abuse, sandbagging effort, financial dishonesty, or leveraging past sacrifice for present leverage. In the long run, the company often loses what could have been a strong contributor because the relational equity was damaged.

Both resentment and entitlement undermine team unity, buy-in, and long-term success.

And here's the key: both reactions are often avoidable.

If leadership had simply honored the individual—valuing them not merely as a function within a system but as a person—the entire trajectory could have been different.

The same principle applies in Kingdom leadership. When people feel used instead of valued, it doesn't just affect production—it affects trust. And when trust erodes, culture eventually follows.

I once asked a staff leader what he thought would be the hardest part of serving under a particular ministry team. He paused for a moment and said, somewhat cautiously, *"I think the hardest thing would be knowing that the leader of that team asks things of people that he wouldn't be willing to do himself."*

If *"Do what I say, not what I do"* is the adopted leadership paradigm on any particular team, then the team is likely to struggle to grow in a healthy way because the leadership itself is unhealthy.

I've often found it remarkable—and deeply troubling—that some leaders who read the same Bible that I do, which clearly calls us to *love our neighbor as ourselves* and to esteem others above ourselves, can still demand sacrifices from their staff in the name of *"ministry"* and *"Kingdom service"* that they themselves would never be willing to make or would consider unreasonable if the tables were turned.

Serving under this kind of leadership can shape a future leader in one of two ways: it can develop a deep conviction to never ask others to do what they wouldn't be willing to do themselves because they've felt the sting of being treated like a *servant* rather than a fellow child of God. Or, it can harden a heart, breeding a prideful mindset that says, *"I've paid my dues— now it's my turn to be served,"* repeating (and maybe even instilling in the next generation) the same unhealthy patterns they once encountered.

Work Hard, Play Hard

Teams often grow resentful when a leader promotes a *"work hard, play hard"* culture—only for the team to realize that the *"play hard"* part seems to apply exclusively to the leader and those closest to him. It's disheartening when staff members notice the leader making time for golf, attending their kids' games, traveling to ministry conferences, or enjoying family vacations while the rest of the team is left to shoulder the workload without flexibility or margin. While there are absolutely healthy ministries out there that genuinely strive to prioritize a healthy work-life balance on their teams, I've also seen many other church organizations that compensate staff modestly, expect high-level output and long hours on a minimal base salary, and then try to make up for it with a Christmas party at the end of the year—convinced that their year-end party checks the box for cultivating a *"work hard, play hard"* environment. In reality, they haven't—and their team feels it.

A leader who operates from a *Kingdom Pyramid* rather than a *Power Pyramid* mentality is intentional about caring for their team—not just in word, but in practice. This doesn't mean every team member receives the same benefits and flexibility as the senior leader, but it does mean the leader actively honors, prioritizes, protects, and empowers the people they're called to lead with intentionality. In the *Power Pyramid*, this kind of care is rare. But under the *Kingdom* model, it should be the standard.

Restore Them Gently

As we close out this chapter focusing on staff perspectives and the impact of PTCD, I want to leave you with a reflection on the role of *correction* in leadership. One of a leader's key responsibilities—when it comes to protecting and empowering those they lead—is the willingness to address misaligned or inconsistent behaviors or character issues.

The way in which a leader delivers correction carries significant weight— it has the power either to wound deeply or to leave a lasting, positive imprint on the heart of the one being corrected.

Years ago, I served as an associate/executive pastor, overseeing staff and volunteer teams. One particular staff member made my role especially challenging. My senior pastor often coached me with the phrase, *"People don't do what you expect—they do what you inspect."* With this staff member, it felt like I had to inspect everything just to ensure things got done. As someone who is naturally self-motivated, this constant oversight became exhausting and frustrating for me as a leader.

Eventually, I hit a breaking point and asked for a meeting with my senior pastor to recommend letting this staff member go. What he said in response has stayed with me to this day: *"Aaron, if you feel we need to let him go, we can. But before we do, I want you to ask yourself something I've always asked myself as a leader— 'Do I have any grace left in my heart to keep working with this person?' If the answer is yes, it's not time to release them. If the answer is no, then we'll move forward with firing them."*

That question challenged me deeply. The staff member's performance clearly wasn't meeting my expectations. But now, as a leader, I had to evaluate my own heart—was I willing to lean in, despite the frustration, and try again to draw something more out of him? Or was I just ready to dismiss him out of convenience? The question challenged my own leadership capacity and pushed me to consider whether my definition of leadership would be about developing people or simply managing performance.

Galatians 6:1-6 (TPT-Emphasis by the author)
*1 My beloved friends, if you see a believer who is overtaken with a fault, the one who is in the Spirit should seek to restore him **in the Spirit of gentleness**. But keep watch over your own heart so that you won't be tempted to **exalt yourself over him**. 2 Love empowers us to fulfill the law of the Anointed One as we carry each other's troubles. 3 If you think you are somebody too important to stoop down to help another (when really you are not), you are living in deception.*
4 Let everyone be devoted to fulfill the work God has given them to do with excellence, and their joy will be in doing what's right and being themselves, and not in being affirmed by others. 5 Every believer is ultimately responsible for his or her own conscience.

Scripture tells us to restore others with a spirit of gentleness. At the time, I honestly just wanted to eliminate the source of my frustration. But my pastor challenged the leader in me—urging me to lead creatively and with grace as long as I still had it in me to do so. And after searching my heart, I realized I did. With intentional effort and open dialogue, that staff member and I were able to find common ground. We ended up working much more effectively together until he eventually moved on to another position with another organization, where he has continued to thrive.

As I reflect back, I wonder what the long-term impact might have been if I had simply given up on him and ignored my pastor's challenge to lead with greater intentionality. Maybe he had never been taught correctly. Maybe no one had ever taken the time to genuinely care for him or invest in his development. Perhaps he just needed a leader who could see the potential in him and draw it out. It's possible that God placed him on our team directly under my leadership because I was meant to show him what a *Godly leader* looks like. And maybe, just maybe, God used him in my life to teach me the very lesson I needed to learn—how to *restore someone with gentleness* when they're falling short of the purpose they were created to fulfill.

I'm sharing these insights because I recognize that many who read this chapter have either worked—or will one day work—for a church and will find themselves in various leadership roles where they're challenged by individuals or leaders who fall short of their expectations. If you've ever been mistreated by a leader, it can shape your own leadership lens in a way that tempts you to respond similarly when it's your turn. And if you're currently leading staff or teams, the frustration you face may make it tempting to *remove* the problem rather than work through it toward resolution. My hope is that this chapter provides a fresh perspective and lenses that may challenge your own and encourage you to approach those people and circumstances with greater grace and intentionality.

PTCD can become a recurring cycle if we don't take the time to learn from our own encounters with it. As the saying goes, *"Those who fail to learn from history are destined to repeat it."* My hope is that sharing parts of my journey will help you process your own—whether past or future—and that together, we can establish more intentional, Christ-centered leadership practices for the generations to come.

Staff leadership is a sacred place of preparation—one where your character is tested, your humility is refined, and your calling is clarified. It's often in these in-between roles, beneath imperfect leaders and within flawed systems, that God does His most formative work. If stewarded well, the staff lens can cultivate in you a kind of leadership that doesn't just carry authority, but also compassion, wisdom, and grace. The goal isn't just to survive hard seasons—it's to let them shape you into the kind of leader others will one day be grateful to follow. In the next chapter, we'll turn our attention to the lens of the volunteer—the often unseen, yet essential backbone of every thriving church—and how their experiences with PTCD can be just as transformative, painful, and redemptive as those in formal leadership roles.

Volunteers are the unsung heroes of the local church—the heartbeat of ministry that keeps everything moving forward. They show up early, stay late, and serve faithfully, often without recognition or reward. And yet, despite their vital role, members and volunteers are also among the most vulnerable to experiencing *Post-Traumatic Church Disorder*. Exploring the unique challenges, expectations, and emotional toll that can come with serving from the pew instead of the platform through their eyes, we'll examine how overuse, underappreciation, and lack of intentional leadership can distort the volunteer experience and lead to sometimes deep wounds—often unintentionally inflicted by the very churches they love.

While it's true that many pastors across the country serve bi-vocationally—working a secular job for income while also fulfilling pastoral responsibilities—many staff pastors, especially in larger churches, are employed full-time by the church and haven't *"punched a clock"* in years. For them, ministry is their primary source of income. When you're getting paid to do what others are volunteering their time to accomplish, it's crucial not to lose sight of the *volunteer experience* lens because that oversight has the potential to create significant PTCD fallout on your volunteer teams.

In every church, the vast majority of people aren't on payroll—they're members and volunteers. Most are juggling full-time jobs, managing households, raising families, attending school events, or pursuing education, all while still finding time to serve their church. That's why it's crucial for leaders to remain mindful of the realities volunteers face outside of ministry. Leading with that awareness helps cultivate a culture marked by humility, gratitude, and emotionally healthy leadership.

A church simply couldn't function without the dedication of volunteers who generously give their time, talents, and treasure (financial resources.) These individuals are the backbone of ministry—teaching Sunday school, caring for infants in the nursery, leading worship, directing traffic, welcoming guests, hosting small groups, chaperoning youth events, serving meals, cleaning facilities, and so much more. And they do all of this on top of full-time jobs, family responsibilities, and personal commitments.

When coaching department leaders on the subject of volunteers, I've often reminded them that churches have a notorious reputation for trying to *"squeeze blood from a turnip"*—in other words, you can't ask more from people than they're capable of giving, and healthy leadership honors and respects that boundary.

When people begin to feel overused and overlooked, it often leads to feelings of being devalued and breeds resentment toward leadership. With authority comes the responsibility to steward people well. In my 30+ years of ministry, I've watched countless volunteers become exhausted and discouraged simply because their leaders lacked the discernment to recognize their weariness.

This is a critical dynamic to pay attention to—once someone starts down the path of burnout and feels invisible, it can quickly become a slippery slope that leads right out the back door of the church.

Over the years, I've come across many volunteers who genuinely love the church and have a sincere desire to invest their time into ministry. They love to serve, and while their excitement is admirable—sometimes even a bit overzealous—it's in those moments they've needed me, as their leader, to protect them from what they didn't yet realize they didn't know. Eager to serve, they often ask to be scheduled multiple times each month, and naturally, the department leader (often a young staff member or volunteer themselves) is thrilled to have someone so dedicated on their team and quickly plugs them in as often as possible. While well-intentioned, this response can unintentionally set both the leader and the volunteer up for disappointment.

A wise and empowering leader must recognize that most people are very uncomfortable with confrontation and will avoid it at all costs. Once a volunteer commits to serving at a high level, they may feel too embarrassed or afraid of letting you down to admit they've overcommitted. That's why it's essential to stay proactive—regularly checking in, maintaining open communication, and watching for early signs of weariness—so you can step in and protect their heart before frustration or offense has a chance to take root.

On the other side of the equation, I've witnessed leaders—lacking either wisdom or a healthy leadership perspective—try to motivate exhausted volunteers by saying things like, *"Ministry is an honor; it's something we GET to do, not something we HAVE to do."* While that sentiment may hold truth in the right context—we should indeed count it a privilege to serve and operate in our God-given role within the Body of Christ—using such blanket statements without discernment can come across as dismissive of people's real-life struggles, emotional capacity, and current season.

When spoken without empathy, the nature of these remarks can easily be interpreted (and often are) as self-serving, guilt-inducing, and even manipulative. Rather than inspiring, they risk shaming people—especially those who are newer in their faith—into service. That's not good leadership. Guilt, shame, and manipulation are terrible team motivators. It's crucial that leaders approach volunteers with both vision and compassion, never disregarding the human side of ministry.

Valuing What God Values

Many times, when people feel disappointed or hurt by church leadership, it's often the result of poor leadership practices. I've witnessed situations where leaders step outside of godly leadership perspectives and prioritize individuals not for who they are but for what they can offer—whether it's their wealth, influence, or fame. While this kind of attention may feel flattering to those being prioritized at first, it eventually begins to feel *transactional* as they develop the sense and awareness that they're being used. That realization is often a turn-off and breeds disconnect.

I've observed occasions where pastors lose credibility with public figures because they couldn't stop *name-dropping* the public figure's name as someone who they know or who attends their church to boost their own social status. I've watched leaders give preferential treatment to generous donors, only for the relationship to shift when the person's financial situation changed. I've even observed leaders metaphorically *rolling out the red carpet* for someone new who pulls into the lot in a luxury car while overlooking a faithful volunteer who has served for years and struggles just to afford gas to get to church.

These kinds of imbalances do not reflect the heart of Kingdom leadership and inevitably cause offense. People aren't blind to favoritism, and trust erodes when they feel unseen or exploited.

James 2:1,8 (TPT-Emphasis by the author)
*1 My dear brothers and sisters, fellow believers in our glorious Lord Jesus Christ—how could we say that we have faith in him and **yet we favor one group of people above another?***
8 Your calling is to fulfill the royal law of love as given to us in this Scripture: "You must love and value your neighbor as you love and value yourself!" For keeping this law is the noble way to live.

Scripture is clear in James 2:1-10—showing this kind of favoritism is a sin. Beyond that, it's also unloving, self-centered, and often manipulative. To any leader who finds themselves prioritizing the famous or influential, I'd offer this challenge: *If you primarily cater to the famous, you'll miss out on learning from the faithful.*

Hurting or High-Profile

While we're on the topic of the lenses of members and volunteers and how they perceive leadership—especially when it comes to how they are valued or treated based on surface-level impressions—I'd like to share a story that recently gave me a fresh perspective. It came out of a conversation with a couple who had been earnestly seeking connection within our church. As they shared their experience at a previous church, something the husband said struck me in a way I hadn't fully considered before.

David told me that he and his wife, Nancy, had been deeply involved in their former church's volunteer culture. He served on the worship team, and Nancy helped lead a small group of teenage girls in the youth ministry. Their church in Nashville, Tennessee, was quite large and well-known. In a city filled with celebrities and affluent individuals, it wasn't uncommon for someone famous to unexpectedly show up at a service. And when they did, even church leaders often couldn't help but act a little starstruck.

The church had a phenomenal outreach program—feeding the homeless, ministering to the underserved, sending prayer teams to hospitals—what he described was all very impressive to me on the surface. He remarked that they often felt unseen despite their heavy involvement, faithfulness, and commitment to the Great Commission. But what David said next hit me like a gut punch when He said, *"We weren't celebrities, and we weren't dying of cancer... so we were invisible."*

That statement has stuck with me for weeks. Sometimes, when you've been on the *"inside"* of church leadership for years—planning, serving, leading—it becomes easy to forget what it's like to feel like an *"outsider"* because you are constantly right in the middle of everything that is happening. David's words reminded me that even the most dedicated volunteers can feel *unseen* if we unintentionally reserve our attention only for the hurting or the high-profile.

That statement carries so much weight for me as a leader—because, sadly, there's a lot of truth in it. Too often, church leaders go above and beyond to make sure that new visitors feel welcomed and seen. If someone shows up looking sharp, driving an eye-catching sports car, or carrying a certain level of influence or status, they're often treated like VIPs. And yes, on the other hand, when someone in the congregation is navigating through a crisis, the church rightly rallies to support them—this is when the *strength of the pack* shows up in force. But it was undeniable to me as a leader that the rule of thumb often holds true: It is *the squeaky wheel that gets the grease.*

Meanwhile, the faithful volunteers—the ones who show up week after week, serve without complaint, don't demand attention, and don't bring any special status to the table—can easily go unnoticed. And yet, these very people are the backbone of any healthy and thriving church. David's perspective is a powerful reminder that, as leaders, we must remain intentional not only with the hurting or the high-profile but with those quietly and consistently carrying the weight of ministry alongside of us. That lens should matter greatly for anyone who truly desires to lead as a Kingdom leader through both protection and empowerment.

As we close this chapter reflecting on the experiential lens of the member and volunteer, it's important to recognize the profound impact church culture and leadership practices can have—both for good and for harm. Volunteers are not just helpers; they are the heartbeat of the Church, and when their service goes unnoticed or their humanity is overlooked, it leaves wounds that often go unspoken. But healing doesn't begin with blaming leadership alone. It begins when we, as volunteers and members, acknowledge our own responses to pain, our expectations, and our role in stewarding our hearts well. In the next chapter, we'll turn the mirror inward and explore what it means to take ownership of our lens—how we see leadership, the Church, and even God—especially after we've been hurt. Because growth isn't just about what happens to us… it's also about how we choose to respond.

Chapter Seventeen
Member/Volunteer Lenses Part II
What Is My Responsibility?

It's often easy to point out leadership *failures* and identify how others have contributed to our wounds, but healing and growth begin when we're willing to ask the harder question: what is my responsibility in all of this? In the story of our own *"church hurt"* and *Post-Traumatic Church Disorder* experiences, our focus often lands on what was done to us—but while Scripture challenges leaders for how they lead, it also challenges us to examine how we responded. This chapter invites you to look inward, not to excuse poor leadership, but to explore how your posture and responses may have also shaped your experience. Because while we can't control what others do, we are always responsible for how we respond—and it's in that response where true spiritual maturity is often revealed.

If that opening paragraph stirred up any defensiveness, please know that wasn't the intent. I truly believe that if you'll keep reading, you'll find this chapter—and the ones that follow—to be not only clarifying, but deeply empowering.

Almost nothing worth having comes without a fight, and personal growth is most often painful. While I've had many enjoyable leadership experiences filled with great memories, the most transformative and enduring lessons I've learned as a leader have often been forged in seasons of difficulty. Following God's direction isn't always easy, and from personal experience, I can tell you there have been times when God asked me to stay silent and submit to leadership, even when I had very strong opinions about another way to handle a situation. There have also been moments where obedience to God meant walking through things that deeply grieved my heart.

God often uses leaders in our lives to stretch and grow us, and I can say confidently that a person who hasn't learned to follow faithfully will typically struggle to lead well. In the Kingdom, promotion is often preceded by submission to the authority God places in our lives for our development. Of course, we're never called to submit to leaders who lead us into ungodliness—that should go without saying. But in many cases, God uses imperfect people in leadership to shape us into the leaders He's called us to be. And herein lies the tension we rarely talk about: we serve a perfect God who sometimes appoints imperfect individuals—those who may even contribute to our PTCD experience—as spiritual voices of authority into our lives. That paradox can create real internal conflict for those trying to follow well.

Through years of faithfully serving both as a leader and under leadership, I've come to realize that some of the most powerful lessons about leadership can come from observing what *not* to do.

As you continue to grow in your leadership journey, it's likely you'll encounter seasons where you're asked to submit to leadership that's far from perfect. How you respond in those moments will play a major role in shaping your growth and preparing you for the doors God plans to open next.

Humility and proper perspective are often developed in the difficult seasons—when God calls you to stay in your lane and honor leadership even when it's uncomfortable. But those who embrace the process and guard their hearts have the capacity to become deeply respected leaders. Why? Because they've been molded not only by good examples but also by learning what not to do from leaders who were still in the process of growing themselves.

Serving under an imperfect—or even poor—leader can actually become a valuable asset to a future high-level leader because it positions you to learn from someone else's mistakes. There's an old saying that a wise man learns from his mistakes, but I don't fully agree. While it's true that a fool may fail to learn even from his own missteps, I believe even a dumb animal can eventually learn from their own pain. A truly wise person, however, is intentional about learning from the mistakes of others. When you serve under a leader who drops the ball in significant ways, insight and wisdom are available—if you're willing to approach the experience with discernment. But it requires resisting offense, disillusionment, or the temptation to replicate those same unhealthy leadership patterns. God never wastes pain, but we must be willing to extract the lesson and use it as an outline for growth.

Perseverance

Perseverance has a way of maturing us and developing character in the life of a believer like few other lessons in life.

Romans 5:3-5 (TPT)
3 But that's not all! Even in times of trouble we have a joyful confidence, knowing that our pressures will develop in us patient endurance. 4 And

patient endurance will refine our character, and proven character leads us back to hope. 5 And this hope is not a disappointing fantasy, because we can now experience the endless love of God cascading into our hearts through the Holy Spirit who lives in us!

James 1:12 (TPT)
12 If your faith remains strong, even while surrounded by life's difficulties, you will continue to experience the untold blessings of God! True happiness comes as you pass the test with faith, and receive the victorious crown of life promised to every lover of God!

Romans 12:12 (TPT)
12 Let this hope burst forth within you, releasing a continual joy. Don't give up in a time of trouble, but commune with God at all times.

Hebrews 10:35-36 (AMPC)
35 Do not, therefore, fling away your fearless confidence, for it carries a great and glorious compensation of reward. 36 For you have need of steadfast patience and endurance, so that you may perform and fully accomplish the will of God, and thus receive and carry away [and enjoy to the full] what is promised.

1 Corinthians 15:58 (AMPC)
58 Therefore, my beloved brethren, be firm (steadfast), immovable, always abounding in the work of the Lord [always being superior, excelling, doing more than enough in the service of the Lord], knowing and being continually aware that your labor in the Lord is not futile [it is never wasted or to no purpose].

Leadership development isn't always easy, but a vital part of becoming the leader God has called you to be often involves learning to work with the authority He has placed over you—even when it's challenging. There will be moments when you believe you have a better idea or hold an opinion that differs from your leaders. But how you respond to their *"no"* or disagreement reveals more about your character than it does about their leadership. Even if you're right and confident in your position, when spiritual authority is established, biblically, it's part of God's divine structure—and learning to honor that (within healthy boundaries) matters.

Romans 13:1a (TPT)
1 Every person must submit to and support the authorities over him. For there can be no authority in the universe except by God's appointment...

If you're not the one in charge, but you know (keywords: "YOU KNOW") God has positioned you in a specific place, at a specific time, under a specific leader, then trust that He has something valuable for you to learn and experience in that season. Be mindful not to derail God's purpose by allowing pride, impatience, or entitlement to take root. Stay humble, stay faithful—because the promise still stands: you will see victory if you don't give up.

Galatians 6:9 (AMPC)
9 And let us not lose heart and grow weary and faint in acting nobly and doing right, for in due time and at the appointed season we shall reap, if we do not loosen and relax our courage and faint.

Position, Proximity, Relational Currency
Since this section of the chapter focuses on your responsibility—and much of the book has already addressed the weight of proper Kingdom leadership—I want to highlight two critical considerations for those who aren't in the top leadership role. Specifically, how you posture yourself and present your perspective to your leader—especially when offering feedback that is confrontational or differs from their current stance—is vital.

If you feel like you have a perspective that could benefit your leader, there are two important things you should take into account before sharing it:

1. **Your Position** – Understand your role in the organization and the authority that comes with it.
2. **Your Relational Currency** – Consider the level of trust, credibility, and relationship equity you've built with your leader.

As someone who has been in ministry for over 30 years, I can confidently say that when it comes to leadership decisions in the church, everyone (and I do mean *EVERYONE*) has an opinion on how things should be done. That constant wave of second-guessing and criticism can be incredibly draining for a leader, especially when they are sincerely seeking God's direction for the organization.

In any leadership structure—particularly in churches—there is typically a chain of command in place that should be respected when raising questions or concerns. For those reading this who haven't held a leadership role in a church (or who may have overestimated their influence within the organization), it's important to understand that ignoring that chain of command is one of the fastest ways to have your perspective disregarded— and to posture yourself for unnecessary offense.

1. Your Position

If you hold an established leadership role within the church—whether as a staff member, board member, team leader, elder, or similar—your perspective naturally carries more weight. Typically, individuals in these roles have demonstrated long-term commitment and meaningful contributions to the church, which lends credibility to their voice. However, even with positional authority, it's critical to honor the established chain of command when expressing concerns or offering input. In larger organizations or churches where the senior leader may have to juggle a lot of staff and people related responsibilities, it's often not feasible for them to personally address every issue. That's why leadership structure and proper communication flow are vital.

2. Your Relational Currency

Relational currency refers to the strength of your relationships—the trust, respect, and credibility you've built with others over time. When you've invested in genuine connections, that emotional capital often gives you the opportunity to speak into situations where others, lacking that trust, may not be as readily heard.

A few years ago, a friend of mine shared a situation with me regarding the church he was attending. The leadership was implementing some changes he strongly disagreed with, and he asked my advice on how to respond. As we talked, I discovered he had only been attending for a short time, wasn't serving on any ministry teams, hadn't built relationships with any of the leadership team, and—most importantly—the issues he was concerned about weren't harmful or dangerous (which might have warranted more immediate action).

So I asked him one final question: *"Do you believe God has called you to be part of this church?"*

He said, *"Yes."*

I told him, *"Then, right now, you haven't built any relational currency in the organization. If you want to have future influence there, wait until God opens the door. If you speak too soon—before earning their trust—you may damage your chance of ever having a meaningful voice of influence with them."*

He paused for a moment, considered what I said, and then thanked me for helping him see things more clearly. Interestingly, I agreed with his perspective on the issue, but I reminded him that being right doesn't automatically grant you the platform to speak. Influence is most often earned through relationship, not just accuracy. Many people don't realize that saying the *right thing* at the *wrong time* can actually be the *wrong thing*. They often only recognize this after they've forfeited their influence by speaking out of turn. While exceptions exist, I would venture to say that this *relational currency* principle holds true in most leadership environments.

Although this wasn't the case with my friend, I've noticed a consistent pattern over the years: when someone new to a church—who hasn't yet built meaningful relationships with the leadership—feels compelled to voice their disagreement or offer direction to senior leaders, it's often rooted in pride, a need to be seen, or an unwillingness to submit to authority.

I've seen this scenario unfold time and time again. While unique circumstances exist, the impulse to be heard without having first earned trust or invested relationally is typically not about the *leadership*—it's about the individual's own critical spirit, pride, or lack of spiritual submission.

These individuals often become church hoppers, moving from one congregation to another, constantly seeking validation, and being easily offended when leaders don't immediately give them a voice of influence. The real issue, however, is that they've never stayed long enough—or submitted deeply enough—to build the trust and relational currency necessary to have their voice carry any weight.

On the other side of the coin, there are individuals who have invested time and effort into the church and developed some level of relational currency— but then overestimate the weight of their influence. It takes discernment to understand that just because your pastor asked for feedback on your child's experience in kids' ministry doesn't mean you now have the authority to offer opinion on how his own children are behaving in that same setting. Trying to spend influence you haven't actually earned often backfires, and instead of gaining trust, you end up losing credibility.

Sometimes, people are genuinely unaware of why their influence seems to diminish. Since this book is about addressing the *elephants in the sanctuary,* this chapter emphasizes that recognizing and accurately assessing one's level of relational currency is essential to maintaining healthy and effective communication within church leadership structures.

When Even Relational Currency Isn't Enough

Still, there is another perspective as it pertains to relational currency that merits consideration. I've witnessed numerous situations in ministry where—even when the right person, with the appropriate amount of relational currency, approached a concern respectfully—things still went sideways. Why? Because the leader's own insecurity couldn't handle being challenged, even by someone qualified to speak into the matter.

There are countless variables in these situations, and it's impossible to address them all here. However, one major source of avoidable conflict could be eliminated simply by understanding and applying the principle of *relational currency.*

Did God Call You There?

Going back to the conversation with my friend about his church. When he came to me for advice about an issue that he strongly disagreed with, the most important question I asked him was this: *Do you believe God has called you to be part of this church?*

When we confront issues of disagreement or discomfort in the church we are attending, we have to ask ourselves the same question… *Do you believe God has called you to be part of this church?* If your answer to that question is *yes*, then you can be confident that God has a purpose for placing you there. As mentioned in earlier chapters, being planted in a local church is not just about what you can receive—but equally or, even more importantly, about what you are meant to give. When you stay connected to the place and people God has called you to, you begin to step into the fullness of who He's created you to be. Fulfillment won't come from what you get but from who you become in the process. That, more than anything, will determine whether you live joyful or bitter.

In any relationship, there will inevitably be moments of disagreement and even painful encounters. Sometimes, the tension may be the result of our own actions—but other times, we're simply caught in the crossfire, bearing the weight of situations we didn't cause. Still, if God has called you to be in that place for a season and hasn't released you from it, then how you respond to the pain becomes your responsibility. To be clear, this is not an endorsement of staying planted under spiritual abuse or heretical teaching. But it's equally important that we don't treat every disagreement, uncomfortable (or even offensive) moment as if it were spiritual abuse or heresy.

Faith in Leaders

I've often heard people say, "I just can't trust Christian leaders after everything I've been through." And while I fully understand where that comes from, especially in the context of PTCD, this chapter is about taking ownership of our responses. It makes me wonder—could it be that the depth of trust we placed in leaders, the expectations we carried, and the lens through which we interpreted our experiences contributed more to our disillusionment than we initially realized?

- Could it be that we've placed more trust in people than we have in God?
- Is it possible that our own insecurities have caused us to respond emotionally rather than being led spiritually?
- Have past wounds made us overly guarded, unintentionally setting ourselves up for disappointment?
- Could we have held unrealistic expectations that made it nearly impossible for leaders to succeed in our eyes from the very

beginning?

- Have we elevated leaders to a place in our hearts that only God should occupy—and when they failed to live up to our standards, were we more devastated than would be healthy?
- Do we carry a fear of rejection that keeps us from fully engaging unless it comes with unspoken conditions?
- Is it possible we've placed too much value on our own opinions and become more easily offended when things don't align with our preferences?
- Have past experiences with failed leadership left us resistant to submitting to authority, even when it's healthy?
- Maybe none of these fully explain our leadership wounds—but could aspects of them be shaping how we see and respond to leadership today?

If we truly want to heal and gain perspective for the future, we must be willing to honestly assess whether we've contributed—at least in part—to our own *Post-Traumatic Church Disorder* experiences. Healing requires us to examine not only what was done to us but also how we responded. Even in situations where we did everything we knew to do and things still unraveled; Scripture still calls us to take responsibility for our response. Whether we were the root cause, a contributing factor, or completely innocent, we are still accountable to respond in a Christ-like way as we move forward.

It's not always easy to do what God asks you to do. Sometimes you want to run, and God says, *FIGHT.* Sometimes you want to quit, and God says, *STAND.* Sometimes you want to fight, but God says, *TURN THE OTHER CHEEK.* Sometimes, you want to resist, and God says, *SUBMIT.* Sometimes, you just have to walk by faith and not by sight when things aren't easy…and God honors your faithfulness when you trust Him even when it doesn't make sense.

In Paul's second letter to the Corinthian church, he wraps up chapter 13 with a strong exhortation: *test your faith, stand strong in it* (verse 5), *so that you may continue on the path of righteousness even if you are **denigrated.*** (verse 7).

I looked up the word *denigrated* and found it interesting that Paul was telling them to hold steadfast to their faith and continue to respond in righteousness even when others *attack their reputation, defame them, speak damagingly of them, criticize them in a derogatory manner, sully them; charge them falsely with malicious intent; and attack their good name and reputation.*

Paul's message was clear: righteousness is still required—even when you're under fire.

It's almost as if Paul anticipated that, as believers, we would need to decide in advance how we'd handle inevitable moments of offense and attack. While the early church certainly faced pressure and persecution from outside sources—like the government—Paul's letters to the Corinthian church focused primarily on how believers treated and responded to *each other* within the church.

It's a sobering reminder that when Scripture says there's nothing new under the sun, that includes *being hurt by fellow believers*. Even if we didn't contribute to the offense, the Bible still gives us clear instructions on how we're expected to respond.

At the end of the day, healing from Post-Traumatic Church Disorder isn't just about what others did wrong—it's also about how we choose to respond when things go wrong. We must be willing to examine our own hearts, our expectations, and our responses through the lens of Scripture and humility. Holding leaders accountable is biblical, but holding ourselves accountable is transformational. The road to spiritual maturity demands that we resist the temptation to become bitter and instead choose the higher road of grace, truth, and Christ-like integrity. In the chapters to come, we'll continue building on this foundation—exploring how healthy church culture can be restored and how leaders and members alike can participate in rebuilding trust, healing wounds, and fostering communities that reflect the heart of Jesus.

Chapter Eighteen

PK Lenses

Growing up as a pastor's kid isn't just a church experience—it's a life experience. For PKs, the church isn't something they attend; it's the environment they're raised in, the backdrop of their childhood, and often the lens through which they first encounter God, people, and pain. From a young age, they are exposed to the beauty and burden of ministry, often without the emotional maturity or language to process what they're seeing and feeling. This chapter on PK's lenses is a compassionate exploration of that experience—the silent pressure, the double standards, the unseen sacrifices, and the deep wounds that can form as a result. But this chapter isn't just for PKs—these lenses have the power to enlighten and bring clarity to anyone who's navigated church life, regardless of their role or background. For those who grew up behind the curtain of ministry, this is a space to feel seen, understood, and maybe, finally, begin to heal.

As many of you know, "PK" is short for *Pastor's Kid* (or *Preacher's Kid*). While preparing to write this book, I sat down with an editor to discuss the content and get her feedback. Almost immediately, she said, *"I have several PK friends who could really benefit from this topic."* She went on to explain that many of them have experienced so much inconsistency in the church that they struggle with *PTCD* more than any other group she's encountered.

Her comment confirmed for me that it was necessary to include a chapter specifically addressing the PK lenses in relation to *Post-Traumatic Church Disorder*. While I wasn't technically a PK—my father didn't become a pastor until I was an adult—many of my childhood friendships were with preacher's kids. Throughout my years in ministry, I've had the privilege of mentoring many PKs. And now, at the time of writing this book, I'm raising a PK of my own—my son has only ever known his dad as a pastor.

As I began to outline the chapter, I discovered that the subjects I would be expounding upon and the lenses I was addressing for *the PK* were much more applicable to a broader demographic than I might have previously assumed. So, PK or not, I think ever reader will find this chapter very enlightening and maybe even healing in your PTCD journey.

The experience of being a PK is unique, largely because they live in close proximity to both the best and most challenging sides of ministry life. This dynamic is especially difficult because they are often forced to process these complex situations long before their emotional maturity or prefrontal cortex has fully developed. It's hard enough for a pastoral husband and wife to navigate the hardships of ministry together as adults, but it's often not acknowledged that when parents endure ministry-related pain, their children often endure it too—without the tools, maturity, or support adults have.

For PKs, church isn't just a place they attend—it's their entire world. When their parents sacrifice for the church, the children do too. When the pastor's closest friends, who regularly shared meals and fellowship, suddenly get offended and leave the church, their children often leave too, taking with them some of the PK's dearest friendships. When the denomination or a church board vote to replace the pastor and sends the family to a new, unfamiliar town, the children are also uprooted from everything familiar. And when a pastor is wounded by congregants, their kids, listening from the backseat, or overhearing late-night conversations, absorb the pain, often carrying secondhand offense, as they become deeply impacted by what their parents are going through.

The most important thing to remember in all of this is: *they're just kids.* While adults might struggle with bitterness or discouragement over church trauma, PKs are left to process the same events with a fraction of the maturity or emotional tools. Unlike most children outside of ministry families, PKs are repeatedly exposed to high-stakes spiritual and emotional pressure, with little preparation or foundation from which to manage it effectively.

And as if the weight of ministry life weren't heavy enough, many PKs also find themselves navigating a confusing spiritual reality—one where what they're taught about God doesn't always align with what they see lived out by His people. The tension between biblical truth and the behavior of those who call themselves Christians can create internal conflict that's hard to untangle, especially for a child. This kind of dissonance often introduces another layer of trauma that I would call: *religious inconsistency.*

Religious Inconsistency

Even Jesus wasn't exempt from the judgment of the religious community around Him. In Mark 2:3, it was the religious leaders who kept a close eye on Him, not to catch some major wrongdoing but to see if He would heal on the Sabbath and break *their* rules or traditions. Unfortunately, that same legalistic, critical spirit still exists in many church environments today through Christians who project that same judgmental, religious spirit upon others.

In particular, Pastor's Kids (PKs) often find themselves under an intense spotlight. They grow up feeling like they live in a glass house, with every move being watched and evaluated. While most families can deal with personal issues privately behind closed doors, that luxury doesn't always exist for PKs, because ministry isn't just a job for their parents, it's their family's life.

So, when a PK hits a rough patch or goes through a rebellious phase, it often plays out publicly, right in front of the same youth group they're expected to be a model for, especially when that rebellion might involve another young person from their youth group. And when a regular church member has a fight with their spouse on a Sunday morning, they can choose to skip service. A pastor doesn't have that option. He still stands on stage, puts on a smile, and delivers a message of hope, even when the family is going through personal pain behind the scenes. PKs see it all. They live behind the curtain and witness both the beauty and the burden of ministry life.

PKs grow up with a constant awareness that their lives are different from those of their peers. From a young age, they recognize that they're part of something unique—something that often requires them to present a version of themselves that feels *safer*, even if it feels *inauthentic*. They watch their families portray one image in public while behind closed doors, life sometimes looks very different. Not from a duplicitous or sinful place, but just from a comfortable *image* perspective, because, as the PK learns very young in life, in many churches, transparency can be costly. This feeling of duality can be deeply confusing and even damaging for children who haven't yet developed the emotional or mental maturity to fully process it.

Beyond feeling like they live in a glass house where every move is scrutinized, many PKs also wrestle with the sense that they've been robbed of a *"normal"* childhood. Some attend private or homeschool settings, while others go to public schools and quickly realize that their life experience isn't like that of their classmates. And it's not just a matter of living by different values—when you factor in all the sacrifices, pressures, and comparisons they deal with, it's easy to see why many PKs begin to feel isolated and sometimes even resentful.

When PKs witness hypocrisy in the church—when the actions of "Christians" contradict what Scripture teaches—it can plant the seeds of resentment. That resentment deepens when they're held to higher standards than their peers or restricted from activities their church friends are freely allowed to participate in. Then there are the personal sacrifices—those moments when church responsibilities pulled their dad away from football games, recitals, or family dinners to tend to a church member instead. When it starts to feel like the congregation gets more of their parents' time than they do, it's unsurprising that many PKs grow up carrying bitterness—not just toward ministry, but sometimes, heartbreakingly, toward God Himself.

While I've known many pastors who've done an amazing job maintaining a healthy work-life balance—raising kids who now have a positive view of ministry—I've encountered just as many, if not more, PKs who, even as adults, still carry resentment toward the church because of how ministry impacted their childhood. And it's not always their parents' fault. Sometimes, the parents did everything they knew to do, and life, people, abuse, and even Satan still found a way to weasel in and cause disillusionment in the PK's life.

I recently watched an interview with a well-known celebrity who was raised as a PK. They described how they never felt free to ask questions that challenged what they were taught. They recalled being prohibited from eating Lucky Charms because the word *"lucky"* reminded their mother of *"Lucifer."* In their household, *"deviled eggs"* were renamed *"angeled eggs."*

While I'm not criticizing the parents for holding to convictions they believed were spiritually important, it was clear that these were just a few of many experiences that this PK struggled to process. When you combine legalistic practices, inconsistencies from people who should've known better, an environment where questions weren't welcomed, and all the unique personal experiences only that family lived through, it becomes easier to understand how this PK ended up conflicted. Their lived Christian experience fell short of the expectations they naturally formed while growing up in a pastor's home, and when they were finally old enough to make their own decisions, church wasn't a priority.

Religious Tradition

The New Testament is filled with examples of religious leaders during Jesus' time who were more focused on preserving traditions, appearances, rule-keeping, and maintaining control than on truly caring for the people they were called to lead. These are the same individuals Jesus openly rebuked— calling them hypocrites and a brood of vipers and even saying their true master was not His Father, whom they claimed to serve, but Satan himself.

Their obsession with strict adherence to religious customs caused them to completely miss the heart behind the rules. They placed higher value on upholding traditions than on showing compassion, prioritizing rigid enforcement over the well-being of those the rules were meant to protect.

In simpler terms: *they majored in the minors and minored in the majors.* They elevated the insignificant and, in doing so, neglected what truly mattered.

In Mark 7, Jesus directly challenges the hypocrisy of the religious leaders.

At the start of the chapter, they confront His disciples—not for breaking a commandment of God, but for eating bread without going through their traditional handwashing ritual. While handwashing is certainly a good hygiene practice, this wasn't a law from Moses; it was a tradition passed down by their elders. The issue wasn't cleanliness—it was that these leaders were treating human tradition as if it held the same weight as God's Word, and they judged others for not following their man-made customs as though it were *"sin."*

When they brought this accusation to Jesus, He didn't hold back. In verse 6, He called them hypocrites, exposing how they honored God with their lips while their hearts were far from Him. Jesus went on to condemn how they used their traditions to manipulate and control people, all while neglecting the more important matters of God's law—especially when it didn't serve their own interests. When I speak with PKs who have been wounded by a PTCD experience, they often point out parallel events.

The Letter vs The Spirit of The Law

When I was in the police academy, we often discussed the difference between the *letter of the law* and the *spirit of the law*. The *letter of the law* refers to the strict, literal interpretation of the law's wording. The *spirit of the law,* on the other hand, focuses on the intent or purpose behind it—the *"why"* it was established in the first place.

In Mark 7, when Jesus confronted the religious leaders, He was highlighting this very difference. He emphasized that obeying the law's literal wording wasn't as important as understanding the heart behind it.

While it's necessary to understand the letter of the law, it's even more important to grasp why it exists. In another similar instance (Mark 2), Jesus was criticized for healing a man on the Sabbath. The religious leaders saw this as a violation of the law. But Jesus responded by saying, *"The Sabbath was made for man, not man for the Sabbath,"* or in other words, *the sabbath was created to serve people, not the other way around*. In this statement, Jesus didn't break the sabbath; HE LOOSED IT! He loosed it from the bondage of tradition in the man-made rules of God.[xliii]

The religious leaders were so fixated on enforcing rules that they completely missed the heart of the God they claimed to serve. Imagine how the people must have viewed God when those who represented Him—these Pharisees and religious scholars—judged, controlled, and mistreated others while claiming to do so on God's behalf. Perhaps this is why Scripture conveys the necessity that Jesus *came to reveal the Father*. People couldn't see God clearly because those meant to represent Him had misrepresented Him so badly.

Few encounter PTCD earlier or more intimately than pastor's kids. From a young age, they often come face-to-face with individuals influenced by the same religious spirits that once drove the religious leaders in Jesus' day. These modern-day Pharisees are so fixated on the letter of the law that they completely miss the heart behind it. And kids—especially PKs—are perceptive. The more they come to understand who Jesus revealed God to be, the more clearly they recognize the gaps between that truth and their own lived experiences. It's in those inconsistencies that resentment begins to grow—especially when the law was imposed on them harshly and hypocritically, without any reflection of the grace or spirit that should have guided it.

Perception Determines Reception

When there's a gap between someone's lived experiences and their expectations, especially within the church, it can deeply affect how they perceive everything tied to that experience. Just as the Pharisees distorted people's view of Jesus' Father, those who misuse their influence while claiming to represent God, the Church, or any trusted institution can shape how others perceive the entire institution. And often, how something is perceived determines how it's received.

A few years ago, I delivered a Father's Day message and was told later about a woman sitting in the back row of the church. With tears streaming down her face, she quietly repeated the words, *"God is not my father."*

It was clear that she was struggling to connect with the idea of God as a father—likely because her own experience with a father figure had been marked by abuse, neglect, or abandonment. That painful association made the concept of a loving Heavenly Father difficult—perhaps even impossible—for her to embrace. I read this quote on the subject from one of my favorite books, And David Perceived He Was King:

I'm convinced that the enemy tries to destroy our relationship with our natural father so that he can dominate our relationship with our heavenly father. The enemy will use our natural father's anger or emotional distance to blind us from seeing what we are called to enjoy with our heavenly Father.[xliv] – Dale Mast

Trauma at any stage of life can hinder development, but the experiences we go through in childhood and early adolescence often have the deepest and most lasting effects. Our personalities, coping mechanisms, and responses to stress are largely shaped during these formative years. That's why so many fully grown adults still seek therapy to work through childhood trauma.

Like the woman with father wounds was struggling to identify with my Father's Day message, for PKs who endure *Post-Traumatic Church Disorder*, it sometimes becomes incredibly difficult to separate their wounds from the *God* their manipulators, controllers, or abusers claim to represent.

Sadly, many of the standards and rules emphasized in church culture aren't grounded in a healthy, accurate interpretation of Scripture. Far too often, what's modeled by leadership doesn't reflect godly character, and the behaviors or traditions upheld can be wildly inconsistent with who Jesus actually revealed Himself to be. For PKs, this disconnect is often experienced up close, leaving a lasting impression. That's why it's so crucial that our understanding of God isn't based solely on people but firmly rooted in the truth of His Word. Jesus came to reveal the true nature of the Father—and while church leaders may try, they don't always get it right.

God's Not Done With You

God's desire was always to have a loving relationship with humanity—it was never meant to be reduced to a religious system. Yes, we've heard that God hates sin, and that's true. But that doesn't mean He hates us because we sin. God loves you—deeply and unconditionally. He knows that one minute of anger, lust, and greed can ruin a decade of hard work,[xlv] and that's why He hates sin. I don't believe for a second that He hates sin just because it hurts Him; I believe He hates it because you are His child, and He knows how much it hurts you!

A parent of a heroin addict doesn't hate the drug simply because it's heroin—they hate it because of the destruction, bondage, and heartache it's caused in their child's life. Similarly, Scripture teaches that sin leads to death, but Jesus came to reveal the love of our Heavenly Father and to give us the power to overcome the bondage and consequences that sin brings. That view of God is radically different from how He is often portrayed—less like an angry judge waiting to punish every mistake and more like a loving Father desperate to rescue His children.

This is why it's so important to understand Jesus' response to His disciples in John 14 when they asked Him to show them the Father. Jesus simply said, *"Look at me…If you've seen me, you've seen the Father."*

He didn't say, *"Look at the religious leaders,"* or *"Follow every tradition and rule, and you'll understand God."* He said, *"Watch me—how I speak, how I act—and you'll understand who your Father truly is."* Then He proved it when a woman caught in adultery—an act punishable by death—was brought before Him. Instead of condemning her, He challenged her accusers: *"Let the one who is without sin throw the first stone."* When they all walked away, He turned to her with compassion and said, *"They're gone—and I'm not here to condemn you either. Go and sin no more."*

Regardless of what may have been misrepresented to you by religious leaders, the image of Jesus standing protectively beside a woman who was clearly guilty—and by the law, deserving of death—is a powerful and true reflection of who God REALLY is. In that moment, Jesus didn't shame her; He covered, protected, and defended her with compassion, even in her guilt.

That paints a very different picture from what many have seen modeled by religious authorities. Jesus didn't say, *"If you've seen the religious leaders, you've seen the Father."* He said, *"Look at Me—I am the exact reflection of My Father."*

PK, if you've experienced PTCD at the hands of those who should have loved and protected you, I want to say I'm truly sorry. It shouldn't have happened, and God does not approve of the way you were treated. But even in that pain, your experience has the potential to become a powerful catalyst for your future—one that brings healing and restores balance for others.

As a pastor's kid, you likely know the Word of God as well as anyone, and you also recognize when it's been misrepresented or misapplied by those in leadership. Your perspective is incredibly valuable to future generations because you've seen firsthand what happens when leaders claim to represent God but fail to reflect His heart. You understand deeply what it means to lead people with authenticity and humility—and what happens when that's missing.

You carry wisdom that the Body of Christ needs. Your story, your insight, and your healing can help shape a healthier model for the Church. You are a vital part of the body of Christ, and we are better and stronger when you walk fully into the role God has created you to fill.

If PTCD has created a distance in your heart between you and the church (or even God), my prayer for you is this: that you would dare to dream with Jesus again. Let Him show you how He sees you—your worth, your calling, and the significance of your purpose in this world. As we've discussed throughout this book, the enemy does everything in his power to disrupt destiny, and he came after you early because he saw the world-changing potential God placed inside of you. But God's not done with you.

I'm simply asking you to reconsider the calling God placed on your life— the one He placed in you before you were born and that He's never taken back. Even if you haven't seen the leader you would have longed for, you can still be that leader for someone else. Your scars don't disqualify you— they prepare you to lead with the kind of compassion, authenticity, and wisdom the Church so desperately needs. As we move forward, let's continue unpacking the individual lenses through which we've seen the Church and God—and begin rebuilding a clearer, truer picture of who He really is and the healing still available to us.

By now, we've unpacked a great deal of truth surrounding church leadership, accountability, and the damaging effects of spiritual abuse and religious systems that misrepresent the heart of God. In Part 1, we laid the foundation of Kingdom leadership as it was intended—anchored in servanthood, humility, and Christ's example. Part 2 pulled back the curtain on the various lenses through which Post-Traumatic Church Disorder is experienced—whether you're a pastor, staff member, volunteer, congregant, or even a pastor's kid—highlighting how those roles shape our perceptions and expectations.

But knowledge alone isn't enough. If we're going to experience healing, it can't just be about what happened to us or what others did wrong. It has to become deeply personal. In Part 3, we begin the sobering but necessary journey inward—examining our own responses to the pain we've endured and asking, *"What now?"* Because while leaders are absolutely accountable for how they lead, we are still responsible for how we respond.

This final section is a call to courageous ownership and hopeful restoration. We'll explore what Scripture says about forgiveness, obedience, and choosing to align our lives with God's truth—even when it's hard. We'll wrestle with honest questions like, *"Where was God when I was hurting?"* and *"Can He still use me after all I've been through?"* Spoiler alert: the answer is yes. He's not done with you. In fact, He's just getting started.

So now, we turn the page from examination to transformation, from what was, to what *can be*. This isn't just about surviving church hurt. It's about thriving beyond it. Because God's plan for your life didn't end with your pain—it continues with your participation. Let's begin this final leg of the journey together… one step closer to healing and one step deeper into purpose.

In earlier chapters, we began exploring the personal responsibility each of us carries when it comes to how we respond to leadership. While many of our painful PTCD experiences have stemmed from toxic or even ungodly leadership styles, we also acknowledged that part of the responsibility lies with us—to remain obedient to the Holy Spirit and respond in a Christlike manner, even when we disagree with those in authority over us.

I was recently having a conversation with a friend in full-time ministry, and I explained it this way: I've learned a lot from the leaders God has placed in my life, but honestly, I've learned more about what *not* to do in leadership than what *to* do from most of them.

People are, by nature, imperfect, and every single one of us needs the Holy Spirit to guide us when our humanity tries to dominate perspectives that only spiritual insight can help us live above.

In today's church culture, it's become increasingly common to approach faith through the lens of personal preference rather than spiritual purpose. Many believers have unknowingly adopted a *consumer mindset*—treating church like a subscription service where the goal is to receive rather than contribute. We pick churches based on programs, personalities, or convenience, and when things get uncomfortable, quit being entertaining, or don't align with our expectations, we move on to chase the next best thing.

This *consumerism* mentality lacks commitment, it lacks connection, and guidance from the Holy Spirit, it lacks power and breeds a lack of depth and maturity in the lives of believers. It runs completely counter to the biblical model of the Church—a place of deep connection, sacrifice, and Spirit-led purpose.

In Acts chapter 2, we see a vibrant, thriving church—but it's important to note that they weren't isolated individuals simply loving Jesus on their own. Instead, they were actively living out their faith in community, not merely pursuing personal comfort.

Acts 2:44-47 (TPT)
44 All the believers were in fellowship as one body, and they shared with one another whatever they had. 45 Out of generosity they even sold their assets to distribute the proceeds to those who were in need among them. 46 Daily they met together in the temple courts and in one another's homes to celebrate communion. They shared meals together with joyful hearts and tender humility. 47 They were continually filled with praises to God, enjoying the favor of all the people. And the Lord kept adding to their number daily those who were coming to life.

If we want to fully live out God's promises—if we truly long to see our families and lives transformed by His power and experience His blessing and favor—we must be willing to follow His leading beyond the boundaries of our own comfort. This means learning to be led by the Spirit, not ruled by convenience.

Galatians 5:16 (AMPC)
16 But I say, walk and live [habitually] in the [Holy] Spirit [responsive to and controlled and guided by the Spirit]; then you will certainly not gratify the cravings and desires of the flesh (of human nature without God).

Bruh, You Gotta Walk in the Spirit

Early in my law enforcement career, I served as a D.A.R.E. (Drug Abuse Resistance Education) officer, speaking in elementary and middle schools about the dangers of drug abuse. One of my training officers during that time was a guy named Andre.

Dre' and I hit it off right away. We were both from the Detroit area and had relocated to Nashville. He was a Michigan State fan, and I rooted for the University of Michigan, so our friendly sports rivalry added some fun to the mix. We shared a background in law enforcement, were promoted to detective around the same time, and were both involved in ministry outside the job.

Law enforcement can take an emotional toll, and it was a gift to have a Christian friend who understood the pressures and could help realign your perspective when needed. One afternoon over lunch, Dre shared a thought that became a *"true north"* moment for me—one I still look back on nearly two decades later.

In most departments, the criminal investigations division is consistently overwhelmed with more cases than there are investigators to handle them, and mine was no exception. I was one of six investigators, and it wasn't unusual for each of us to be assigned multiple new cases every day. The sheer volume of work kept us in a constant state of triage, where only the most serious cases could receive immediate attention. While every victim understandably views their case as urgent, a vandalized mailbox simply couldn't take precedence over a home burglary, and a burglary would take a back seat if a homicide came in.

That week, I had been assigned a case that I spent several days working on until the Assistant District Attorney (ADA) called and told me to place it on the back burner—he needed me to focus on a different matter. The very next day, that same ADA called again, this time sounding unusually anxious, and insisted I shift my attention back to the original case. By that point, I had already started making calls and organizing my schedule around the new assignment, so the sudden shift left me frustrated and in a bit of an emotional tizzy as I headed out to meet Dre' for lunch.

We sat down, and it was clear to Dre' that something was bothering me. He asked what I was working on, and as I started walking him through everything that had happened over the past 24 hours, the frustration and stress were written all over my face. Dre', with a knowing half-smile, looked down at the table and shook his head.

Curious, I asked, *"What's so funny?"* He looked up at me and said, *"Bruh, you gotta walk in the Spirit."*

I heard the words, but they didn't quite sink in. Still venting, I went on, *"You know how it is! The ADA probably got a call from someone who donated to the DA's campaign and—"* Before I could finish, Dre' cut me off—still smiling but now more serious. He looked me straight in the eye, leaned in, and said slowly and with emphasis on each word, *"BRUH. YOU. GOTTA. WALK. IN. THE. SPIRIT."*

Those words have stuck with me ever since. Even now, years later, whenever I find myself getting emotionally wrapped up in a frustrating situation, I can still hear Dre's voice echo in my mind—*"Bruh, you gotta walk in the Spirit!"*

Choosing to Walk in the Spirit

We are instructed throughout Scripture to rise above our natural tendencies and live empowered by the Spirit of God. *"Walk by faith, not by sight," "walk in the Spirit, and you won't gratify the desires of the flesh,"* and *"trust in the Lord with all your heart and don't lean on your own understanding"*—all of these verses point to a higher way of living. And the truth is, it's a choice. We actually can choose to walk in the Spirit. It requires intentionality, but it is the Godly path.

Human nature tends to focus on what we lack rather than what we have.

Think about Adam and Eve. As mentioned earlier in the chapter on discontentment and deception, they lived in Eden—a literal paradise. They walked with God daily, were free from sin, and yet still managed to become dissatisfied. A single suggestion that perhaps God was withholding something from them was enough to plant seeds of doubt and lead them to act outside of His plan. As I stated in that chapter, I believe it was always God's intention to teach them about good and evil—but they took it upon themselves to rush the season and produce something in their lives before its proper time.

So, I question, how often do we do the same? How often do we try to rush through a season of discomfort before God has finished teaching us what we need to know? Our fast-paced, consumer-driven culture pushes us to crave quick solutions and immediate relief, but God's process often calls for patience, trust, and surrender. And I think it is safe to assume that every one of us has wrestled with that at one point or another.

When it comes to PTCD and our overall church experience, many find themselves tempted to rush God's process. Sometimes, it happens when they believe they're ready to lead—or even think they should already be the one in charge. Other times, they convince themselves it's time to leave a season prematurely because they assume they've already learned all there is to learn from a particular leader or environment.

I've seen discontentment arise in the hearts and minds of people when they become frustrated by a lack of information about a situation happening within the church that they believe they should be privy to, or when they're offended by a decision the pastor makes that doesn't align with what they would've chosen. It might even surface when a sermon challenges them, stirs discomfort, or confronts their personal views. Maybe it's when the pastor holds a different opinion—spiritually, doctrinally, or even politically. Whatever the trigger, the temptation is the same: to walk away or disengage rather than lean in and ask God what He's trying to form in them through it.

Assignment vs Attendance

If you believe that God led you to your church, then it's likely He placed you there with a purpose. There are lessons to learn, experiences to gain, and growth to be had in the season you're in. When you approach it as an assignment from the ultimate Teacher, your perspective shifts from passive attendance to intentional engagement.

Viewing church as just a place you *"attend"* leads to a consumer mindset, and you ask questions like: *"What do I get out of this?* and *"How does it make me feel?"* But when you see it as an assignment, your questions change to: *"What can I give?" "How can I serve?" "What has God placed in me that this community needs?" "What's missing if I'm not here?"*

Consumerism feeds our natural tendencies, but God has called us—and empowered us—to live above those tendencies and walk in intentional purpose with a Kingdom mindset.

I can't begin to count the number of times in my ministry journey that I pleaded with God for a new assignment. It hasn't always been an easy pill to swallow. I've served in churches where legalism, judgment, small-mindedness, division, deception, exclusion, and even degrees of spiritual abuse were present—and there were times when all I wanted was to move on to the next season. But time and time again, God said, "Stay."

Believe me when I say I understand what it feels like to remain obedient when everything in you wants to walk away. I've been there. But I can also tell you with absolute certainty that the hardest seasons of ministry were the ones that shaped me the most. They prepared me to lead with wisdom, empathy, and purpose. Sometimes, I had to stay because one person still needed something I was there to give. Other times, God was forming in me a perspective I could never have gained any other way—except by walking through the fire and staying faithful.

I won't claim to have always gotten it right, but I do believe this: when you remain faithful through the hard seasons God has called you to *endure*, it brings honor to Him.

James 1:2-4 (The Passion Translation – Emphasis by the author)
*2 My fellow believers, when it seems as though you are facing nothing but difficulties, see it as an invaluable opportunity to experience the greatest joy that you can! 3 For you know that when your faith is tested it stirs up in you the power of **endurance**. 4And then as your endurance grows even stronger, it will release perfection into every part of your being until there is nothing missing and nothing lacking.*

I really love how these verses in James are worded. While some Bible translations say that trials produce *patience,* both the Amplified Classic and The Passion Translation use the word *endurance* in verse 3—and I really connect with that.

So many believers—maybe even the majority—show up to church each Sunday, viewing it more as a place of *attendance* than an *assignment*. And when things become uncomfortable, it's easy to fall into a *consumer* mindset instead of seeing ourselves as Kingdom contributors. But when that happens, everyone misses out. If God led you to be there, it's for a purpose—and until He releases you, there's still more He wants to do in and through you in that place.

In Acts 20, Paul says something truly powerful. In verses 18–23, while addressing leaders, he basically says (paraphrased), *"You know I've never shrunk back from doing the hard things, even when it's cost me beatings and time in prison."*

Then, he shared how the Holy Spirit was leading him toward Jerusalem, fully aware that suffering and imprisonment awaited him there. In verse 24, Paul says something incredible about his assignment that deeply challenges and inspires me.

Acts 20:24 (The Passion Translation – Emphasis by the author)
"But whether I live or die is not important, for I don't esteem my life as indispensable. ***It's more important for me to fulfill my destiny and to finish the ministry*** *my Lord Jesus has assigned to me, which is to faithfully preach the wonderful news of God's grace.*

This mindset is one that I believe many in the Body of Christ today would struggle to fully grasp. Paul essentially tells the leaders, *"I'm probably going to die; they aren't going to accept me, but it's more important for me to be obedient, endure to the end, and finish this race that God has placed before me than to preserve self."*
That's a radically different level of commitment to endurance, and it's recorded in Scripture for a reason. The road to God's promises sometimes requires us to walk through hardship. We don't have to live there. We don't have to settle there. But sometimes we do have to walk through there. And when those tough seasons come, it's our responsibility to pursue God's way of doing and being, then follow the Holy Spirit's leading, even if it's difficult, uncomfortable, or doesn't seem to directly benefit us.
I've heard pastors preach (and until I had my own revelation of it, I too have used the quote in conversation and maybe even the pulpit): *"Go where you're celebrated, not where you're tolerated…"* But this is a completely unbiblical mindset. *Where you are celebrated* carries no bearing on your calling or direction from the Holy Spirit. Sometimes, the assignment is just bigger than your comfort, and it's your responsibility to be faithful to the call of God until you are released from it. I'm not saying it's easy, but it's right.
Our Western, *consumerism* culture has significantly influenced how we view the church. For many, church has become more like a gym membership than a spiritual family—something you join for personal benefit and leave when something more appealing comes along. If preferences aren't met or a *"better"* option appears, the instinct is often to move on. But the truth is, while there are moments when it's appropriate to transition, there are also times when staying planted is the right and necessary choice.
With that in mind, I want to share something I came across on this topic— five valid and five invalid reasons for leaving a church. I'm not presenting these as absolutes, nor is the list exhaustive, but when I read through it, I felt it offered some worthwhile perspective and was worth passing along for your consideration.

Five Valid Reasons to Leave a Church:
1. You've relocated to a different city, state, or country.
2. The church has strayed from essential, non-negotiable biblical doctrine.
3. The environment has become emotionally or spiritually abusive, and even after addressing it, nothing changes.
4. Persistent sin and a lack of holiness are tolerated or overlooked.
5. You genuinely feel led by the Holy Spirit to serve elsewhere, and you've prayed about it and sought counsel from your current pastor.

Five Invalid Reasons to Leave a Church:
1. Someone in the church offended you, and you don't want to deal with it.
2. You're simply bored and want something new or more exciting.
3. You have a gift but aren't willing to submit it to leadership, and you're searching for a place that will use you on your own terms.
4. You're chasing a doctrine that aligns with your preferences—even if it's biblically unsound.
5. You were challenged in an area of sin or character, and instead of growing, you chose to walk away.

You won't grow spiritually if you're always hopping from one church to the next. And you'll never truly love a church until you commit to loving its people—especially when times are tough[xlvi].

Sometimes, we do everything we know is right, yet things still don't turn out how we expected or hoped. Sometimes, we align ourselves with visions or leaders who stumble, and it leaves us feeling disoriented, hurt, or even betrayed. We may serve with faithfulness and integrity, only to be mistreated by those who should've known better. The truth is, we're all imperfect people on a personal journey with God, and sometimes situations simply don't go our way. But no matter what others do, their actions can never cancel the promises God has spoken over your life.

Scripture reminds us that *God is not mocked—whatever a person sows, that is also what they will reap* (Ephesians 6:7). We're also promised that *God is faithful to complete the good work in us that He began* (Philippians 1:6).

As you reflect and we close this chapter, I urge you to remember that when disappointment or betrayal comes, don't take it personally, and don't let it shake your faith. Disillusionment leads to distraction, and distraction opens the door to deception. Don't allow pain to drive a wedge between you and God—or between you and the Body of Christ, which is meant to be a source of connection, strength, and refuge. People will sometimes let you down, but God never will. If you run to Him instead of pulling away, He is always faithful to restore and renew.

Consumerism may be the culture we live in, but it was never meant to be the culture of the Church. We were created for community, called to commitment, and commissioned to contribute—not just *consume*. My hope is that this chapter brings clarity to the consumer mindset that has crept into the Church and inspires those who may have unknowingly adopted it to pause and reevaluate, shifting from viewing church as a service to *consume*, to embracing it as a spiritual family we've been called and assigned to. Your presence matters. Your obedience matters. And your willingness to stay planted—especially when it's hard—can bear fruit in ways you may not even see yet. So, resist the urge to move on when things get uncomfortable. Instead, lean in, walk in the Spirit, and trust that even in the messiness, God is forming something in you that will last.

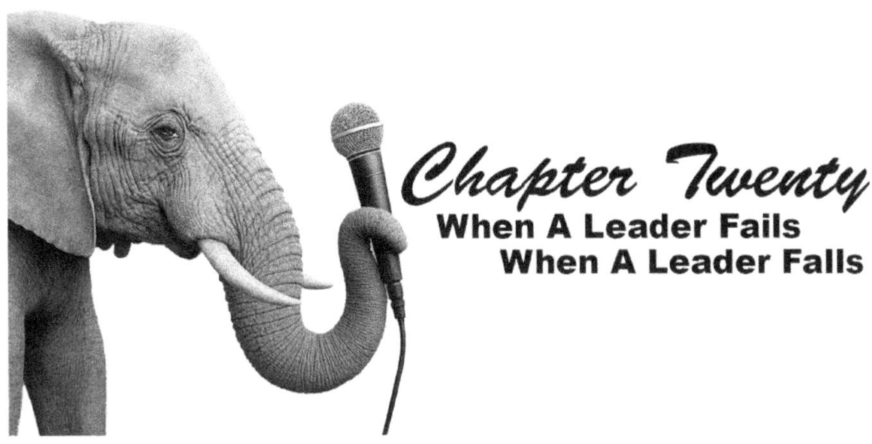

Few things hit harder than watching a spiritual leader stumble—especially when that leader was someone you trusted, followed, or loved. In those moments, the shockwaves don't just shake your view of them—they can rattle your sense of security, belonging, and even your faith itself. Whether it was a public fall or a private betrayal, the pain cuts deep because it touches something sacred. And while leadership failure may not be a new reality, its impact is always deeply personal. In this chapter, we are going to address that pain honestly and process it intentionally. Because how we respond in these moments has the power to shape our healing or harden our hearts.

Looking back to my childhood, I've witnessed more than my share of leadership breakdowns. I clearly remember the fallout from the high-profile televangelist scandals—moments etched in my memory not just because of the headlines but because of the tears I saw in the eyes of family and friends as the details of the stories unfolded. I've heard other's stories of betrayal and heartbreak, often caused by a leader's moral failure or affair when many had invested so much of themselves; their time, finances, emotions, and trust into a vision they believed was God-ordained, only to feel abandoned when it all came crashing down.

For many, when the church family scattered and the dream they had supported disappeared, what remained was a painful realization: their identity and sense of belonging in the body of Christ had been shaken and, in some cases, turned completely upside-down by the very person they trusted to lead them with integrity, humility, and submission to the Kingdom principles they once preached.

Experiences like these can be deeply discouraging and disorienting—sometimes to the point of redefining one's entire religious perspective, as the thought of starting over after so much was invested and lost in the wake of a leader's failure can feel like an impossible concept.

The reality is that most of us either already have, or eventually will, walk through something like this—maybe more than once. And when it happens, it's only natural to want to protect your heart moving forward and to build walls so that you're never hurt like that again.

There's no question that PTCD (*Post-Traumatic Church Disorder)* moments—when a leader fails or falls—can deeply impact and even redirect the course of your life. And while we may not be able to control the decisions those leaders make or have the relational equity to influence their outcomes, we are far from powerless. We still have the ability to shape our response and impact our personal outcomes—before, during, and after their failure.

Before the Failure Before the Fall

During my childhood and early adolescent years, I encountered several life-altering events that became the root of deep-seated foundations of fear and insecurity in me. But as I moved into my mid and late teen years, I discovered that by leveraging my physical stature and channeling anger, sometimes even rage, I could feel a sense of strength, and others would cower in situations that would normally trigger those insecurities and fears.

Anger eventually became my go-to defense mechanism against fear, but it also grew into a stronghold in my life. It wasn't a healthy response, and there were seasons when it became difficult for me to control. As I've grown and matured, and by directly confronting those strongholds, I've learned how to better manage my emotions and submit to the leading of the Holy Spirit. Still, the soil of my flesh has often proven fertile ground for anger to take root. Because of this, I've noticed that when the enemy targets me, it's usually through situations that provoke anger—his most familiar point of successful attack in my life. It's undeniable that the enemy cultivated this stronghold early on in my life with the intent of using it against me to limit my impact in the Kingdom of God.

Case in point, several years ago, I lost a close friend in a tragic and unexpected way. He had been my pastor for 16 years. We traveled together, I supported his vision wholeheartedly, and I even vacationed with him. We shared countless meaningful—sometimes even miraculous—moments throughout our years of friendship and ministry.

But toward the end, without unnecessarily diving into all the compounding complexities, I found my heart pretty deeply wounded. And as has often been my default in the face of that pain, I turned to anger as a coping mechanism.

I know the truth—*we don't wrestle against flesh and blood.* I know we're called to *take every thought captive and submit it to the obedience of Christ.* I understand that behind every earthly challenge, there's a spiritual root. I know who the real enemy is and where my strength is supposed to come from. But in that season, I lost sight of all of it... and I gave in to the hurt.

Even though the circumstances we faced would have inevitably changed the nature of our relationship—God was clearly shifting my path—I allowed offense, fueled by anger, to harden my heart. I gave up on someone I had once called a dear friend.

What makes it worse is that I knew he was going through his own battles, facing some serious health issues that desperately needed God's intervention. But my anger validated my offense, and the offense gave me permission to distance myself. I stopped reaching out. I even stopped praying for him.

And my friend died.

I'm sharing this story with raw honesty and transparency because I've spent my entire life immersed in ministry. I haven't just studied the Bible and its principles—I've devoted the majority of my life to teaching and guiding others in them. And yet, when the situation turned painful, I allowed my emotions to take hold in the midst of a spiritual battle manifesting in physical form, and I didn't respond in a way that reflected the heart of God.

Despite all my years in leadership and ministry, I wasn't exempt from reacting in a way that failed to reflect the love I knew I was called to walk in. I felt justified in my anger—because the offense was real. And as time passed, more layers of hurt and betrayal continued to emerge, uncovering things I hadn't initially known and further validating my reaction in my own mind. But looking back now, I can see that—regardless of the circumstances—I could have, and should have, responded differently.

I'm not claiming that my friend passed away solely because I stopped praying—but I also can't ignore the fact that my emotions played a significant role in causing me to give up on someone. I stopped interceding for him. Even when I don't just believe that prayer is powerful—I *know* it is.

While some view prayer as a last resort, I'm convinced it's the most powerful thing we can offer. Through prayer, the impossible becomes possible—where God's supernatural power meets our natural reality. Yet, in my anger, I believe I walked away from an assignment to pray for my friend before God ever released me from it.

I don't know whether or not my prayers would have changed the outcome. But the truth is, I never will know… because I quit.

Leaders often live under constant spiritual attack because the enemy knows that the sheep will often scatter if he can strike the shepherd. While we tend to evaluate our leaders through the lens of their roles and what we expect from them in leading us, I don't believe that many churchgoers and members often stop to consider their own role in protecting and covering their leaders in intentional prayer.

Ask yourself honestly—how often do you intentionally reflect on how you can be a blessing or source of support to your church, your pastor, or the leadership team? I know in my own life, it's been less than I should. But, as our *consumerism* chapter pointed out, far too often, people attend church solely focused on what they or their families can receive, when they have so much more to contribute.

When considering the number of moral and relational failures among leaders worldwide, I can't help but wonder how much those outcomes might have changed if the Body of Christ consistently and intentionally prayed for their pastors.

This is not to excuse any leader's personal responsibility to walk with integrity and godly character. But if we truly believe there is a real enemy actively working to steal, kill, and destroy—and if we believe in the power of prayer to push back against those attacks—then could it be that we've sometimes made it easier for the enemy and his attacks by failing to raise a spiritual shield against him through intercession and prayer? I'm not shifting blame, but I do think there are times when the weight of responsibility might be more complex and, at least in part, shared.

Scripture tells us that it's the *small foxes that spoil the vine* (Song of Solomon 2:15)—meaning that it's often the seemingly minor issues that, when left unchecked, can cause significant damage to relationships and spiritual growth. Major failures rarely begin with big, dramatic events; they often start with small compromises—seeds of pride, insecurity, resistance to correction, or an unwillingness to submit to spiritual authority. These small openings give the enemy a foothold in a leader's heart and mind, eventually derailing their long-term calling and purpose. I truly believe that many of these *"small foxes"* could be eliminated before they even become a problem if our leaders were surrounded by people committed to shielding and lifting them up through prayer, intercession, and godly relationships.

David fell into sin with Bathsheba because he wasn't where he was supposed to be. Likewise, before many leaders experience a public fall, there's usually a series of smaller, avoidable missteps that gradually take them out of alignment with their calling. In an effort to maintain appearances, leaders may project strength while privately sinking into emotional and spiritual despair. When these spiritual issues aren't confronted early and with intentionality, many leaders resort to fleshly means—like addictive behaviors or unhealthy coping mechanisms—to dull the internal pain. But as Scripture says, when we sow to the flesh, we reap destruction. That's because God never designed us to fight spiritual battles with natural weapons, and we also were not intended to fight alone.

Before a pastor fails or falls, we as the Body of Christ have a responsibility to faithfully operate in our role—being the part of the team God has called us to be—and, most importantly, to consistently cover our leaders in prayer. We should be praying for their protection, their families, their emotional well-being, their strength, and for divine wisdom to lead us well. We should be praying that *no weapon formed against them or their families will prosper*. If we know the enemy's strategy is to divide the Church, then we must be just as committed to intentionally and proactively intercede for our leaders—rather than waiting to pray only after the damage has been done.

During the Failure During the Fall

I've been in that situation more than once—receiving the text or call for an urgent leadership meeting involving staff, deacons, board members, and elders to address a leadership failure within the church structure.

The goal of the meeting is to ensure that all key leaders are informed and aligned, ready to answer questions from the congregation before rumors spread and phones start blowing up. It's never a call you want to receive, but the longer you're involved in ministry and the deeper your leadership role becomes, the more likely it is that you'll experience moments like these.

Sometimes, even when we've done everything right—loving our leaders, praying for them, serving faithfully, supporting the vision, and standing behind them in their calling—we can still find ourselves dealing with the painful consequences of a spiritual leader's ungodly decisions. And when that happens, the wounds can cut especially deep.

When we talk about spiritual leaders, it's important to remember that leadership in this context isn't limited to someone with the title of *"pastor."* Maybe your grandmother served as your spiritual leader, but shamed you for something that wasn't even a sin. Maybe your father, who raised you in church, was your spiritual leader—until his affair shattered your family. Or maybe it was a counselor, someone you trusted spiritually, who crossed a boundary with an inappropriate comment. I've witnessed countless situations where individuals in positions of spiritual influence—people meant to lead us toward Christ—fell short of that calling. And when that person has been a personal voice of spiritual guidance in your life, the impact can be just as devastating, if not more, than when a public *pastor* falls.

When the leaders we've looked up to fall short, it can leave us feeling powerless—sometimes even hopeless. Thoughts begin to swirl: *"If they couldn't live with integrity and a passion for Christ, what chance do I have?"* or *"They were my example—was any of it even real?"* or *"They were the only one who ever truly showed up for me… now that they're gone, where do I turn?"* These questions have the potential to shake the very foundation of our faith.

In the immediate aftermath of a leader's failure, the enemy often seizes the opportunity to sow division and disillusionment. Emotions run high, and that's when the enemy loves to whisper toxic, unbiblical thoughts. He'll try to get you to generalize and mistrust entire groups of people: *"See? All*

Christians are fake." or *"You were foolish to ever trust church people."* or *"This whole Christianity thing is a lie—why bother when even the leaders can't live it out?"*

And when you're in the middle of the emotional chaos, those thoughts might even seem reasonable. But that's exactly how the enemy works— using your pain to try and pull you away from faith, urging you to walk by what you see and feel rather than by faith in what God has said.

It's okay to admit that you were hurt. It's okay to recognize the wrong that was done. It's okay to call out the hypocrisy. Accepting that the person you looked up to wasn't who you thought they were is okay. But in the middle of all of that, when the emotions are high, don't be deceived into believing a lie—because *when you choose to believe a lie, you empower the liar.*

I've been married for 30 years. Overall, it's been a beautiful journey with an incredible woman—someone far better than I probably deserve. But let me be honest: there have been times when we have had some arguments. And during those difficult moments, the enemy was always nearby, ready to whisper lies designed to tear us apart. That's what he does—he tries to sow division by planting doubt and feeding off our emotions. Maybe you've had some thoughts like these yourself when you've been in disagreeable moments with your spouse:

- *If she truly loved you, would she have acted that way?*
- *If he actually respected you, there's no way he would've said that.*
- *What you tolerate, you authorize to exist; if you don't leave, you are just encouraging this!*
- *Maybe the love is gone, and divorce would be the best way forward.*
- *That guy at work who's always been nice to you would never treat you like this.*

When emotions are running high, the enemy is quick to flood your mind with lies, and if you dwell on them, the spiral downward can be intense. He understands that *what happens in the mind will happen in time,* as thoughts shape actions, so he strikes hardest when you're at your weakest. The same is true when a leader fails or falls—those vulnerable moments are prime time for his spiritual attack.

There's an old saying that still rings true, especially when someone we love or admire lets us down: *Don't forget in the dark what you learned in the light.* When God met you in your lowest moment, that was real. It was real when He used that leader to help you through that dark season of pain. When you sat in that service, overwhelmed by the tangible presence of the Holy Spirit—it was real. When you witnessed those miracles, when that message pierced your heart and marked a turning point in your life, when you felt like you heard directly from the throne of God as He spoke to you in those amazing services at the church—it was all real.

The enemy will do everything he can to make you second-guess those moments when your emotions are stirred, but you *know* the truth deep down. Don't let him steal what God deposited in you through those encounters. People are human—they fail—but what God did through them in your life was undeniably real!

Run *Too* (Also) or Run *To* (Toward)

There are countless ways a leader can stumble or fall—but when it happens, my encouragement to you is simple: do the opposite of what the lies are urging you to do. In your most painful and fearful moments, the enemy will work to divide, isolate, and scatter. And in those moments, when others feel the onset of panic, you'll feel the urge to *run too*. Don't!

That impulse to retreat is exactly what your enemy hopes you'll follow. Just like a predator seeks to scatter the herd to isolate its prey, the enemy wants to separate you from your place of safety, strength, and covering. So when everything in you screams that self-preservation means *running too*, I urge you—defy the fear, silence the lies, and by faith, *run to* the God who never fails.

Run to the One who promises never to leave you or forsake you. *Run to* the Friend who sticks closer than a brother. *Run to* the One who cherishes you so deeply that He collects every tear you've cried. *Run to* the One who loves you so much; He's counted every hair on your head.

Run to the Way-Maker—the One who opens paths where none exist. *Run to* the Truth and the Life, especially when lies have left you broken and betrayed. *Run to* the One who knew you before you took your first breath and chose to love you anyway.

Run to the One who specializes in healing what's been shattered and making all things new.

When everything in you wants to follow the herd in the midst of the chaos and *run too*, *run to* the only One who will never leave your side. *Run to* the living God—your source of strength when yours is gone, your peace in the middle of the storm.

You don't have to have it all figured out. When the pain feels unbearable and the questions are too big, just *run to* the One who knows what to do even when you don't.

During the Failure, During the Fall (for Leaders)

As a leader, one of the most difficult tensions you may ever have to navigate is what happens when another leader falls. In moments like that, you are not only trying to process your own pain, disappointment, and confusion, but you also find yourself in a position where others are looking to you for strength, clarity, and protection while they are hurting too.

That alone is heavy. But it becomes even heavier when integrity collides with loyalty.

Scripture tells us that to whom much is given, much is required. Leadership carries a higher standard of integrity because leadership is not just a title. It is a calling. And if it is truly a calling, then you do not have the luxury of claiming Kingdom leadership while living as though Kingdom standards are optional.

For example, imagine serving as the Executive Pastor of a church where one of your closest friends on staff is the Associate Pastor. You have done years of life together. Ministry together. You have stood shoulder to shoulder in the trenches.

Then one day, he comes to you privately and confesses that he has been unfaithful to his wife with someone on the worship team. He tells you he has come clean to his wife, that they are trying to work through it, and that he has asked God and his wife for forgiveness.

But then he asks something of you.

He asks you to keep it quiet.

In his mind, this is now a private matter. He does not want to lose his position. He does not want the church to know. He does not want the fallout, the embarrassment, or the cost that would come if this was brought into the light. He wants to deal with it at home and keep functioning in ministry like nothing happened.

But the moment he told you, it stopped being only private.

Now you are carrying something he no longer carries alone.

And now you are stuck in one of the hardest tensions a leader can face.

On one side, there is *loyalty*.

Your friend. Your history. Your relationship. The trust he placed in you by telling you the truth.

On the other side, there is *responsibility*.

The integrity of the leadership team. The trust of the congregation. The biblical standard required of those who lead.

And there is another layer that makes it even more complicated. The person involved is someone on the worship team. Someone inside the ministry. Someone connected to the very leadership structure you are responsible to help protect.

Meanwhile, from the outside, everything still looks normal.

He is still preaching.

Still leading.

Still being trusted by people who have no idea what has gone on behind the scenes.

So whatever judgements are made will be by people who do not have access to the whole story.

If you stay quiet, you preserve the friendship in the short term, but you compromise the integrity of leadership and risk greater harm to others.

So, you go back to him and tell him plainly that this cannot stay hidden. He needs to bring it into the light. He needs to come clean to the Senior Pastor and the board, or you will have to.

And that is where it gets even harder.

He looks at you and tells you that if you bring it forward, he and his wife will deny it.

Now the very trust that pulled you into the situation becomes the thing that puts you in the crosshairs.

What started as a *confession* has become a *threat* of contradiction.

And suddenly, you are no longer just carrying the weight of what he did. You are now dealing with the reality that doing what's right may cost you your credibility, your relationships, and the benefit of being believed by people who do not have the full story.

Your motives will be questioned.

Your loyalty will be questioned.

Your integrity will be questioned.

And the painful reality is that many of the people judging you will do so with incomplete information and no understanding of the weight you are carrying.

If you stay silent now, you may protect yourself, but you fail the people you were called to protect.

If you move forward, you may lose the friendship, damage your reputation, and stand in the lonely place that often comes with real leadership.

There is no easy version of that moment.

There is only the decision to walk in integrity, protect what has been entrusted to you, and honor the calling on your life as a leader even when it costs you more than anyone around you will ever fully understand.

Because in moments like this, leadership is not proven by what you *"cover"* for your friends.

It is revealed by what you are willing to protect for the people.

And if you ever find yourself in that place, understand this: doing what is right will come at a cost, and sometimes that cost is far greater than anyone around you will ever see.

While the story above is hypothetical, the tension in it is not. I have had to walk through situations in my own life that carried parallel painful conflicts. Different details, same weight. Different circumstances, same cost. More than once, I have been placed in situations where I had to choose loyalty to God and commitment to my calling over loyalty to friendships, relationships, and people I genuinely loved. And I didn't always do it as quickly as I probably should have.

When you are positioned as a leader over God's children, or over His Bride depending on the lens through which you are viewing it, protecting those entrusted to your care is not optional. It is part of the calling.

That part is easy enough when you are protecting the *sheep* from *wolves*.

It becomes far more painful and complex when you are forced to protect people from someone you love, someone they love, or someone who once carried legitimate spiritual authority but has since lost their way, stepped into sin, or moved outside the boundaries of biblically aligned leadership. In some cases, leadership responsibility carries not only spiritual weight, but legal accountability as well. When a leader knows harm is being done and chooses not to act, they can become complicit in the very actions they were responsible for addressing and legally liable for the fallout.

If you have never had to stand in the place to have to protect at that level, be thankful.

It is brutal.

In my own life, choosing integrity and remaining committed to my calling in moments like that has cost me dearly. It has cost me relationships. Influence. Finances. Position. It has also cost me the privilege of being understood by people who did not have the full picture and could not possibly have understood the complexity of what I knew that they did not.

And that is one of the hardest parts.

Because when you do what is right in those kinds of situations, especially when you do it quietly, prayerfully, and in love, people will still make judgments about your motives, your heart, and your character without ever knowing the whole story. The problem is, wisdom and integrity often will not let you tell the whole story.

So, while others are forming conclusions about you, you are left carrying the weight of obedience, the pain of loss, and the reality of being misunderstood all at the same time.

Self-preservation is not part of the assignment.

Trusting God to be your defender is.

That means there will be seasons in Kingdom leadership when you have to obey God without explaining yourself, walk in integrity without clearing your name, and let people believe things about you that are unfair because protecting what is sacred matters more than protecting your image.

That is not easy. But it is real. And it is part of the weight of this calling.

Welcome to Kingdom leadership, my friend. This too is part of the cost.

Perseverance Through the Pain

I want to be vulnerable and transparent in what I'm about to share, while still remaining honorable toward those involved.

There is a part of me that would rather protect myself from revisiting the emotion connected to these events. Not because I am trying to hide the truth, but because this level of emotional transparency is uncomfortable. But I also believe there are leaders reading this book who will one day walk through similar valleys, and I do not want you to feel alone, confused, condemned, or blindsided by the depth of pain these moments can carry.

As stated on the previous pages, sometimes choosing integrity hurts far more deeply than you expected it would.

Sometimes doing the right thing costs more emotionally than you were prepared to pay.

And when those moments come, they create unique opportunities to lean into God in ways other seasons never will. Painful seasons like these can shape, refine, expose, strengthen, and mature you in profound ways if you allow God to meet you in them instead of allowing the pain to push you away from Him or the assignment He has placed on your life.

I remember crying out to God, *"Yet will I trust You."*

My heart was deeply grieved. There were many moments during that season when I wept under the weight of disappointment, loss, confusion, betrayal, and the overwhelming ache that comes when relationships you treasured suddenly become fractured.

But even in those moments, the *pain* was not the highest *truth*, His faithfulness was.

By the time I faced the pain of this season, years of walking with God through heartbreak, injustice, betrayal, loss, and personal suffering had already established something deeper inside of me. I had seen His faithfulness too many times through too many difficult valleys to question it now. Even when life was painful, God had always proven Himself faithful.

In especially hard seasons, there is a rare invitation to draw closer to the Lord and discover His strength at a deeper level than you may have ever known before. In those moments, you are faced with a choice: allow God to *prepare a table before you in the presence of your enemies*, or withdraw and isolate yourself inside your pain.

I love what David says in Psalms 23 as he confronts his own season of pain:

Psalm 23 (TPT)

1 Yahweh is my best friend and my shepherd. I always have more than enough.

2 He offers a resting place for me in his luxurious love. His tracks take me to an oasis of peace near the quiet brook of bliss.

3 That's where he restores and revives my life. He opens before me the right path and leads me along in his footsteps of righteousness so that I can bring honor to his name.

4 Even when your path takes me through the valley of deepest darkness, fear will never conquer me, for you already have! Your authority is my strength and my peace. The comfort of your love takes away my fear. I'll never be lonely, for you are near.

5 You become my delicious feast even when my enemies dare to fight. You anoint me with the fragrance of your Holy Spirit; you give me all I can drink of you until my cup overflows.

6 So why would I fear the future? Only goodness and tender love pursue me all the days of my life. Then afterward, when my life is through, I'll return to your glorious presence to be forever with you!

What a perspective. What a promise!

But it is essential to understand what David is really communicating in this passage. In order to actually receive from God's table—"You become my delicious feast"—during those dark moments, we have to choose to partake. It is always our choice whether we partake of His provision or run from it.

During that season, it felt as though God kept asking me:

"Will you let Me feed you?"

"Will you let Me strengthen you?"

"Will you let Me defend you?"

When people I genuinely loved, and believed loved me, chose to stand against me, and I discovered they had lied to me or about me, the grief cut incredibly deep. In those moments, I had a choice to make: would I partake of what God was offering me in that valley, or would I reject it because of the pain I was carrying?

Would I trust Him anyway?

Would I worship anyway?

Would I allow Him to build and strengthen me while my heart was literally breaking under the weight of loss, misunderstanding, and injustice?

Looking back now, I realize something powerful: while I could not escape the pain of that season, I also could not escape what God deposited into me because I chose to sit at His table in the middle of it.

My three highest personal values in life are integrity, loyalty, and justice. So, when I found myself forced into situations where integrity and loyalty collided, it shook me deeply.

I was angry.

Angry at the people who should have stepped forward in honesty and transparency. Angry that leadership decisions placed innocent people in vulnerable and confusing positions. Angry that silence and self-preservation forced others into impossible situations they never wanted to be in and weren't equipped to navigate.

There was almost nothing I wanted more in those moments than to remain a loyal friend, support everyone involved, protect relationships, and help everyone come to a place of clarity and healing.

But leadership does not always offer outcomes where everyone walks away unscathed. Sometimes doing what is right presents varying degrees of perceived loss.

Sometimes loyalty to God and loyalty to righteousness require you to lay personal loyalty on the altar.

And that hurts.

The wounds from that season ran very deep.

Knowing my motives were being questioned by people who did not know the full story. Knowing that some who *did* know the full story should have been the ones carrying the weight of leadership responsibility themselves. Knowing that confidentiality, wisdom, and integrity would prevent me from explaining myself while others formed conclusions based upon incomplete information.

If you are not aware of the attack, that kind of pain has the potential to make you want to withdraw.

It can make you cynical.

Defensive.

Guarded.

Distrusting.

And that is exactly where the enemy wants leaders to live after PTCD events, where trauma becomes the catalyst for further calamity.

Because if he can wound your heart deeply enough, he can tempt you to disconnect from the very presence of God that could heal you, mature you, and prepare you for the next phase of your calling.

But God promises throughout Scripture that He is our protector, vindicator, healer, and sustainer.

And in those moments, I had to make a decision.

Would this season be defined by the pain?

Or would this season be defined by my faith in God?

I could have stayed silent. I could have protected myself. I could have avoided the misunderstanding, criticism, and fallout, and maybe even saved face by remaining the loyal friend who stayed behind to help pick up the broken pieces when everything fell apart.

But there were too many variables in that scenario that left innocent people vulnerable to continued hurt. And eventually, I had to come to terms with the reality that loyalty could not be allowed to override integrity.

I protected people and reputations for as long as I possibly could. But eventually, I had to make a choice between protecting reputations and protecting people who were being wounded without understanding why things were unfolding the way they were.

And as painful as it was, I chose integrity.

Moments like these leave wounds in everyone they touch. Leaders grieve. Congregations grieve. Relationships fracture. Trust gets shaken. And those carrying the responsibility of navigating the fallout often walk away wounded themselves. But even in the aftermath of failure, collapse, exposure, and loss, God's grace still remains available. Failure does not have to be the end of the story. And no matter how painful the fallout may be, restoration is still possible for those willing to walk honestly before God in humility, repentance, and surrender.

After the Failure After the Fall

When processing the pain of leadership failure, many people mistakenly believe that God is somehow directly or indirectly responsible for the pain they've endured. It's as if, in their minds, every hardship is tied to God's will in some cosmic sovereign plan. But I believe this is one of the enemy's most effective deceptions—convincing us to run from the only One who can actually rescue and heal us. Because if you're convinced that God caused your pain, why would you trust Him to comfort you in the midst of it?

Satan despises God, and I believe one of his tactics to wound God is by hurting us—God's children. As a father, I can't think of anything more painful than someone harming or abusing my child and then convincing them that it was somehow *my will* or all part of my warped plan to cause them unbearable pain to teach them a lesson. Tragically, that's exactly the lie many have come to believe about God—sometimes even because of what they've been taught by well-meaning but misguided Christian leaders.

Scripture is full of God's promises. As we discussed previously, Jesus told us in His Word that He is the exact representation of the Father, and *"if we've seen Him, we've seen the Father."* When we study Jesus' life, we see He clearly reflects the heart of a compassionate and loving God. Yet, in moments of deep pain, the enemy is quick to insert a lie when emotions are high. In those vulnerable times, we can be tempted to *rewrite our theology to accommodate our tragedy*—simply because we can't make sense of what we're walking through.

I actually believe this is Satan's most effective strategy against the lives and progress of believers. He orchestrates division, pain, and death and then deceives us into believing that God played a part in it. After all, it's nearly impossible to wholeheartedly trust someone you believe has harmed you. Satan knows this, which is why he works to distort our perception and redirect our faith by casting suspicion on the very One we're meant to trust.

Throughout Scripture, we see countless moments where God takes what the enemy meant for harm and transforms it for good. But this doesn't mean that God was complicit in your tragedy; it just means that He is not content to allow tragedy to have the last word in your life—because He is faithful.

When you accept a lie, you give power to the liar—and believing lies about God can keep you from walking fully in faith. Since faith is what moves mountains, the enemy's strategy is simple: if he can get you to doubt God, your mountain becomes a permanent barrier between you and your breakthrough.

After the failure or fall of leadership, it is essential that we recognize that the enemy will use this situation to try to influence our faith and attempt to derail our destiny. We must be proactively aware of his attacks and devices so that we don't allow him to steal any more ground than has already been taken by his ability to deceive our spiritual leader into making ungodly choices.

From this place, we can also seek the Lord and listen for the Holy Spirit's guidance on how we might play a part in God's plan moving forward. Philippians 1:6 reminds us that *it is God who began the good work in us, and He is faithful to bring it to completion.* Even though a leader's failure or fall may shift your course onto alternate tracks, their actions do not change God's love for you or His unwavering faithfulness to fulfill His purpose for your life.

Matthew 11:28 (AMPC)
28 Come to Me, all you who labor and are heavy-laden and overburdened, and I will cause you to rest. [I will ease and relieve and refresh your souls.]

Run to Him.

When a leader falls, the impact can be disorienting, heartbreaking, and faith-shaking. But it doesn't have to define your future or derail your calling. While we can't always control what others do, we can take ownership of our response and anchor our healing in the truth of who God is. He is not the author of our pain—but He is the Redeemer of it. So instead of running from the hurt, run to the One who heals, restores, and finishes what He started in you. Don't let the failure of someone else become the ceiling of your spiritual growth. Let it become the catalyst that drives you deeper into the arms of the only One who will never fail you.

In opposition to the temptation to isolate yourself, I encourage you to resolve to make this your personal declaration of faith in God's sustaining power for your life regardless of whether or not a leader fails or a leader falls: *I will not live my life bound by the opinions or failures of others. I will choose to see people through the eyes of grace, not prejudice, and I will live with an open heart, willing to be poured out for others. Yes, that kind of vulnerability carries the risk of being hurt—but I believe that the love of God within me is strong enough to sustain me through it. Fear builds walls, but love builds bridges. I won't let the pain from my past dictate my openness in the future. Every person deserves a fresh start—I will not withhold myself from the next season because of what transpired in the last.*[xlvii]

Chapter Twenty-One
Judged

*J**udgment* is one of the most painful and misunderstood forces in the Church. It wounds deeply when it's misused and has the ability to distort our perception of both people and God. Many who walk away from faith aren't rejecting Jesus—they're fleeing from those who claimed to represent Him while casting stones. Whether it's harsh criticism, spiritual shaming, or being condemned for struggling, the impact is real. In this chapter, we will explore what it means to be judged, how it affects our spiritual identity, and why it's so important to separate God and His love for us from the actions of people who misrepresent Him. Because healing from judgment starts when we begin to see God clearly, and trust that He sees us fully and loves us anyway.

While walking through the mall, I noticed a young man wearing a shirt that boldly read, *Only God can judge me.* It struck me as a reflection of the times we're living in—where so many push back against anything or anyone they associate with harshness, hypocrisy, or control. As I watched him, his body language seemed to exude toughness, but his eyes told a different story—one that felt more like insecurity than strength.

It made me wonder what pain he had walked through that led him to wear such a pointed statement across his chest. Was it really about judgment, or was the message beneath the message something deeper? Maybe it was: "*My grandmother, who raised me, doesn't understand me.*" Or, "*My father abandoned me.*" Or, "*I feel out of place, even among the people who were supposed to love me.*" Maybe he had questions about God and faith that he was never allowed to voice. Maybe the spiritual leader he looked up to fell, and now he just feels lost. Maybe the church he once attended emphasized the wrong things—majoring on the minors and minoring on the majors—and left him feeling jaded and disillusioned. Or maybe he simply made a mistake and found himself exiled from a community that once called him *family.*

It's common to hear both believers and unbelievers quote Jesus from Matthew 7:1 — *"Judge not, lest you be judged."* This verse is often used as a defense against criticism, but I've admittedly observed a concerning pattern within the Church—a culture where judgment, often unrighteous, unloving, and un-Christlike, has been projected. This is not to excuse sin in any way in the person who may have been confronted by another believer for ungodly behavior, but rather to highlight the imbalance we've allowed to fester between cause and effect.

So, on one end, we see what I would refer to as this *Pharisaical spirit* at work — one like the Pharisees of Jesus' day that seems more interested in pointing fingers and condemning than in restoring and loving. But just as dangerous is the opposite extreme, where, in an effort to avoid appearing judgmental, some have stopped addressing sin altogether. In doing so, they fail to warn those they lead about the very actions that can destroy their lives. Neither approach reflects the heart or the standard of God.

Loving Correction

While no one *"loves"* to be corrected, loving correction has its place—but far too often, within the body of Christ, people misuse their influence or platforms to tear down fellow believers simply because they disagree with them. The reality is that someone can be wrong in a certain area and still bear fruit. And while you may be right in pointing out their misgivings, your response can still be completely wrong if it lacks love.

I recently heard someone say, *"Who am I to cut down a tree that's still bearing fruit?"* In other words, it's not our place to tear down something or someone that still holds potential to grow and thrive. There may be times when God uses us to lovingly confront someone about something in their life that could lead to destruction—something they may not even see. But the way we approach it often matters more than whether we say anything at all. Correction, when necessary, must be rooted in love. As 1 Corinthians 13 reminds us, no matter how gifted we are, if love isn't at the center, then our words and actions lose their value and impact.

If not for the grace of God, where would any of us be?

Still, it is imperative that we understand that the most loving thing you can do for someone is to warn them when you see danger ahead. But realize this, there's also a personal responsibility for them to receive that warning.

I can stop a blind man from stepping into traffic and explain the oncoming cars he can't see—but if he chooses to ignore the warning, accuse me of judging him, or insist I'm wrong, then continues walking into the street… that's not bravery, that's reckless arrogance. And if he gets hit, it's not because he wasn't caringly warned—it's because he refused to listen to someone who could see what he couldn't.

Whether it's a hypercritical, unloving, *Pharisaical* spirit or a passive, *"turn-a-blind-eye"* attitude from someone too afraid to confront what's out of alignment in another's life, I've come to this realization: many who profess to follow Christ have never actually seen a true reflection of who God is modeled for them. Instead, they perceive Him through a lens shaped by their own assumptions—formed more by imagination or experience than by the biblical truth of His character.

What Does Love Look Like?

1 John 4:8 reminds us that anyone who doesn't love doesn't truly know God—because God is love. In today's culture, I believe the enemy has worked relentlessly to twist and confuse the meanings of both love and hate. There are few things more isolating than being perceived as someone who hates others, and few challenges more painful for believers than being labeled *hateful* simply for standing on lovingly biblical truth. This distortion creates tension for Christians who are called to live in love while also remaining faithful to God's standards.

There was a time when people could engage in meaningful debate, share differing perspectives, and still respectfully *agree to disagree*. But today's cultural climate has shifted toward extreme, black-and-white thinking—where *love* is often defined as full affirmation of someone's beliefs, and anything less is labeled as *hate*.

While I won't deny that some who claim to be Christians do harbor genuine hatred toward those with different beliefs or values, the more subtle and dangerous deception is the belief that disagreement automatically equals disdain. I believe the enemy uses this mindset to block people from receiving the love that God—and those who genuinely reflect His heart—want to offer. Many assume they're being *hated* simply because a biblical perspective doesn't align with their personal values. As a result, they develop a distorted view of God's people, which tragically prevents them from experiencing God's love through the very community meant to represent Him. Believing that disagreement equals rejection, they conclude that if God's people don't affirm their choices, then God must not love them either.

This mindset isn't exclusive to *unbelievers*—many *believers* have unknowingly adopted aspects of this distorted view as well. If I were to poll the readers of this book, I'd imagine a large percentage would admit that at some point in their Christian journey, they've struggled with this very issue: believing that because God hates sin, when they themselves sinned, it became difficult to separate and differentiate between how God feels about *sin* and how they believed that God feels about *them*. But this confusion is part of a deeper, darker strategy—an intentional tactic of the enemy designed to keep us distant, ashamed, and running from the very God who loves us most. Yet God, through His Word, has already defined what real love looks like—no matter what others may have taught, modeled, or implied.

Jesus Is Perfect Theology

Mankind is a poor representation of the Father, but as we touched on in an earlier chapter, the Bible tells us that a major reason that Jesus came to earth was to *reveal the Father*. Another scripture states that He was the Father's *mirror image*. The Greek word for *mirror image* is *Icon, which means a* visible representation and expression of God the Father, allowing humanity to understand and experience God's nature through his Son.

For those who've experienced PTCD, it's easy to see how the image of God can become distorted when viewed through the lens of a leader who caused them pain. But here's the good news—we're not left to form our understanding of God based solely on the flawed examples of His followers. If you want to know what real love looks like and who God is from a theological standpoint, look to Jesus. His life is the perfect expression and icon of God. Jesus is perfect theology.

Jesus came as the perfect reflection of God's character. His life revealed the true nature of the Father, especially in contrast to what the leaders projected when they misrepresented Him. When the disciples asked Jesus to show them the Father in John 14:9, He responded, *"If you've seen Me, you've seen the Father."*

We also briefly referenced the story in John chapter 8, where a woman caught in the act of adultery was dragged into the street—completely exposed and shamed. In that culture, her sin carried a sentence of death by stoning, according to the law.

Let's read this story from the bible:

John 8:3-11 (NKJV)
3 Then the scribes and Pharisees brought to Him a woman caught in adultery. And when they had set her in the midst, 4 they said to Him, "Teacher, this woman was caught In adultery, in the very act. 5 Now Moses, in the law, commanded us that such should be stoned. But what do You say?" 6 This they said, testing Him, that they might have something of which to accuse Him. But Jesus stooped down and wrote on the ground with His finger, as though He did not hear.
7 So when they continued asking Him, He raised Himself up and said to them, "He who is without sin among you, let him throw a stone at her first." 8 And again He stooped down and wrote on the ground. 9 Then those who heard it, being convicted by their conscience, went out one by one, beginning with the oldest even to the last. And Jesus was left alone, and the woman standing in the midst. 10 When Jesus had raised Himself up and saw no one but the woman, He said to her, "Woman, where are those accusers of yours? Has no one condemned you?"

11 She said, "No one, Lord." And Jesus said to her, "Neither do I condemn you; go and sin no more."

This account is especially powerful when viewed through the lens of today's distorted love/hate narrative that labels disagreement as hatred. Scripture tells us that God is love, and Jesus, being the exact representation of the Father, reveals what that love looks like in action. When Jesus encountered the woman who was caught in adultery and about to face religious and legal judgment, notice what He didn't do: He didn't defend her behavior, affirm her choices, justify her sin, or explain it away by appealing to her human nature and telling her that *God created her with a sexual drive* or by condoning all the reasons that it may have been in her human nature to gratify her desires. Instead, He *revealed the heart of the Father*. First, He protected her—rescuing her from the immediate threat of death. Then, He extended grace when the law demanded punishment, saying, *"I don't condemn you."* Finally, He gave her a loving but firm call to transformation: *"Go and sin no more."* Every part of this interaction—from protection to grace to correction—was an authentic expression of divine love.

John 3:17 (TPT)
17 "God did not send his Son into the world to judge and condemn the world, but to be its Savior and rescue it!"

Just like the men who stood ready to stone the woman, every one of us reading this book has sinned—and if placed in that moment, we, too, would have to drop our self-righteous stones. Jesus was the only one who was sinless and qualified to throw a stone, and He chose not to. That truth captures the essence of the verse we opened this chapter with: *"Judge not, lest you be judged."* There's a clear distinction between godly accountability and critical fault-finding. What Jesus modeled at that moment reveals the loving nature of the Father: He didn't ignore the sin, but knowing that sin leads to death, He extended grace and followed it with a call to change. His loving accountability wasn't to condemn but to protect from the very thing that threatens to destroy—sin. *Jesus releases us from the bondage of our past, religion, and traditions. The truth and reality of Christ brings freedom*[xlviii].

Rules Are Not for Rules Sake
When we view God as a strict enforcer who's more focused on discipline and *rule-keeping* than a loving Father who sees the bigger picture and is trying to protect us from harm, it becomes easy to resent the boundaries He's set. But what we fail to recognize is that to God, the issue isn't the rules—

it's our misunderstanding of their purpose.

To make this point, I'd like to challenge you with a question:

Is it possible that God knows more than you do and that there may be elements and variables surrounding what He has asked of you that you are completely unaware of?

In my book *Quantum Christianity*, I asked a similar question and used the following example:

Ancient Hebrew purification laws instructed God's people not to touch anything dead, and outlined specific steps for cleansing if they did.

Thousands of years later, with the invention of the microscope, we now understand the existence of harmful bacteria that thrive on decaying matter—something completely beyond human comprehension at the time. Yet, God's instruction had already accounted for it.

To protect mankind from what they could not intellectually fathom at the time, He tells Moses that if the people touch anything dead, they have to cleanse themselves by washing their hands and anything they have touched seven times. Which would seem like a dumb rule without the advanced knowledge of micro-organisms and cross-contamination. But imagine this human rationale playing out in these fictional events set in the ancient Hebrew world:

Young Benyamin was the first-born son of his family, named intentionally because, as his name was defined, he was, to them, "the son of their right hand." Overall, Benyamin was a pretty good kid, but like any teenager, he went through a stage where he was a bit of a know-it-all and began to question why some of the things he was taught within his religion were even necessary, particularly as it pertained to all of the laws and rituals.

As the firstborn son of a firstborn son and inheritor of the family birthright, Benyamin had a special bond with his grandfather, Gedaliah, the patriarch of their family.

Because it was the harvest season and all the young men were working, Benyamin had not seen Gedaliah in several days. His mother, Eliana, sent him to the house of his grandfather Gedaliah just to check on him and bring him some food that his mother had cooked for him.

When Benyamin arrived, he discovered his grandfather, whom he so adored, had likely died days before, and in his grief and mourning, he ran to his grandfather's dead body, embraced him and kissed him as he wept, and disregarding the knowledge that he was not supposed to touch the deceased.

Within days, Benyamin became deathly ill himself, and within a week's time, the family lost not only a patriarch but also a son.

In a hypothetical scenario like this, I can hear a grieving mother screaming out to God about how *good her son was* and how *unfair it was that God would take his life simply because he failed to obey a stupid cleansing ritual.* As is human nature, the rule would become the focus, and for no other reason than ignorance, Benyamin's family and all who knew him would assume that Benyamin was a tragic victim of a failure to adhere to God's law regarding the dead, and God killed him! But, from a twenty-first-century perspective, we know it wasn't the law or God that killed young Benyamin but the microorganisms that entered his body when he kissed his grandfather.

Once we understand the totality of the circumstances, what could never make sense to an ancient Hebrew mother makes perfect sense to us today as we realize that the rule was never about a rule for the sake of rules but for the sake of preservation and protection from man's own ignorance. Microorganisms have always been a part of the scenario; it's just that man's understanding of them was not.

Until history and science revealed the advancements of the microscope, allowing us to see life at a cellular level, understanding the complexities of cells, bacteria, and microorganisms would have likely been beyond man's realistic capacity to process this information properly and within the scales of balance.

So, in this case, there was a significant divide between what was instructed and what was understood in the overall complexity paradigm of the law of cleansing and understanding why the law was even necessary.[xlix]

The truth is, we won't always fully understand why God gives certain instructions. But I am absolutely convinced that our loving Father isn't obsessed with rules—He's focused on us. When He gives a command, it's never to restrict us but to protect us.

That said, like the religious leaders in Jesus' day, people often miss the heart behind God's instructions. In their effort to enforce the letter of the law, they sometimes misrepresent the very God they claim to serve.

Most of the time, the difference between judgment and godly accountability doesn't come from Scripture itself—it comes from the condition of the heart delivering the message.

When accountability is rooted in love, it sounds like Jesus: *"Neither do I condemn you. Go and sin no more."* But when it stems from a judgmental spirit, it seeks to accuse—like those watching Jesus closely, hoping to catch Him healing on the Sabbath just to be able to bring an accusation against Him.

I have been unfairly judged by people who claimed to represent God, and it's very likely that you have, too. But, to put things in perspective, Jesus was the perfect Son of God and was also unfairly judged by people who claimed to represent His Father. I guess the point is that we have to push past the obstacles of *imperfect people* misrepresenting God and pursue God for ourselves regardless of how people fail to live up to the standards that God has set for them.

Scripture is clear—each of us will one day stand before God and give an account for how we lived our lives. If others misrepresented Him, they'll answer for that. But we won't be able to deflect, shift blame, or point fingers when it comes to our own obedience. The failures of others won't excuse our own choices, especially when it comes to whether or not we responded to God's direction in our lives.

Rationalizing Sin

One of the Ten Commandments says, *"Thou shalt not covet"*—which, in today's language, could be understood as *"Don't compare."* Comparison is one of the enemy's most effective deceptions. It leads believers to tolerate or justify sin by thinking, *"At least I'm not as bad as someone else."*

As we've emphasized throughout this book, the standard for a believer's life must be the Word of God—not the behavior of a parent, leader, or friend. You can't excuse sin by pointing to someone else's failure.

In Mark 9, Jesus uses powerful, hyperbolic language, saying that *if your hand, foot, or eye causes you to sin, it's better to remove it than to be thrown into hell with your whole body intact.* The message is clear—whatever compromises your righteousness is not worth holding on to.

Yes, when we make Jesus our Lord and Savior, His grace covers a lifetime of sin. But that grace also calls us to live differently. Just as Jesus told the woman caught in adultery to *"go and sin no more,"* we, too, are called to live in alignment with God's ways. Through the power of the Holy Spirit, that life is not only possible—it's expected.

2 Corinthians 5:17-18 (TPT)
17 Now, if anyone is enfolded into Christ, he has become an entirely new person. All that is related to the old order has vanished. Behold, everything is fresh and new. 18 And God has made all things new, and reconciled us to himself, and given us the ministry of reconciling others to God.

God Has Made You New

All of us were born into sin and at times, will battle the desires of our flesh. But as we read a moment ago, in Christ, God has made us a completely new person! Jesus conquered sin on the cross, and through the Holy Spirit, we have been given the power to walk in victory over it.

In order to walk in power and authority over sin, we have to shed the victim labels of our past! Quit excusing and agreeing with the nature of sin and start identifying and agreeing with your new victorious nature in Christ Jesus.

What happened to you (even in PTCD events) is only one chapter of your journey—it doesn't have to define your ending. God specializes in redemption. He can restore everything, but it starts with surrender. If you will trust Him with the broken pieces, He will make all things new.

Romans 8:28 (NKJV)
28 And we know that all things work together for good to those who love God, to those who are the called according to His purpose.

The verse above from Romans doesn't say that *everything that happens is good*—it says that God will cause all things to work together *for your good.* That means even if you've been judged unfairly, it can become part of your testimony of victory. If you've been trapped in sin, that, too, can be woven into your redemption story. If you've suffered deep wounds or abuse, those experiences can be transformed into powerful chapters of your healing journey—because God truly can make all things new.

Romans 8:33,35-38 TPT
33 Who then would dare to accuse those whom God has chosen in love to be his? God himself is the judge who has issued his final verdict over them— "Not guilty!"
35 'Who could ever divorce us from the endless love of God's Anointed One? Absolutely no one! For nothing in the universe has the power to diminish his love toward us. Troubles, pressures, and problems are unable to come between us and heaven's love. What about persecutions, deprivations, dangers, and death threats? No, for they are all impotent to hinder omnipotent love,
37 Yet even in the midst of all these things, we triumph over them all, for God has made us to be more than conquerors, and his demonstrated love is our glorious victory over everything!
38 So now I live with the confidence that there is nothing in the universe with the power to separate us from God's love. I'm convinced that his love will triumph over death, life's troubles, fallen angels, or dark rulers in the heavens. There is nothing in our present or future circumstances that can weaken his love. 39 There is no power above us or beneath us— no power that could ever be found in the universe that can distance us from God's passionate love, which is lavished upon us through our Lord Jesus, the Anointed One!

Romans 8:33 reminds us that while others may try to pass judgment, they have no true authority to do so. God's Word declares that if you belong to Him, He has already given the verdict—*not guilty*! He's not holding your sins over your head. He loves you deeply and wants you to live in the freedom of that truth.

Judgment may have been the weapon used against you, but it was never God's heart toward you. His desire has always been restoration, not rejection; redemption, not ruin. Yet when we've been wounded by those who claimed to represent Him, it's easy to confuse their voices with His and assume their actions reflect His nature. But the truth is, no matter what others have said or done, God has never left you—not in your failure, not in your pain, not even in your wandering. And in the next chapter, we'll go even deeper, asking a question many of us have wrestled with in our darkest moments: *Where was God when it all went wrong?* The answer might surprise you—and it might just begin to heal something you thought would always remain broken.

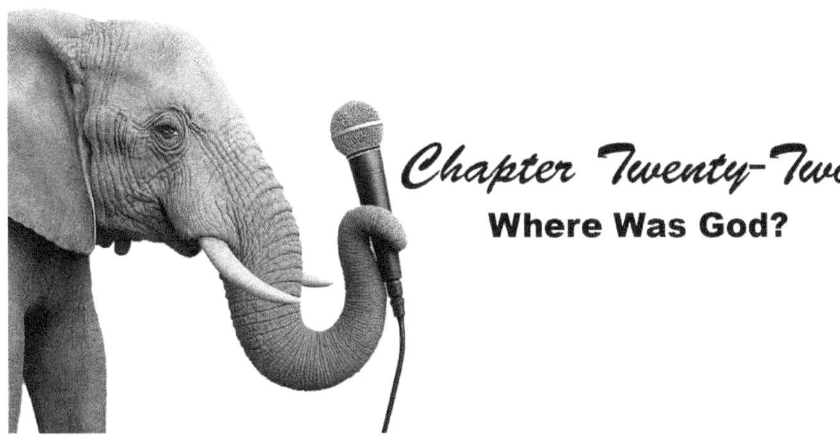

Chapter Twenty-Two
Where Was God?

At some point in nearly every story of PTCD spiritual pain, there comes a question that goes deeper than the betrayal of people or the breakdown of systems—a question that reaches into the core of our faith and our understanding of God Himself: *Where was He?* Where was God when it all fell apart? When people we trusted failed us? When prayers seemed unanswered and pain appeared to have the final word? These aren't just emotional reactions—they're real, honest cries from wounded hearts trying to reconcile God's promises with their human experiences. And if we're going to heal from *Post-Traumatic Church Disorder*, we have to be willing to go there. We have to wrestle with what we believe about God when our reality doesn't seem to match our expectations.

It's a valid question—wrestling with where God was in the midst of their trauma and whether He was somehow responsible for, complicit in, or at least allowed—the pain they endured.

There are so many factors that play into how we process this equation, including the theology we were raised under, traditional perspectives, what our leadership has taught us, and even just our cause-and-effect assumptions based on our experiences.

Often, well-meaning pastors—especially during moments of personal grief themselves or while trying to comfort others in tragedy—sometimes make statements about God that may sound compassionate or reasonable but aren't always aligned with solid biblical doctrine.

It must not be God's will to heal your mother...
God must have needed another angel in heaven...
Everything happens for a reason...
God is sovereign and works in mysterious ways...

To be fair, many of these leaders likely formed their conclusions through the lens of their own unmet expectations of God. Instead of abandoning their faith entirely, they've tried to reconcile their experiences by assuming those moments were simply part of God's *"mysterious plan."*

Even when offered with good intentions, these kinds of explanations can unintentionally lead hurting people to believe that God is the source of their pain. It's a black-and-white lens that many believers adopt—one that assumes if something happens, it must have been God's will. But when held up against the full counsel of Scripture, that viewpoint becomes much harder to defend as an absolute truth.

Consider the story from the Old Testament book of Daniel. The prophet prays to God and then waits for weeks without receiving a response. When an angel finally appears, here's what he tells Daniel:

Daniel 10:12–13 (NKJV – Emphasis by the author)
*"Do not fear, Daniel, for from **the first day** that you set your heart to understand, and to humble yourself before your God, your words were heard; and I have come because of your words. But **the prince of the kingdom of Persia** withstood me twenty-one days; and behold, Michael, one of the chief princes, came to help me, for I had been left alone there with the kings of Persia."*

It was obviously *God's will* that Daniel would receive an answer from Him in regard to what he prayed, yet there was something other than *His will* standing in the way of Daniel receiving what God released to him 21 days before. This opposition was directly connected to the establishment of another kingdom in the earth with some form of spiritual leadership and authority that could contend with the progress of an angel of God reaching Daniel with the answer to his prayer. In this case, it was the *"prince of the kingdom of Persia."*

The fact that this spiritual prince was capable of thwarting God's spoken Word and will from reaching Daniel for twenty-one days presents at least a dozen additional questions, not the least of which is, *how in the world was evil able to delay the commanded movement of the Word of God?* I believe that the answer is undeniable from a spiritual perspective—**there are other kingdoms besides those established for God that directly influence mankind and his reception of the manifested *will of God* in the earth.**[1]

Many of us have been told by religious voices—or even well-meaning leaders—not to ask questions. We're told to just accept what happened, chalk it up to "God's ways are not our ways," and move on. But when the promises of God's Word don't seem to line up with our lived experience, especially for those in covenant relationship with Him, shouldn't it be not only acceptable, but healthy to wrestle with that tension? What if, like in Daniel's story, there are unseen spiritual dynamics at play that delayed the answer? What if something broke down—not in God's faithfulness, but in our perception or understanding? What if there's more going on than we realize beneath the surface?

Many will blame God's *"sovereignty"* on their experiences but I'm convinced that God's will is sovereignly revealed THROUGH His Word! God was sovereign when He made those promises; He sovereignly had those promises recorded in His Word for us to know who He is and His desires for us, and He sovereignly sent His Son to provide us with a new covenant that entitled us to much more than any of us are fully experiencing. If God's sovereign Word tells us that He is a covenant-keeper and *not a man that can lie*, then if my experience differs from what He has promised me in His Word, maybe something external or maybe even oppositional (as in the case of Daniel 10 from above) may be interfering with the fulfillment of God's promises in my life.[li]

We've explored throughout this book how Satan works to manipulate us through deception. Repeatedly, I've highlighted how he aims to isolate us, separating us from the strength of community, so we become more vulnerable to his attacks. He exploits our pain to further his agenda: to steal, kill, and destroy. He deliberately drives a wedge between God and us—or distorts our view of Him—so that we hesitate to run to the only One who can really help us in our greatest moments of need. Every move is calculated with one ultimate goal in mind: your destruction.

Side note: If you've ever wrestled with understanding how God sees you or question where you stand in your relationship with Him, I want to encourage you to check out my book Limitless: You Can Experience the Freedom, Power, and Potential You Were Created For. It's broken into five key sections: Who is God? Who am I? Where have I been? Where am I now? Where am I going? This book dives deeper into the themes we're exploring in this chapter and offers a more extensive look for anyone wanting to grow in this area.

Balancing God's Will and Our Tragedy

When we choose to view God through the lens of His promises and His deep, unfailing love for us, it forces us to confront and re-evaluate many of the perceptions—or misperceptions—we've held about Him. And in doing so, it naturally raises some honest, very legitimate questions about *why* our experiences sometimes pan out the way they do.

If God is good and He loves us, why have some things happened the way that they have?

I've heard people say, *"God gave me a brain tumor to teach me to obey Him, and now that the tumor is gone, I'm better for it."* In their mind, it was all a part of God's master plan to *pain* them into submission and teach them a lesson in order for them to be better in the long run. But what about the other guy who died from the same type of tumor? What was his lesson? Was God good to one but failed the other?

These are the real, raw questions we wrestle with when trying to reconcile our faith with our reality.

It's hard to completely rationalize God from this perspective because what makes sense on one end of the spectrum doesn't from the other. Of course, then the common Christian and religious excuses and clichés are presented to explain our lack of understanding. *Well, God's ways are not our ways, and we just won't understand until we get to the other side.* Or, *God's plan was to use this death to bring more people to Him; after all, God works everything together for our good, so this must just be a part of His plan.* This leaves us with the only logical conclusion from this perspective, which is that it must be that God is playing favorites by doing good for one and leaving another questioning, *why not me?* In those events, you find yourself feeling like the poor kid next door who Santa Clause overlooked as he went down the street on Christmas Eve.

Jesus never operated that way. He never told one person to stay blind because it would teach them humility while offering healing to someone else. That just wasn't His way. In every account, Jesus healed to reveal God's heart and draw people closer to Him. There is no scriptural record of Jesus using sickness or tragedy as a tool for teaching the masses a lesson. Instead, time and time again, we read that *He healed them all,* and as people witnessed those miracles, they believed.

I understand the struggle. When life doesn't make sense, we grasp for answers. And often, in an attempt to protect our faith, we blame things on *"God's will."* But if we're being truly honest, those explanations don't always bring peace—especially when they don't line up with what Jesus actually said and did in the bible. So maybe the problem isn't the circumstance itself. Maybe it's the lens we're using to try and make sense of it.

The Wages of Sin or the Will of God?

Let me offer a different perspective. What if we live in a world deeply affected by sin, and many of the hardships we face are actually the consequences of sin—not necessarily the direct *will of God?* What if much of our pain stems from people choosing to live by their own standards (or sin's way) rather than God's? The Bible says that the wages of sin is death—so what if it's not God causing the pain, but rather the natural result of sin in a broken world? What if, more often than we realize, it's a mix of our decisions and our lack of understanding that's shaping our experiences—not God's divine plan?

In 1986, there was a nuclear powerplant meltdown in the Ukraine, known now as the Chernobyl disaster. The city of Pripyat was evacuated as a result and remains a ghost town to this day. Radiation has completely immersed the structures and even the soil of this region, and it is uninhabitable unless, of course, you are okay with suffering the consequences.

If you were to be dropped off in Eastern Europe today and wandered into the abandoned city of Pripyat, unaware of the dangers of invisible radiation upon the environment, you might assume that you had *hit the jackpot* by discovering your own abandoned city! But your ignorance would not protect you from the nuclear fallout of radiation silently impacting your body. In time, because of your proximity to it and emersion in it, the unseen radiation would have its effects upon you and eventually produce death in you.

The kingdom of sin has much the same effect on our environment. The wages of sin still produce death, and man's choices toward sin (which include the choices of others) impact all of our realities.

For example, if a man sneaks away from his wife and family and visits a prostitute who is carrying a sexually transmitted disease when he too contracts the disease, it's not because God was *mad at him*, nor did it have anything to do with *God's will*, but rather the contraction of the disease was simply part of the fallout associated with his choice to sin.

Furthermore, when he goes home to his wife and passes this disease on to her, even though she had nothing to do with his sinful choice, because of her proximity to the one who has chosen badly, the fallout of her contracting the disease then becomes an unfair repercussion that she suffers but had no direct participation in. That scenario has nothing to do with *God's will* and everything to do with the fallout of sinful submission.

So many scenarios that we question, from a drunk driver killing an innocent family and walking away unscathed himself, to starving children in Africa, to diseases that plague our bodies, often come back to human choices to either do things in agreement with God's will or rebellion against it.

I've heard it said that the entire world could be fed on the food produced in Texas alone. But for reasons ranging from greed to callousness, choices are not being made toward these types of efforts. And medical science has proven that most cancers and heart disease are a direct result of the food that we place on the end of our fork or the chemicals we intentionally place in our bodies. In the example of the drunk driver, I would ask, *what part of that scenario was God's will? The man drinking to excess? Choosing to drive while intoxicated? When he crossed the median into oncoming traffic? The innocent being tragically killed?* Or are these just the fallout consequences of a man's choices toward sin?

What if *God's will* rests not in man's choices toward sin and the fallout we all experience, but rather in we who were created in the image of God seeking His rule in our lives to the point where we can hear His voice and follow His leading to the fullest, where we impact our spheres of influence and avoid the tragedy a few miles up the road altogether?

I would never argue against God in His faithfulness, working everything together for our good. He certainly has an amazing way of turning tragedy to triumph. But what if the reason He does it has little (if anything) to do with His participation (or will) in your tragedy, but rather because, in His immense love for you, God is not content to allow tragedy to be the last word in your life?[lii]

I realize these thoughts may challenge much of what you've been taught (maybe even by people you have greatly respected) about God's role in our trauma or tragedy, but when you compare them to His Word and what Jesus modeled when He said, "W*hen you've seen Me, you've seen the Father*," God's nature seems much more clearly defined.

I can absolutely relate to the tension of believing God's promises while not always experiencing them the way we hoped, even after doing everything we knew to do. I've felt the pain of watching situations unfold in ways that didn't align with what I believed God had spoken, even when I was walking in as much faithfulness as I knew how. I've wrestled with the confusion of seeing ministries operate in miraculous healing, only to lose a close family member to the very disease they've seen healed in countless others. I've struggled with the reality of a minister who has witnessed the deaf receive their hearing time and again when he prayed for them while still living with near complete deafness himself.

There is sometimes an apparent contradiction between God's promises and the fulfillment of those promises in believers' lives, and it's not always easy to rationalize.

What I've come to realize is that sometimes, we simply have to live in the tension of unanswered questions until clarity comes. It's okay to admit when something doesn't make sense. Even the disciples faced moments like that—take Matthew 17, for example. They had previously cast out demons and healed the sick many times before, yet when they came across a particular demon-possessed boy, they couldn't help him. It wasn't until they later asked Jesus in private that they discovered the missing piece—*unbelief*, which, He explained, *would only come out through prayer and fasting.*

John 17:19-20a (NKJV)
19 Then the disciples came to Jesus privately and said, "Why could we not cast it out?"
20 So Jesus said to them, "Because of your unbelief..."

It wasn't that they lacked authority or that it wasn't *God's will* to heal him – we see it was absolutely God's will because Jesus eventually healed the boy himself. The issue was a missing component in their approach that needed to be addressed in order for their experience to align with the promise.

Daniel had no idea that his answered prayer was being held up by demonic resistance in Persia. The disciples didn't realize their unbelief was why they couldn't heal the possessed boy. And considering we have a real enemy who is constantly plotting our downfall, it makes me wonder—how many times are there unseen or misunderstood variables influencing our disappointments and unmet expectations? How often are our outcomes shaped by factors we don't even know are in play?

Imagine how the disciples might have interpreted their failure to cast out the demon if Jesus hadn't been there to clarify what was actually missing. Left to their own understanding, they might have concluded that *some demons were simply too strong—even for the name of Jesus—*or that perhaps *it wasn't God's will for everyone to be healed and set free.* They might have even blamed the boy or his father, assuming *their lack of faith was the reason he wasn't delivered.*

Does this sound familiar? That kind of reasoning mirrors much of what we still hear from leaders today when trying to reconcile God's promises with disappointing outcomes. But that's not what Jesus said. When they asked Him why they failed, He pointed to their unbelief—not God's will, not the demon's power, and not the boy or his father's faith. Something was blocking the promise, and it wasn't *God's sovereign will.*

Maybe, just maybe, sometimes our human reasoning can actually oppose the truth of God's Word and be *enmity against God* —because, according to scripture, that's exactly what it does.

Romans 8:5-11 NKJV (Emphasis by the author)
*5 For those who live according to the flesh set their minds on the things of the flesh, but those who live according to the Spirit, the things of the Spirit. 6 For to be carnally minded is death, but to be spiritually minded is life and peace. **7 Because the carnal mind is enmity against God**; for it is not subject to the law of God, nor indeed can be. 8 So then, those who are in the flesh cannot please God.*
9 But you are not in the flesh but in the Spirit, if indeed the Spirit of God dwells in you. Now if anyone does not have the Spirit of Christ, he is not His. 10 And if Christ is in you, the body is dead because of sin, but the Spirit is life because of righteousness. 11 But if the Spirit of Him who raised Jesus from the dead dwells in you, He who raised Christ from the dead will also give life to your mortal bodies through His Spirit who dwells in you.

Even when we don't fully grasp why certain things unfold the way they do, one truth remains unshaken: we must be careful not to rewrite our theology to accommodate our tragedy. God's Word is truth—unchanging and eternal. If we're not walking in the fullness of what He has promised, it's not because the promise is flawed or untrue. Like the disciples who couldn't cast out the demon until Jesus pointed out what was missing, there's likely something we've yet to understand or apply—not a fault in God or His Word.

God never promised that the storm wouldn't come, but He promises to never leave you nor forsake you. And He'll walk you through it.[liii]

God's Word assures us of His never-ending love, yet there will be moments when you don't *feel* loved. Though He promises never to leave or forsake us, there will be seasons when you feel painfully alone. Scripture declares that we *reap what we sow*, but sometimes it seems like you're harvesting pain from seeds you never planted. The Word says, *those who call on the name of the Lord will be saved*, yet there are days when you may not *feel* saved. Jesus paid for your peace, but fear will still try to take root. He bore stripes for your healing, yet sickness may sometimes attack.

So, the question is: do your feelings define truth—or does God's Word?

I was recently counseling a man who was wrestling with his personal experiences in light of God's promises. I asked him, *"Are you saved?"* He said, *"Yes."* So, I followed up with, *"How do you know?"* He confidently quoted chapter and verse, referencing what Scripture says about the conditions of salvation. Then I asked, *"Do you always feel saved?"* That question gave him pause. I continued, *"When you stub your toe or get cut off in traffic, do you feel saved in that exact moment?"* Looking a bit confused, he eventually replied, *"No…"* I asked one more question: *"Are you any less saved in that moment because you don't feel it?"* That's when he started to see where I was going. When you walk by faith and not by sight, you have to put your faith in the promise of God, regardless of what things look or feel like around you. Either the Word is all true or none of it is. The same Word that defines our spiritual promises for salvation also outlines the promises for our healing, peace, and freedom.

Everything that we understand about our relationship with God, our covenant with Him, how He feels about us, what we are entitled to, and our eternal destination is directly and unequivocally substantiated by the Word of God and His promises in His Word. Could it be that faith means holding to the promises of God's Word even when everything around you seems to tell a different story? Is it possible that God's will is fully expressed and defined by His Word, and yet sometimes we have to *fight the good fight of faith* in order to stand on His promises or fully experience them?

Keep On Keeping On

To close this chapter, I'd like to leave you with a reflection on a well-known verse—Matthew 7:7-8.

When most people quote this passage, they usually say:

Ask and you shall receive, seek and you shall find, knock on the door and it shall be open to you...for everyone who asks, receives. And those who seek, find. And those who knock will have the door open to them.

The problem is that the commonly quoted words *ask, seek, and knock* are presented as singular events. But that's not actually properly interpreted from the original text and further substantiates the point of this chapter, which is to highlight that everything we have been *taught or thought* is not always the whole *truth.*

Properly interpreted, the scripture should read:

Matthew 7:7-8 (AMPC – Emphasis by the author)
7 **Keep on asking** and it will be given you; **keep on seeking** and you will find; **keep on knocking** [reverently] and [the door] will be opened to you. 8 For everyone who **keeps on asking** receives; and he who **keeps on seeking** finds; and to him who **keeps on knocking**, [the door] will be opened.

Over the years, whenever I've taught from this passage, I've often used the analogy that our responses often reveal what we truly believe. As I mentioned earlier in this book, *you don't need to tell me what you believe—your actions will show me.*

For example, if I called you and told you that I was at home and asked you to come over to my house, and I would give you a check to pay off all of your debt. The way you respond from that moment on would reflect what you truly believe about me and my word. Driving to the house and knocking on the door would initially express what you believed. At that point, you may still be in that realm of *hoping* that it's true, and you would be simply doing what I instructed, with maybe a *half-expectation* that I would do it.

If you came to my house, knocked once, waited briefly, and then left when I didn't immediately answer the door, that response would reflect the depth of our relationship and what you truly believed about my word. Maybe you know me a little; maybe past experiences have left you feeling let down by others, and you were *hoping* I might be different. But by walking away without the check for your money, what you're really showing is that while you had some *hope* that I was telling you the truth, you didn't have full confidence or *real belief* in what I promised.

Now, if I told my son the exact same thing, it would be a completely different story—because that boy *knows* his father. He knows I don't make empty promises and that when I say something, I mean it. If he showed up at my house for the check I said was his, he would come fully confident he was walking away with it. In fact, he'd already be picturing how his life was about to change once he cashed that *promise* from his dad.

If I didn't answer the door right away, it wouldn't shake him in the slightest. Because he knows me and trusts me, he'd just knock louder. If there were still no answer, he'd try the window, the back door, the garage—he'd even start calling my phone nonstop or yelling up to the second floor. He wouldn't question whether I meant what I said; he'd assume there was just something in the way. And knowing how determined he is, he'd probably start kicking the door down if he had to—because he knows his father and knows I do not break my word.

Do you see the parallel? Even if when you first came to my house, you were simply *hoping* I'd follow through on my word, there comes a moment when *hope* shifts into *faith*—when your actions prove you're not leaving because you trust the promise. That's when you *"keep on asking, keep on seeking, and keep on knocking."* According to verse 8, the one who keeps doing those things will receive, will find, and the door will be opened to them.

Mark 11:24 (AMPC)
24 For this reason I am telling you, whatever you ask for in prayer, believe (trust and be confident) that it is granted to you, and you will [get it].

James1:5-8 (TPT)
5 And if anyone longs to be wise, ask God for wisdom and he will give it! He won't see your lack of wisdom as an opportunity to scold you over your failures but he will overwhelm your failures with his generous grace. 6 Just make sure you ask empowered by confident faith without doubting that you will receive. For the ambivalent person believes one minute and doubts the next. Being undecided makes you become like the rough seas driven and tossed by the wind. You're up one minute and tossed down the next. 7-8 When you are half-hearted and wavering it leaves you unstable. Can you really expect to receive anything from the Lord when you're in that condition?

Through years of pursuing and living out God's promises, I've come to realize that when my experience doesn't align with my expectations, there are often additional factors at play beyond simply *God's sovereign will* that can influence my outcomes.

In those challenging seasons, the enemy's goal is to get you to give up—to *quit knocking*—to convince you that what you're facing must simply be God's will, leading to frustration, disappointment, or even anger toward God. His hope is that you'll settle for living beneath God's promises—or worse, that you'll abandon your pursuit of a relationship with Him altogether because of disappointment or unfulfilled expectations.

Just remember this, when you believe the lie, you empower the liar! Satan absolutely desires to take you out, and if you quit, he wins. Never forget that God promises that if you refuse to quit, you will win!

Galatians 6:7-9 (Emphasis by the author)
*7 Do not be deceived, God is not mocked; for whatever a man sows, that he will also reap. 8 For he who sows to his flesh will of the flesh reap corruption, but he who sows to the Spirit will of the Spirit reap everlasting life. 9 And let us not grow weary while doing good, for in due season **we shall reap if we do not lose heart**.*

Even in seasons of silence, frustration, or seeming contradiction, God has not forgotten you. The pain you've endured, the questions you've wrestled with, and the tension between your expectations and reality have not disqualified you—they've shaped you. Though the enemy wants your trauma to be the end of your story, God specializes in redemption. He's not finished with you. The same God who walked with you through the fire is the One who still calls you by name and invites you forward. So, as we turn the page, let's shift our focus from the weight of what was to the hope of what still can be—because your story isn't over, and His plans for you are still unfolding.

Chapter Twenty-Three

God Isn't Done

After walking through the fire of betrayal, disappointment, and spiritual trauma, it's easy to wonder if there's anything left of your calling—or if God still wants to use you at all. When your trust has been broken and your heart left wounded by those who were supposed to reflect Him, it can feel like everything you once believed in has been reduced to ashes. But make no mistake—God is not done. Your story isn't over. What feels like an ending may actually be the ground where God is preparing to rebuild something stronger, deeper, and more enduring than before. As we begin this chapter, I invite you to consider a hard but freeing truth: just because you've been burned doesn't mean you've been broken beyond use.

As we've discussed in earlier chapters, it's common for people who go through PTCD experiences to begin processing life through a lens of absolutes, leading to firm inner vows such as:

- *"I'll never trust a leader again."*
- *"I'll never be part of a church again."*
- *"I'll never again subject myself to organized religion."*
- *"I prayed, and God didn't show up the way I expected—so I'll never let my guard down with Him again."*

While these *"never again"* declarations might feel like reasonable inner vows of self-protection, they are often emotional reactions to deep wounds—

and more importantly, they're deceptions planted by the enemy to keep us from ever walking into the fullness of what God has planned and promised for our lives.

It's a reality we all face—life brings painful moments that leave us longing for different outcomes. We live in a world filled with broken people, many of whom are driven by selfish ambition and willing to hurt others in their pursuit of personal gain.

For those of us who genuinely care about people and seek to be a blessing to others, encounters with individuals who don't share that heart can be deeply painful—especially when those individuals identify as Christians, sit next to us at church, or even hold positions of leadership in our lives.

The Power of Agreement

The enemy's goal behind every distraction from God and His promises is ultimately your destruction. When he uses people and situations to try and derail your destiny, it's not random—it's a calculated strategy. Behind the scenes, he's the puppet master pulling strings, manipulating circumstances, and feeding lies to both sides, persuading them to surrender their will to his deception. And make no mistake—he is a master at it.

When my son was in middle school, I began asking him strategic questions to help him think like his enemy, so he could better anticipate the attacks he might face.

Son, if you were the devil, knowing that the devil comes to steal, kill, and destroy, and knowing what has caused you to mess up in the past, how would you attack you to get you to mess up again?

Son, your enemy doesn't have the power to make you do anything, but he does have an uncanny ability to deceive you into doing things his way. If you were him, what thoughts would you try to get you to believe to deceive you into making the wrong decisions or come to ungodly conclusions?

As mentioned several times in earlier chapters, *when you believe the lie, you empower the liar.* Satan is a master theologian who has spent millennia studying human behavior—learning how to exploit our vulnerabilities, plant deceptive thoughts, and orchestrate circumstances in an attempt to lead even those who pose the greatest threat to his schemes to side with his lies rather than align with God's truth about their lives. Never forget he walked with God and interacted with Him face to face. If anyone can twist the facts about God to try to convince you to believe a lie, it's Satan…he did it with one-third of the angels in heaven.

To show you how he works, consider this: have you ever argued with someone you know truly loves and cares for you? Just the other day, my wife and I were reflecting on the fact that in nearly 30 years of marriage, we've only had a handful of serious disagreements. Sure, we've argued from time to time and often decided to simply agree to disagree—but only on rare occasions have we been genuinely upset with one another.

I remember one moment in particular—standing in the shower, playing out an argument in my head that hadn't even happened yet. I was mentally rehearsing my response to something she hadn't said, but that I imagined she might. It was a hypothetical continuation of a disagreement still lingering beneath the surface. And the strange part was, deep down, I knew the truth: I loved her, and she loved me. But in the emotion of it all, I lost sight of that truth and gave space to thoughts that didn't reflect it. Even though I knew I loved her, love wasn't the emotion I was feeling. And even though I knew she loved me, the words I was meditating on in that moment were anything but loving. Looking back, I can see it more clearly: we don't wrestle against flesh and blood. And in that vulnerable space, I have no doubt that something spiritual was at work—whispering, fueling the narrative, feeding the thoughts that pulled me further from the truth I already knew.

James 3:16 KJV
For where envying and strife is, there is confusion and every evil work.

The Spirit of Strife

To illustrate how the enemy subtly infiltrates our relationships in hopes of getting us to agree with his lies and invite disorder into our lives, I want to share a lighthearted story. And just for the record—my wife has given me full permission to tell you this, so there is no need for concern later! If you can't tell it from the tone, I'm smirking as I type this.

During one of our more minor disagreements, my wife, Lisa, was pretty irritated with me over something that, from my perspective, wasn't a big deal. In fact, I can't even recall what the disagreement was about—I just remember she was frustrated, and as we went to bed that night, she was still giving me the cold shoulder.

Don't get me wrong, I had told her what the bible says about not letting the sun go down on your wrath, but she was in complete rebellion…(for you literal readers out there, this entire paragraph is *tongue in cheek*) Looking back, I'm guessing I might've used her as an example in a sermon to make a point—kind of like I'm doing now—and she probably didn't love that.

Okay, back to the story.

As I turned off the light to go to sleep, she made a slightly snarky remark and rolled over with her back to me. One thing we've dealt with over the years is my tendency to express my feelings, let them go, and move on quickly—whereas she sometimes sees that as me *"not caring as deeply about the issue as she does."* That's exactly what happened that night: I drifted off to sleep without a second thought while she stayed wide awake, stewing in her emotions.

Our bedroom was on the second floor of our house, and on her side of the bed, there was a window. It was not uncommon for me to stand gazing out that window into the moonlit field behind our house when I couldn't sleep at night. On this particular night, as she lay facing the window, she noticed a silhouette standing there, quietly staring outside. Annoyed and confused, she asked, *"What are you doing?"* When there was no response, she asked again, a bit louder, *"Aaron, what are you doing?"*

Things quickly turned unsettling when I didn't respond but instead leaned down, just inches from her face, and continued to stare. Panic set in... and just as her mind went into overdrive, she suddenly felt me shift in the bed behind her.

Screaming and startling me awake, she yelled, *AARON!!!! SOMEBODY IS IN THE ROOM!!!!!*

In one swift motion, I rolled out of bed and had my Glock in hand from the nightstand before my knees even touched the floor. Instinct took over, and in full S.W.A.T. mode, I rose into a crouch, scanning the darkened room through the glow of the Trijicon night sights on the slide of my pistol. I swept the room, then flipped on the lights, while Lisa—still shaken—insisted that someone had been crouched beside the bed just moments earlier, silently staring at her.

I searched the entire house, room by room. There was no one there.

When I came back to our room, she unlocked the door, and I explained that no one was in the house, and every door and window was locked. She was still in full *fight-or-flight* mode, having completely forgotten in the chaos that she was supposed to still be angry with me. She asked, *"Aaron, I know what I saw! If no one is in the house, what do you think that was?!"*

Without thinking—or perhaps filtering my response with even an ounce of wisdom—I blurted out, *"That was the Spirit of Strife... and you invited him here."*

I'm sure every guy reading this story just laughed out loud, while most of the women probably got secondhand offended on my wife's behalf—but this was one of those rare moments I just couldn't let pass. Still visibly shaken, she looked up at me and asked, *"Are you serious right now?!"* And the truth is... I was. That moment actually sparked some meaningful conversations and deeper reflection for both of us about the Word of God and, specifically, what Ephesians 6 tells us about spiritual warfare.

Ephesians 6:12 (AMPC)
For we are not wrestling with flesh and blood [contending only with physical opponents], but against the despotisms, against the powers, against [the master spirits who are] the world rulers of this present

darkness, against the spirit forces of wickedness in the heavenly (supernatural) sphere.

I share that story as a tangible example of a spiritual truth that's just as real as the air we breathe—even if it feels abstract or hard to grasp. Like air, most of us believe in the existence of the unseen spiritual realm, even though we don't remain constantly aware of it the way we do with what we can physically observe. We tend to notice the air only when breathing becomes difficult. Similarly, the spiritual realm often fades off our radar—until something happens that demands we face it directly.

Some of you aren't fighting demons – you're entertaining them, excusing them, and calling it "just who I am." What you refuse to confront will eventually control you.[liv]

It's important to realize there are always spiritual catalysts at work in our physical experience, and those forces are as real as the air that we breathe. We have an enemy that, while we often remain relatively unaware of him and his devices, he is prominently aware and primarily focused upon us. As we discussed in previous chapters, his modus operandi is to steal, kill, and destroy his primary target – you. His most effective means of your destruction takes place when he deceives you into believing that your enemy is not the *spirit* behind the chaos, but the *physical one* that you can see with your eyes. When your crosshairs are on anything besides him, he's winning because you're missing the real target with every misplaced physical shot.

He'll tell you:
- *Your wife doesn't respect you,*
- *Your husband doesn't appreciate you,*
- *Your pastor doesn't care about you and your family,*
- *Your leader isn't leading well,*
- *You're failing your family,*
- *You'll never be anything more than you are,*
- *You're a loser,*
- *You're worthless,*
- *You'll never win…*

Wherever the enemy has built a stronghold of fear, insecurity, or offense in your life, he will continually feed lies into that area, trying to get you to come into agreement with him. Because he knows that, *as a man thinks in his heart, so is he…*and once he has your agreement, he has you. When you believe his lie, you empower him in your life as the liar.

If you believe you're weak, you'll behave as though you are. If you see yourself as a failure, your actions will reflect that belief. Your thoughts—what you dwell on, and what you truly believe—will eventually shape your reality. A mentor once told me, *"What happens in the mind will happen in time."* Henry Ford echoed this sentiment: *"Whether you think you can, or you think you can't—you're right."*

This is why it's absolutely vital that we anchor our faith and belief in the truth of God's Word above every other voice. The enemy deliberately plants seeds of doubt and unbelief in our minds, hoping to distract us from the very truth that has the power to set us free.

John 8:31-32 (TPT)
31 Jesus said to those Jews who believed in him, "When you continue to embrace all that I teach, you prove that you are my true followers. 32 For if you embrace the truth, it will release true freedom into your lives."

The Power of Agreement

A significant aspect of the power of prayer in our lives is found when we read the promises of God in His Word and then release our faith in prayer and agreement with His Word. This act of agreement forms a spiritual connection between heaven and earth, intertwining our faith with divine intention. While this may not always make sense to our natural understanding, Scripture reveals that aligning our belief with God's Word is what ushers us into the reality of His promises.

Matthew 18:18-20 (TPT)
18 "Receive this truth: Whatever you forbid on earth will be considered to be forbidden in heaven, and whatever you release on earth will be considered to be released in heaven. 19 Again, I give you an eternal truth: If two of you agree to ask God for something in a symphony of prayer, my heavenly Father will do it for you. 20 For wherever two or three come together in honor of my name, I am right there with them!"

2 Corinthians 10:3-5 (AMPC)
3 For though we walk (live) in the flesh, we are not carrying on our warfare according to the flesh and using mere human weapons.
4 For the weapons of our warfare are not physical [weapons of flesh and blood], but they are mighty before God for the overthrow and destruction of strongholds,
5 [Inasmuch as we] refute arguments and theories and reasonings and every proud and lofty thing that sets itself up against the [true] knowledge of God; and we lead every thought and purpose away captive into the obedience of Christ (the Messiah, the Anointed One)

As 2 Corinthians 10:5 indicates, a crucial aspect of spiritual warfare is discerning when a spiritual force is at work behind the battles we face and then confronting the lies and arguments it raises against *the true knowledge of God*. It's our responsibility to take those deceptive thoughts captive and bring them into alignment with the truth and authority of Christ.

Praying in alignment with God's Word is a powerful weapon designed to tear down spiritual strongholds, false arguments, and deceptive thoughts—especially when the enemy is feeding you lies that contradict God's true nature. When we agree with God's Word, we release the authority and power of His truth to work in our lives. But I also believe the reverse is true: when we put our faith or agreement in the lies of the enemy, we empower his influence instead.

Satan frequently uses confusion, doubt, and fear because he knows that if he can get you to speak from that place, you'll unknowingly begin to align your agreement with his plans rather than God's. In fact, complaining can become a form of giving praise to the enemy—by agreeing with his lies instead of standing on God's truth. The enemy plants a lie in your mind, like *"you'll never get ahead,"* and then waits for you to water that seed with your own words, saying things like, *"I'll always be broke,"* or *"I'll never be able to do that."* When you speak these words, you reinforce agreement in his deception rather than in God's promises.

When you start to recognize how the enemy can manipulate your own thoughts and emotions as weapons against you, the battles you face begin to look a lot different—and a lot more beatable. As you process your own PTCD experiences, it's potentially liberating to realize that behind the behavior of that insecure leader who manipulated, judged, or hurt you, there was always a spiritual force at work, strategically aiming to lead you (and possibly them) toward destruction. What once felt confusing or senseless begins to come into focus. The things your mind struggled to understand before now make more sense in light of the spiritual forces influencing the physical issues. Though the pain unfolded in the physical realm, it all makes more sense when you realize that the real battle—the root of it all—was spiritual from the beginning.

The Strategy Revealed

The enemy's plan has always been to use your pain to serve his agenda. You do not get to choose everything that happens to you, but you do get to choose what you come into agreement with. Some people will judge your actions. Some will misrepresent who you are. Some will respond in ways that are completely ungodly. You cannot control any of that. But your agreement still matters. Your life will move in the direction of whatever you choose to agree with.

He carefully orchestrated circumstances to distract you from the truth and lure you into agreement with his lies. He used broken people, battling their own demons, to wound you in the places he knew would hurt the most, hoping it would cause you to lose focus, give up, or distance yourself from the very One who could heal and empower you to fulfill your God-given purpose. But when you come to the realization that it was not God behind your pain, but the enemy working in the background, manipulating your thoughts, and twisting the truth—clarity begins to break through. That's the moment when you can reclaim your life and experience the freedom that only Truth can bring.

Don't Quit

For anyone who's walked through the pain of *Post-Traumatic Church Disorder,* it's vital to remember—God is not finished with you. Even if you've been through the fire, felt burned, discarded, or overlooked, His purpose for your life still stands.

Romans 11:29 (AMPC)
29 For God's gifts and His call are irrevocable. [He never withdraws them when once they are given, and He does not change His mind about those to whom He gives His grace or to whom He sends His call.]

To close out this chapter, I'd like to share a story from Israeli history to drive home this point.

In 600 B.C., during the reign of King Nebuchadnezzar, the Babylonians tore down and set fire to the protective walls surrounding Jerusalem, and the people of God were exiled to Persia. Years later, after their return from exile, the Jewish people found their city still vulnerable and without defense. During this time, God called Nehemiah to rise up and lead the people in rebuilding the walls that once safeguarded Jerusalem.

What stood out to me in this story is how the biblical account specifically highlights that Nehemiah used the *charred stones from the rubble* of the destroyed walls to rebuild. When a foreign leader named Sanballat saw this, he mocked Nehemiah, scoffing, *"Are you really going to rebuild the wall with those burned stones?[lv] "*

I see this story as a spiritual metaphor for many of us who, after experiencing deep disappointment, found ourselves in a season of exile—emotionally, mentally, or spiritually—feeling as though our confidence, security, and sense of protection had been shattered by a PTCD moment, leaving us trying to make sense of it all in unfamiliar territory.

Yet even in the midst of that chaos and loss, our faithful God still loves us and has a plan to restore what the enemy tried to destroy. That restoration just requires a season of rebuilding. What's powerful about the stones Nehemiah used is that they were not ordinary stones. Jerusalem's walls had originally been constructed with limestone—known as *Jerusalem stone*—which usually crumbles and turns to dust when exposed to intense heat. But the stones Nehemiah rebuilt with had endured the fire and remained intact.

Though his enemy mocked him for rebuilding with burned stones pulled from the rubble, Nehemiah understood something deeper—those stones had been through the fire and didn't crumble. They were proven, resilient, and capable of withstanding more than the others that had cracked under the pressure.

When we draw a parallel between our own lives and those stones, it's crucial to realize that God wasn't the one who set the fire or burned the stones—Babylon did. The people of Jerusalem didn't ask for the attack. They never wanted to be driven from their homes, burned out of their city, or forced into exile. But Babylon crept in anyway—uninvited—and disrupted everything they knew.

In many of our PTCD experiences, it wasn't the Kingdom of God that inflicted the damage—it was *Babylon* that infiltrated the church and sparked the destruction that left us burned. It was *Babylon* that slipped into the structure of leadership. It was *Babylon* that found its way into the heart of the leader who let you down. It was *Babylon* that drove you into a season of exile, and it was *Babylon* that attacked your heart and mind in the middle of your pain. That wasn't God—it was the enemy doing what he does to steal, kill, and destroy.

So many believers have been content to leave themselves on the burned rubble pile of their PTCD experience after *Babylon* has convinced them that the fire rendered them useless. But here's something worth reflecting on: you made it through the fire—and you're still here!

While you've probably heard the mocking voices—like Sanballat—trying to convince you to remain in the rubble, know this: Jesus wants to restore you to your place in the wall. He's not finished with you. In fact, He desires to use those who have been refined and strengthened by the fire to stand in the gaps in the defenses—fortifying the most vulnerable places against the enemy's attack.

Your time in exile is over; it's time to get out of the rubble heap and back to your place in God's Kingdom, tested and refined by fire!

Galatians 6:9
9 Let us not become weary in doing good, for at the proper time we will reap a harvest if we do not give up.

God's not done with you, just don't quit!

You've walked through the fire, you've wrestled with questions, and you've carried wounds that most will never see. But here's the truth: the fire didn't destroy you—it proved you. And now, with a renewed understanding of your value and a deeper grasp of the spiritual reality behind your pain, the only question that remains is—what will you do with what remains? God is not only rebuilding what was broken; He's inviting you to step forward with boldness, to move from survival into surrender, and from restoration into purpose. As we move into the closing chapters of this book, we'll explore what it means to step fully into God's will—refusing to let Babylon define your future and choosing instead to walk in the destiny God always had in mind for you.

Chapter Twenty-Four
It's A Choice

After the dust of pain and disappointment settles, after the questions and emotions have run their course, we're left with something far more powerful than we realize: the ability to choose. Healing, growth, and transformation don't happen by accident—they happen on purpose. And while we may not have chosen the pain or the betrayal, we absolutely get to choose how we move forward from it.

Life is filled with choices that fuel our outcomes, and, as you know, it's not always our own choices that have changed the trajectory of our lives. I'm convinced that so much of what creates the *Post-Traumatic Church Disorder* that we have experienced could be avoided if those who call themselves *believers* simply believed enough in Jesus' words and teachings to pursue them with their actions intentionally. Imagine if those who say they love Jesus simply followed His commandments.

John 14:15 (AMPC)
15 If you [really] love Me, you will keep (obey) My commands.

The way we lead is a choice. Who we give our ear to is a choice. What we permit to shape us is a choice. The leadership approach we adopt is a choice. Whether we accept correction is a choice. The leaders we model ourselves after—that, too, is a choice. Choosing to grow, to mature, to prioritize—each of these comes down to a choice. And those choices don't just reflect what matters to us; they expose what we truly believe, because our actions reveal the values and belief systems we live by.

Just to be clear, this isn't to say we never veer off course from what we genuinely believe—especially in emotionally charged moments. I fully believe self-control is a fruit of the Spirit, and most of the time, I feel like I walk that out pretty well. But let's be honest: when I slam my toe into the bedpost on a midnight trip to the bathroom, that jolt of pain can cause a sudden, emotional reaction that doesn't quite reflect my core values. Sometimes, those slip-ups can reveal what's simmering just beneath the surface—things that might need to be addressed. I'll just leave that for you and the Holy Spirit to unpack, especially in light of this scripture:

Matthew 12:34b (NKJV)
...For out of the abundance of the heart the mouth speaks.

There's a saying I've heard: *"The juice comes out in the squeeze."* In other words, pressure reveals what's really inside. In leadership circles, it's often said that you don't truly know a person until you see how they react when they're told *"no."* Jesus taught this same principle in His own way. He said that His true followers would be known by their love (John 13:35), and that those who only appear to be believers—but are actually deceivers—can be recognized by the fruit their lives produce (Matthew 7:15-20).

It's absolutely important to be discerning and observe how people respond—every reaction tells a story when we understand that actions reflect character. However, there's another side to that truth. When we've been wounded by our own *Post-Traumatic Church Disorder* experiences, we can easily become overly cautious, excessively critical, and at times, more self-reliant than biblically grounded.

We've already established in this book that leaders in the Body of Christ are held to a higher, biblically defined standard—and rightfully so. That standard should be clearly recognized and evaluated. However, there are also spiritual expectations and responsibilities that apply to every believer, not just leaders, and those cannot be ignored or dismissed—even in the wake of a leader's failure.

When each of us stands before God, He won't ask us about the decisions our leaders made or why they chose the paths they did. They'll be responsible for their own actions. We won't be able to justify our own choices by pointing to someone else's greater failures. And we won't get away with the kind of reasoning we used as teenagers—deflecting responsibility by comparing our actions as *less severe* than our peers. In God's Kingdom, the failures of others, even those in leadership or authority, never give us a free pass to lower our own standards or walk outside His will.

Philippians 2:12 urges us to *"work out your own salvation with fear and trembling,"* reminding us that every believer is responsible for cultivating their personal relationship with God. This means intentionally embracing His ways, living out His teachings, obeying His commands, reverencing His ways, and reflecting His character in our daily lives—even if no one else around us is doing the same.

By design, a relationship with God is personal. With that personal relationship comes the expectation of personal responsibility and accountability—seeking out, understanding, and applying His instruction and guidance in our lives.

Ignorance Is a Choice

At no point in history has access to information been more abundant than it is today. In this era, ignorance is also *a choice.* Unlike the days when people depended solely on priests to read and interpret Scripture, we now have the freedom to read the Bible for ourselves. A simple internet search can yield countless resources, offering insights from diverse perspectives on any passage of Scripture. And with tools like AI, you can generate detailed reports and even receive sourced material for deeper study on virtually any topic.

I recently heard someone say something I can't stop thinking about. He said: "We're not biblically *illiterate*, we're biblically *aliterate*. *Illiterate* means you can't read. *Aliterate* means you can; you're just unwilling.[lvi]

In light of this, a lack of understanding of God's Word is no longer a valid excuse. *Choosing* not to live according to His Word is, ultimately, just that— a choice.

In the example of stubbing my toe on the way to the restroom in the middle of the night, a painful event transpired that created an emotional response. Some people respond to pain with tears, some people fall on the floor and scream and moan, and some people internalize pain and make odd displays with their facial expressions. When I experience pain, it ignites anger in me. That emotional anger catalyst in the experience of a less disciplined man may trigger a less than Godly response, where they might say something like, *"Oh, sugar!"*

In truth, depending on the damage to my toe, I might have had extended amounts of pain-filled, emotional expressions until the initial pain subsided. Then, depending on the severity of the injury, I might have to get some professional help to stitch the gash or reset the toe if it was broken. I might need a splint or a cast and might have to limp and hobble through the pain until I became more functional – as we all know, healing doesn't always happen overnight. But, over time, the pain should lessen, and I should get back to a more centered state of balanced reaction and response. It doesn't mean it doesn't still hurt, but my response to the pain should become less emotional and, if I'm a Christian, more *Christ-like.*

In the same way that physical trauma provokes a range of emotional reactions, a PTCD moment can trigger vastly different responses depending on the person. Some react with anger, others with tears. Some go silent and shut down, internalizing their pain. There's no one-size-fits-all response to trauma, and depending on the severity of the wound, it may be wise—

sometimes even necessary—to seek professional help as part of the healing process. And just like someone nursing a physical injury might walk with a limp for a season, we may move forward with caution, careful to guard ourselves against being hurt again.

But over time, healing should be progressive. The pain may not disappear entirely, but the intensity of our emotional reaction should begin to subside. That doesn't mean what happened wasn't real, or that it doesn't still affect us, but our response to the pain should become more balanced. As followers of Christ, that means responding not just from a place of emotion, but from a place of maturity—one that reflects His nature in us.

So, what's the takeaway for those of us who've been deeply wounded on our spiritual journey? It's this: we may not have seen it coming, and we may not have chosen the pain, but we do have the power to choose what comes next. Healing doesn't always begin with a feeling. Sometimes it begins with a decision—a choice to respond, not from the wound, but from who God is calling us to be on the other side of it.

It's Not a Feeling, It's a Choice

What are you going to do with that pain? Will you let it define who you are, shaping your identity around what hurt you instead of what God intended for you? Will you keep replaying the events, justifying a life that settles beneath your calling? At some point, you have to decide—will you choose to be pitiful or powerful? Will you cling to the pain or reach for the promise? You've carried it long enough. Now the question is: what are you going to do with it?

I'm not downplaying your pain and certainly not dismissing it. I'm not saying God caused it—but I am convinced He won't waste it. If we'll allow Him to shape us through the pain instead of letting the enemy twist it into bitterness and powerlessness, then what the enemy meant for harm can be transformed by God into strength. The very thing that was designed to drive you away from God, from the church, and from the strength of community, can become the fire that forges you into a lion—one who devours adversity and rises up to train the next generation to do the same.

Choosing to do things God's way often goes against what our flesh desires. While our flesh craves revenge, God says, *"Vengeance is Mine."* When we feel like fighting, God tells us to *"turn the other cheek."* When we want to give up, He tells us to *"press on in your calling."* Our flesh longs for control, but God says, *"Give it to me."* We instinctively try to protect ourselves, but He invites us to find *"rest in His protection."* The flesh wants to be bitter; God commands us to *"forgive."* When our emotions lead us, God calls us to *walk by faith, not by sight.* Our flesh may say, *"Follow my lead,"* but God says, *"Follow My Word."* Because true victory isn't found in our feelings—it's found in the choices we make to trust and obey Him.

UGH!!! This is one of those scriptures that makes my flesh squirm. It's uncomfortable, no doubt, but it's still the Word of God. These aren't just abstract ideas; they're direct instructions Jesus gave to His disciples and followers. And let's be honest, it's so much easier to critique leadership when you're not the one leading. We can quickly spot their flaws and slam down the gavel of guilt from the bench of self-righteousness. Don't get me wrong—they may very well be guilty. There's no denying that we're facing a global epidemic of PTCD, and I firmly believe that ungodly leadership standards have played a major role in fueling it.

But here's the hard truth: even if leadership failed you—failed to lead from a place of humility, holiness, or Godly purpose—that doesn't give you license for your own disobedience. Their shortcomings don't excuse you from pursuing your own salvation and living out your calling. We are each responsible for how we respond to God's Word, our pain, and how we walk out our faith. God doesn't want to *shame* you; He wants to *show* you who He really is, even in your most painful experiences.

You are promised in God's Word to be an overcomer, but unless you never face an adversary, what are you an overcomer of? Doing things God's way is not a feeling; it's a choice. When we choose to follow His leading even when it hurts, even when we don't understand, even when we feel let down, I believe we learn more about God, His faithfulness, and *walking by faith instead of by sight* in those moments than at any other time in our Christian lives.

At the end of the day, we can't always control what's been done to us— but we do get to decide what we'll do with it. Will we let the pain dictate our path, or will we choose to align with God's Word, even when it challenges our emotions and instincts? God's truth is not just meant to comfort us—it's meant to shape us. And stepping into healing, purpose, and lasting transformation requires more than just knowing what His Word says. It requires choosing to obey it. In the next chapter, we'll dig deeper into what it truly looks like to follow God's instruction—how submitting our lives to God's Word leads to the freedom, clarity, and power we've been searching for all along.

Chapter Twenty-Five

It's A Choice Part II
Forgiveness

If walking in obedience is hard, walking in forgiveness can sometimes feel nearly impossible—especially when the wound was inflicted by someone who claimed to represent God. For many recovering from church trauma, reading scriptures about *forgiveness* feels less like a spiritual virtue and more like an unfair demand. In this chapter, we're going to take a closer look at what that choice really means, how it plays out in both everyday offenses and life-altering betrayals and why choosing to forgive, even when we don't feel like it, can be one of the most freeing and faith-filled decisions we can ever make.

Choice is the foundation of free will. Whenever we're faced with whether or not to follow God's way, that decision always involves a personal choice. While our relationship with God *should* influence that choice, it's not always the determining factor. Consider Adam and Eve—despite having the most direct and intimate connection with God imaginable. God Himself formed Adam, breathed life into him, walked with him, taught him, and entrusted him with meaningful purpose. Adam didn't need a sermon or a prophet to know who God was—he had firsthand experience. And yet, even with that level of closeness, the enemy was still able to creep in and convince them to break the one command God gave— *"Don't eat from that one tree!"* I can hear the meme writers exclaiming, *Adam, you had ONE JOB!*

2 Corinthians 11:3 (TPT)
3 But now I'm afraid that just as Eve was deceived by the serpent's clever lies, your thoughts may be corrupted and you may lose your single-hearted devotion and pure love for Christ.

We're all familiar with the consequences that came from Adam's sin, but thank God for the truth found in Romans 5, which tells us that *where sin increased, God's grace abounded even more through the sacrifice of Jesus!* Still, it's worth noting that Adam had the most perfect leader imaginable and still chose to disobey. Jesus Himself had twelve disciples, and even one of them betrayed Him for money. The religious leaders of His day, who were supposed to know the most about God, were the very ones who condemned the Son of God to death. This isn't to excuse their choices, but it does highlight a pattern: throughout Scripture and history, people often make decisions that contradict God's Word, even while claiming to follow Him.

James 1:22 (AMPC)
22 But be doers of the Word [obey the message], and not merely listeners to it, betraying yourselves [into deception by reasoning contrary to the Truth].

Christianity is not for the faint of heart. Walking in God's will sometimes means obeying His direction even when it defies logic. At times, it requires choosing what's right—even when it's painful or comes at a personal cost. There are moments when pursuing His Kingdom and righteousness (His way of doing and being) demands you lay down your own desires or, in some cases, your life. If your obedience to God depends on whether it feels good or makes sense, chances are you'll give up before His purpose for that season is revealed or fulfilled. It's not always easy, but it's always worth it.

Luke 9:23-25 (TPT- Emphasis by the author)
*23 Jesus said to all of his followers, "If you truly desire to be my disciple, you **must** disown your life completely, embrace my 'cross' as your own, and surrender to my ways. 24 For if you choose self-sacrifice, giving up your lives for my glory, you will discover true life. But if you **choose** to keep your lives for yourselves, you will lose what you try to keep. 25 Even if you gained all the wealth and power of this world, and all the things it could offer you, yet lost your soul in the process, what good is that?*

A Whale of a Problem

As a kid in Sunday school, I vividly remember hearing the story of *Jonah and the whale.* In this dramatic account, God commands Jonah to go and deliver a message to the Assyrians—a brutal enemy of Israel known for their idolatry, violence, and ruthless destruction of Israeli cities. Jonah, by his own admission, despised them.

The twist in the story comes when God specifically sends Jonah to Nineveh, the heart of Assyria, to call them to repentance. What's almost comical is Jonah's response—he didn't run away from God's command because he feared failure or opposition; he ran because he knew he'd succeed. He knew that if he preached, they would repent, and God would show them mercy. Jonah even confessed he'd *rather die than witness God extend forgiveness to people he hated.*

That level of bitterness and unforgiveness is intense—but for some of you reading this, your *Post-Traumatic Church Disorder* experiences may have pushed you to a similar place. Like the friend I mentioned earlier in this book who was raped by his youth pastor, maybe you've endured deep wounds inflicted by those who claimed to represent God—leaving you not hoping for their redemption but rather wishing for God's judgment to fall on them. If that resonates with you, I share the story of Jonah to remind you that—even in Scripture—you are not alone in that struggle.

Still, identifying with a biblical prophet doesn't remove our personal responsibility to confront the areas in our hearts that are out of alignment with God's truth and will for us. Even Jonah, after wrestling with his own anger and resistance, ultimately obeyed God's command. He just had to process some inner turmoil before reaching that point of surrender.

Forgiveness

Living according to God's ways includes walking in forgiveness, but let me be honest with you: what you may have been told forgiveness is, or what you've assumed it to be, probably isn't the full picture. Sometimes, forgiveness isn't just for those who've experienced deep wounds. Sometimes, it's about letting go of things we took more personally than we should have.

Yes, some people have endured deep, significant wounds, while others are still harboring resentment over minor offenses they simply never released. No matter the depth of the pain, forgiveness is essential—and it must be addressed in every form and situation.

When many people hear scriptures about forgiveness, they interpret them as *excusing the offense* or saying what happened was *okay*. Let's be clear— forgiveness is NOT saying that what someone did to you was acceptable. Abuse, manipulation, betrayal, or being taken advantage of is never *okay*. It wasn't okay when it happened, and it never will be.

Even from a psychological perspective, genuine healing begins when we have the courage to face and acknowledge both the reality of what happened and the weight it carried. That moment of recognition is where restoration truly begins. In fact, admitting that what happened was wrong is a crucial and necessary step in the healing process.

Forgiveness isn't about minimizing the pain—it's about shifting the weight. It's not telling the offender their actions were acceptable; it's telling *yourself* that it's alright to let go and release it to God, trusting Him to carry what you were never meant to hold onto forever.

Psalms 55:20-23a (TPT)
20 I was betrayed by my friend, though I lived in peace with him. While he was stretching out his hand of friendship, he was secretly breaking every promise he had ever made to me! 21 His words were smooth and charming. Yet his heart was disloyal and full of hatred—his words soft as silk while all the time scheming my demise.
22 So here's what I've learned through it all: Leave all your cares and anxieties at the feet of the Lord, and measureless grace will strengthen you. 23 He will watch over his devoted lovers, never letting them slip or be overthrown...

I often hear the phrase *"forgive and forget"* tossed around when people talk about healing from deep wounds. But let's be honest—if you're waiting until you feel *okay* about what happened or until you can *forget* it completely, you may be waiting forever. Feelings are unpredictable, and when it comes to traumatic experiences, there will likely never be a day when you feel like it was *"okay."*

Furthermore, as it pertains to forgetting, that's not even something we're wired to do. While it's true that Scripture says God chooses to *forgive and forget* our sins, that divine ability doesn't translate to a requirement for us. Forgiveness isn't about erasing the memory—it's about choosing to release the hold it has on your heart. Forgetting isn't a prerequisite for forgiving. You can remember and still release forgiveness.

Hebrews 8:12 (AMPC)
12 For I will be merciful and gracious toward their sins and I will remember their deeds of unrighteousness no more.

Psalm 103:11-12 (AMPC)
11 For as the heavens are high above the earth, so great are His mercy and loving-kindness toward those who reverently and worshipfully fear Him.
12 As far as the east is from the west, so far has He removed our transgressions from us.

I'm incredibly grateful that it's God's nature to no longer remember our sins, but that doesn't mean we, as human beings, won't still have to work through the emotions and pain connected to our own memories. The reality is that we're going to feel things—unpleasant, painful, lingering emotions tied to what we've experienced.

As we've explored in this chapter and the one before, there's a consistent theme: *the power of choice*. And forgiveness, at its core, is exactly that—it's a choice, not a feeling. Just because the act of forgiving doesn't feel like what you imagined forgiveness should feel like, it doesn't mean you're not walking in it.

When you choose to forgive, even if it's purely an act of obedience, you're aligning yourself with God's Word and His command to forgive. It's not about what you feel—it's about what you choose to do in faith.

Matthew 18:21-22 (TPT)
21 Later Peter approached Jesus and said, "How many times do I have to forgive my fellow believer who keeps offending me? Seven times?"
22 Jesus answered, "Not seven times, Peter, but seventy times seven times!

After responding to Peter in this passage, Jesus went on to explain that an unwillingness to forgive actually creates a barrier between you and your ability to receive what you need from God.

Every Deed is a Seed

In another scripture in Matthew chapter 5, Jesus instructs us not to even give an offering at church if we remember that someone has an offense against us.

Matthew 5:23-24 (TPT)
23 So then, if you are presenting a gift before the altar and suddenly you remember a quarrel you have with a fellow believer, 24 leave your gift there in front of the altar and go at once to apologize to the one who is offended. Then, after you have reconciled, come to the altar and present your gift.

I found this scripture puzzling until a few years ago. *Giving your offering at church* when someone else had an issue with you seemed insignificant to me until I realized that *every deed is a seed*. Deeds sown in obedience produce the fruit of obedience, and deeds sown in disobedience produce weeds that choke out the fruit of the good seeds planted.

Just like tending a garden, if we want to see the fullest yield, we have to first clear the soil of weeds before planting. And even after the good seeds are sown, we must stay watchful, pulling up the weeds that try to grow alongside and strangle what God has purposed to flourish.

The Bible tells us that when we give, God gives back to us in abundance (Luke 6:38). If giving an offering is a seed of obedience sown in faith, then, like a garden, we may need to be aware of weeds in that garden that could choke out the good fruit of that seed. This is why I believe in Matthew 5:23-24 Jesus says, *don't even plant the seed (give your offering) until you uproot that weed of strife and unforgiveness that might try to choke out the blessing God has for you when you obediently give.*

When the bible tells us to walk by faith and not by sight, even those words imply difficulty, and I believe one of the most challenging and uncomfortable tests of our faith is revealed when we face events where forgiveness is necessary because we've experienced betrayal. Betrayal cuts deep—and it's in those moments we're immediately faced with the decision: will we respond based on what we feel and see, or will we choose to trust God and walk by faith?

Choosing Forgiveness

Not everyone has a story as extreme as mine—where someone literally tried to take my life—but maybe by sharing how I walked through my own life-altering experience, it will help you process your own trauma. On the very day I was attacked, I made the conscious decision to forgive the two young men who tried to kill me. Just an hour after being admitted to the hospital, lying there in that bed, I looked at my wife and said, *"I choose to forgive them."*

The deeper truth behind that initial decision is this: I didn't feel a wave of peace wash over me in that moment. In fact, as the reality of my injuries set in—months of daily physical therapy, intense psychological counseling to deal with PTS, medication to manage panic attacks, and the eventual loss of my job, business, and financial stability—there were countless moments when forgiveness felt like anything but *peace*. At nearly every stage of that journey, there were no warm or affirming feelings to accompany what I had imagined forgiveness might feel like. But I can still recall countless moments when anger or bitterness would start to rise within me, and I'd speak it out loud: *"No! I chose to forgive them—and I choose it again right now!"*

Proverbs 4:23 (TPT)
23 So above all, guard the affections of your heart, for they affect all that you are. Pay attention to the welfare of your innermost being, for from there flows the wellspring of life.

You see, that event had already stolen so much from me financially. When it was all said and done, it cost me more than a million dollars in lost wages between the loss of my career and personal business, but I wasn't willing to allow it to steal any more than it already had!

After years in ministry, I'd seen the people who lived and dwelt in the misery of bitterness and unforgiveness. I've observed how the growth of those *weeds* of bitterness in their lives not only influenced their perception of the past but continued to choke out the promises of their future. I'd read in the scripture about how the enemy comes to steal, kill, and destroy, and seen over my lifetime countless numbers of people who had unlimited potential capped by a ceiling of unforgiveness and an inability to move on in life as their enemy daily reiterated their most painful moments. I'd experienced the blessing of doing things God's way and the setbacks associated with falling into the traps of the enemy, and I wasn't willing to allow tragedy to have the last word as it pertained to my destiny, so I chose forgiveness.

When rage tried to creep in during my tenth hour of physical therapy that week, I made the decision once more to forgive—I said it out loud: *"I choose to forgive them again."* And just minutes later, when grief or fear tried to overwhelm me, I repeated it: *"I choose to forgive them."* Again and again, every time my emotions clashed with my decision, I reinforced that choice— not because it was easy, but because I refused to let the weeds produced by injustice strangle the seeds of my destiny.

I can assure you, emotionally, I felt nothing warm or positive in my heart toward these men as I forgave them repeatedly. But in those moments, I was choosing to live by faith, not by how I felt. Over time, those painful emotions started to lose their grip, and my feelings began to align with the decision I had already made—to forgive.

To forgive is to set a prisoner free and discover that the prisoner was you.
– Lewis B. Smedes

I believe one of the most effective deceptions the enemy uses to derail a believer's destiny is convincing them to embrace the identity of a victim, and then trapping them in a cycle of reliving that pain daily through bitterness and unforgiveness.

We often fall for the lie that if we don't hold our abuser or betrayer accountable, no one will. But that's simply not true—and it's not biblical. God is a just and righteous judge, and He calls us to cast our burdens on Him, trusting Him to handle justice in His perfect way and timing.

Because I've personally walked out deep levels of forgiveness in my own life, I believe God has entrusted me with a unique authority to help guide others on that same journey. I've witnessed physical miracles occur in people's bodies moments after they chose to surrender their will, trust God fully, and forgive those who had wounded them.

There's Healing in Forgiveness

I remember ministering at a church in Edmonton, Alberta, Canada, where we saw several miraculous healings during a time of prayer. As I began praying for one woman who had endured years of intense pain, I noticed something different—unlike the others, there was no immediate change. Despite the miracles we had already witnessed that day, nothing seemed to be happening in her case.

I stepped back and quietly asked the Holy Spirit, *"Is there something hindering this woman from receiving her healing?"* Almost instantly, I heard one word: *"Unforgiveness."*

I turned back to her and gently asked if she might be holding onto bitterness or unforgiveness toward someone who wounded her deeply in her life. At that moment, she collapsed to the floor, letting out a sound between a scream and a moan, and began to weep uncontrollably. I knelt down on the floor with her and spoke with her about what forgiveness really means, and led her through a forgiveness exercise and a prayer to release it. Once she made the decision to forgive, I prayed for her again, and she was instantly and completely healed of all her pain.

In this case, I believe the weed of unforgiveness was choking out the miracle that God's will and promise had for her... but she had to choose to release bitterness and forgive first.

In the story I just shared, I mentioned walking her through a forgiveness exercise. One of the tools I regularly use to help people make the decision to forgive is a simple yet powerful visual exercise that I developed as part of the two-day *Walking in Freedom* seminar I teach. This exercise is designed to help individuals break free from strongholds, like unforgiveness, where the enemy has gained influence in their lives. I begin by asking them to bring to mind the person who caused them pain—whether through abuse, betrayal, neglect, or abandonment. I always emphasize that this exercise isn't about excusing or justifying what happened. It's about releasing that weight to God so they don't have to carry it any longer.

I instruct them to make a closed fist and whisper that person's name into their hand. I then have them stretch their hand and arm out in front of them where they can clearly see it and ask them to say out loud, *"I am not defined by what has happened to me; I am who God says I am, and I choose to forgive you and release you."*

As they speak those words, they open their hand—visibly and symbolically letting go of what they have held onto for so long.

Several powerful things happen when someone walks through this forgiveness exercise:

1. **They align themselves with God's Word** by choosing obedience and responding to His command to forgive.
2. **They hear truth coming from their own mouth**—declaring agreement with God's Word rather than reinforcing a narrative of victimization. For many, past thoughts or conversations about the event have always come from a place of pain or powerlessness.
3. **They establish a new visual and auditory memory tied to that experience.** Previously, recalling the person or event brought only

pain. Now, they created a new memorial when they look back and remember the moment they declared their identity in Christ, took authority over their emotions, and chose to take back their power and release the offender.

While making the decision to forgive and walking through this exercise isn't a one-and-done, cure-all fix for the struggle with bitterness or unforgiveness, it does mark a powerful starting point. With a clearer understanding of what forgiveness truly means, why it matters, and the intentional choice to align with God's Word, the forgiver begins to uproot the weeds the enemy planted to choke out their blessings—and take intentional steps toward God's purpose for their lives.

2 Corinthians 13:11 tells us to be cheerful! *Repair whatever is broken among you, as your hearts are being knit together in perfect unity. Live continually in peace, and God, the source of love and peace, will mingle with you.*

Jesus Prays for You
Forgiveness is a powerful prerequisite for progress in the Kingdom of God, while bitterness is a major obstacle hindering the spiritual growth of many believers. Throughout Scripture, we see many events where Jesus prayed for people, but only one where He specifically prayed for you! And the focus of that prayer was *unity*.

John 17:20-23 (TPT)
20 And I ask not only for these disciples, but also for all those who will one day believe in me through their message. 21 I pray for them all to be joined together as one even as you and I, Father, are joined together as one. I pray for them to become one with us so that the world will recognize that you sent me. 22 For the very glory you have given to me I have given them so that they will be joined together as one
and experience the same unity that we enjoy. 23 You live fully in me and now I live fully in them so that they will experience perfect unity, and the world will be convinced that you have sent me, for they will see that you love each one of them with the same passionate love that you have for me.

I fully understand that certain PTCD experiences can significantly alter the dynamics of relationships to the point where continuing to run together in the Kingdom in close connection is no longer possible. In my own life, I can recall a few relationships where we once worked side by side closely, but due to differences in perspective, direction, or— in one case—deeply broken trust, we are no longer directly connected in ministry. However, there's no unforgiveness or bitterness separating us. I can still look back fondly on the seasons we shared, and when we do cross paths, there's no animosity—just the understanding that our callings led us down different paths based on the priorities we each embraced. It didn't become that way overnight, but with intentionality, God was able to work everything out for the good.

We see a similar situation unfold in the Bible with Paul and Barnabas, who experienced what the bible calls a *"sharp disagreement"* over whether to bring John Mark along on their second missionary journey. The disagreement was so significant that they parted ways, each choosing a different path for ministry.

Although they were later able to reconcile and restore their relationship, the intensity of their disagreement at that moment made it extremely difficult—if not impossible—for them to continue working together during that particular season.

Amos 3:3
3 Can two walk together, unless they are agreed?

There are times when resolving differences and continuing together on the same path just isn't possible in a given season—and that's okay. Life is filled with both mountaintops and valleys, and not all relationships are meant to last through every season. Some are temporary, while others are long-term. What truly matters is that we remain intentional about including God in our process and avoid giving the enemy space to plant seeds of offense or bitterness that can derail God's purpose for us.

While people can be inconsistent, fickle, flaky, judgmental, or even abusive, God remains steadfast, faithful, and unchanging. Even when those who were meant to represent Him have failed, God's character and promises have not. He is far greater than any person's failure or the pain it may have caused. He is a redeeming God who can take even the messiest situations and bring beauty and restoration. He is still in the business of making all things new.

When we look at the negative events in our lives, we need to see beyond the person and the event—discerning the hand of the enemy. If we keep giving honor to the Lord and to others, we will receive it from the Lord and from others—and the enemy cannot stop us. It is also very important to realize that some people are not safe to have a trusted place in your life. David honored and served King Saul, but he realized that he couldn't trust him.[lviii]

When you experience pain from PTCD events, it is so important to resist the temptation to completely disconnect. Just because you can no longer stay connected to a certain part of the vine doesn't mean you're cut off entirely. God can graft you into another place where you can heal, grow, and bear fruit again.

When Pain Lies

I want to close this chapter by offering one final perspective on the topic of forgiveness. While there are certainly PTCD experiences that are a direct result of leaders failing to lead from a godly, biblical, Kingdom-centered perspective, that's not always the full picture. Sometimes, after being wounded in one season, we begin to filter our new experiences through the lens of past offenses.

Back in the chapter on *Charisma vs. Character*, we said, *"If you don't heal from what hurt you, you'll bleed on people who didn't cut you."* That truth doesn't just apply to leaders—it applies just as much to followers. Too often, people carry wounds from past seasons into new ones, and without realizing it, begin holding current leaders to tests they didn't know they were taking—and to expectations they never agreed to—all because they're being viewed through the lens of someone else's failure. In those moments, unresolved trauma from the past begins to distort your present reality.

It's like stepping into a new relationship after a painful divorce. If those emotional wounds are still raw, it's easy to project past pain onto someone who had nothing to do with it—undermining a healthy connection based on assumptions that don't belong in the current story. And when that happens, you risk sabotaging your future because you haven't fully released your past.

Those who are looking for something to be offended by will always find it, and holding current relationships accountable for pain caused by someone else is unfair and unsustainable. The insecurity and pain inflicted by others may not be your fault, but healing from it is your responsibility.

Make the decision today that you won't allow offense or unforgiveness to keep you from the destiny God has for you. He has so much more in store! And you don't have to come to Him perfectly put together—bring your hurt, your questions, even your anger. He will meet you right where you are. It's normal to experience seasons of pain and uncertainty, but don't let them become permanent places. Let them be part of your journey, not your destination.

When you've walked through pain, betrayal, or spiritual trauma, choosing to forgive can feel like you're surrendering your only remaining form of justice. But forgiveness isn't about surrendering justice—it's about surrendering control. It's trusting that God sees, God knows, and God will deal rightly with what we've endured. More than anything, forgiveness is the key that unlocks the door to our own healing. And once that door is open, we're able to step into something greater. Because God never intended for your story to end with pain. He's a God of restoration—of resurrection—and He specializes in making all things new. As we step into the final chapter, we'll begin to explore how, even after deep wounds and devastating experiences, God is not only able but eager to breathe new life into what once felt lost.

If you have struggled to release forgiveness, I would encourage you to repeat this prayer:

Prayer of Forgiveness and Surrender
Dear Heavenly Father,
Today I choose to live my life in alignment with Your will.
I reject the lies the enemy has whispered to me—lies that tell me I'm a victim, that holding onto bitterness will protect me, or that justice won't be served unless I carry this pain alone.
Thank You for giving me the power, through Christ, to overcome every scheme and stronghold of the enemy.
Because of Jesus, I am not defined by what has happened to me—I am defined by what You say about me.
Right now, I choose to forgive those who have hurt me—deeply and unfairly.
Not because they deserve it, but because You have commanded it, and because I refuse to let the weeds of bitterness choke out the fruit of my destiny.
I release them into Your hands and trust You as my perfect Judge.
I let go of my right to hold onto offense, and I pick up Your invitation to walk in freedom.
Even if my emotions haven't caught up to my decision, I declare it by faith: I choose to forgive.
Again and again, as often as needed, I will declare it—until my heart aligns with Your truth.
Please purify my heart, renew my mind, and restore the places in me that have been fractured by betrayal, offense, or pain.
Help me to uproot the weeds the enemy planted in my soul and replace them with the seeds of Your Word, love, and purpose.
I choose to forgive—not just once, but as a way of life.
I choose to walk by faith, not by what I feel.
And I choose to believe that You are not finished with me yet.
What the enemy tried to use to destroy me will be the very ground You use to grow something new.

In Jesus' name,
Amen.

Chapter Twenty-Six
All Things New

After everything you've read, everything you've processed, and everything you've endured, the idea that God could still want to use you—or even restore what was broken—may feel difficult to grasp. But the truth is, restoration is not just something God does; it's part of who He is. He doesn't discard what's been damaged—He rebuilds it with greater purpose. As we close this book out, my prayer is that you are beginning to see your story through a new lens. Not one shaped by pain or disillusionment but by promise. Because no matter how deep the wounds or how long the detour is, God is still in the business of making all things new.

Throughout this journey, we've clearly established that *Post-Traumatic Church Disorder* is very real. The countless stories that have been shared with me over the years—and the fact that you've made it this far in this book—serve as undeniable proof. Whether you're a leader left questioning your calling after a painful church experience, someone raised in a legalistic or controlling environment, a minister-in-training seeking wisdom before jumping into ministry with both feet, or simply a faithful church attender who watched your family suffer under unhealthy leadership—I want you to hear this loud and clear: the local church was, and still is, God's idea. And His desire hasn't changed. He longs for you to be a whole, healthy, thriving part of the body of Christ, walking in the identity He designed for you and living out the calling He placed on your life long before the pain ever entered your story. Yes—He truly can make all things new.

The most valuable things in life are often forged in the fires of adversity. *"Hardship often prepares an ordinary person for an extraordinary destiny."*[lix] That truth is echoed throughout Scripture, particularly in the lives of those God called His own. You were created with a divine purpose. Your unique personality, skills, and spiritual gifts are intentional reflections of your Heavenly Father's image displayed through you. And it's precisely those God-given traits that the enemy targets in you, because you remind him of the One he hates most—God…and, as you have likely experienced, Satan doesn't fight fair.

Satan Even Attacks the Children

How many of us experienced deep disappointment, confusion, or even abuse long before reaching adolescence? Just like Moses and Jesus, those who are called according to God's purpose are often targeted by the enemy from a young age. The attack on your destiny likely began before you ever knew you had one.

I imagine many reading this book had dreams for the future and began to demonstrate leadership qualities early in life, only to find that the very people closest to you seemed determined to crush your spirit. Like Joseph, you may have carried a God-given dream in your heart while navigating seasons that felt more like a pit or a prison than a path to the palace God promised.

Some of you might still be processing the confusion of your early leadership experiences—clearly anointed, yet placed under leaders who, like King Saul with David, used their position and authority not to equip you but to wound you. And yet, even in that pain, you held onto the call because deep down, you knew that God's hand was still on your life.

Side note: I could write an entire book on David, but my friend Dale Mast already has, and it is the most powerful book on identity and calling I've ever read. It's titled, And David Perceived He Was King. I highly recommend you order it for your next book. It's brilliantly written, and I believe it would be very inspirational for anyone reading this book.

The stories of these influential leaders throughout Scripture remind us that the journey toward our God-given destiny is rarely smooth. But when we respond with faith, refuse to give up, and continue trusting Him through every hardship, God redeems even the most painful and devastating attacks of the enemy. He doesn't just restore what was lost—He uses those very experiences to shape us into leaders who reflect His nature, carry His heart, and exemplify what godly leadership is meant to be. Leaders who have been through the fire and remained faithful can now model strength, humility, and trust for the next generation.

We serve a God of justice, and His Word consistently shows that those who respond unjustly toward others will ultimately face the consequences of their actions. Our role in that divine order is to follow Christ's example— blessing those who curse us and praying for those who mistreat us. But don't be mistaken: sin has a cost. Scripture is clear that the wages of sin lead to destruction—and this applies just as much, if not more, to those who have misused the authority entrusted to them by God.

Luke 12:48b (TPT)
For those who have received a greater revelation from their master are required a greater obedience. And those who have been entrusted with great responsibility will be held more responsible to their master."

God's favor and anointing departed from King Saul when he hardened his heart, refused to repent, and stepped outside the boundaries of God's assignment. Tragically, I've witnessed this same pattern unfold in the lives of unhealthy church leaders time and time again. Scripture does not make exceptions for those in leadership—if anything, it holds them to a higher standard. When the Bible warns that *"the wages of sin is death"* and that *"your sin will surely find you out,"* these truths don't bypass those in positions of authority.

This isn't to say that grace doesn't extend to leaders—God's mercy is available to all. But when pride, abuse, and rebellion are left unchecked in the heart of a leader—when they excuse sin instead of confronting it— destructive consequences inevitably follow. Willful rebellion against the clear instruction of God will produce ungodly, destructive outcomes in anyone's life, and that does not exclude leaders. Not as a result of God's punishment, but *because sowing and reaping will also remain as long as the earth remains.*

Jesus didn't mince words when speaking with and confronting religious leaders who misrepresented His Father. In fact, He was more direct and offensive with those who were teachers of God's Word than any other people recorded in the New Testament, even accusing them of adhering to the traditions of men and serving their master, Satan, when refusing the instruction of God.

Luke 11:42-47, 52-54
42 "You Pharisees are hypocrites! For you are obsessed with peripheral issues, like paying meticulous tithes on the smallest herbs that grow in your gardens. Of course, these matters you should do, but when you unjustly cheat others, you ignore the most important duty of all: to walk in the love of God. Readjust your values and place first things first.
43 "You Pharisees are hypocrites! You love to be honored before others with titles of respect, seeking public recognition, aspiring to seem more important than others.
44 "You Pharisees, what hypocrites! Your true character is hidden, like an unmarked grave that hides the corruption inside, defiling all who come in contact with you."
45 Just then a specialist in interpreting religious law blurted out,

"Teacher, don't you realize that your words insult us?!"
46 Jesus responded, "You are also hypocrites, you experts of the law! You crush people beneath the burden of obeying impossible religious regulations, yet you would never even think of doing them yourselves. 47 What hypocrites! You build monuments to honor the prophets of old, yet it was your murdering ancestors who killed them. The only prophet you'll honor is a dead one!
52 "You are nothing but hypocrites, you experts of religion! You take away from others the key that opens the door to the house of knowledge. Not only do you lock the door and refuse to enter, but you also do your best to keep others from the truth."
53-54 All that Jesus said enraged the religious leaders and experts of the law and they began to oppose him furiously. They harassed Jesus all the way out the door, spewing out their hostility, arguing over everything he said—wanting nothing more than to find a reason to entrap him with his own words.

John 8:43-44 (TPT – Emphasis by the author)
*43 Why do you not understand My speech? Because you are not able to listen to My word. 44 **<u>You are of your father the devil</u>**, and the desires of your father you want to do. He was a murderer from the beginning, and does not stand in the truth, because there is no truth in him. When he speaks a lie, he speaks from his own resources, for he is a liar and the father of it.*

It's undeniable that those who are entrusted to lead and interpret the Word of God are held to a high standard—to represent Him with integrity and character. But that accountability isn't theirs alone. As followers and learners, we also carry the responsibility to put that Word into action—to not just hear it, but to live it.

James 1:22 (AMPC)
22 But be doers of the Word [obey the message], and not merely listeners to it, betraying yourselves [into deception by reasoning contrary to the Truth].

Whether we are leading entire churches, teams, families, or just trying to figure out how to lead ourselves, being a *disciple* of Christ is not about following or adhering to traditions or rules; it's about following Jesus. A *disciple* is not a *rule follower*; he's a *Jesus follower*.

Repentance and Redemption
When religious leaders attempt to reduce our faith to rituals and rule-

keeping, they're echoing the same spirit that Jesus confronted in the Pharisees of His time. Jesus never came to enforce tradition—He came to destroy the works of the devil and restore our relationship with God.

In Luke 19, when Zacchaeus, a corrupt, dishonest man known for cheating others, encountered Jesus, everything changed. Jesus met Zacchaeus exactly where he was at, without demanding that he first clean up his life or meet certain religious expectations. He simply accepted the invitation to come to his home. And in that one moment of authentic connection, Zacchaeus' heart was pierced by truth. Without being pressured or lectured, he repented, pledged to give half of his wealth to the poor, and promised to repay four times what he had stolen. His transformation wasn't the result of legalism or religious structure—it came from a personal encounter with the living God. That one moment of revelation shifted the trajectory of his life, showing us that when Jesus enters our story, it's not about perfection—it's about surrender.

One of the story's most powerful and touching moments is when Jesus tells him, *"Today, salvation has come to your whole household."* Why? Because Zacchaeus' decision to turn from sin and follow Jesus didn't just change his life—it altered the legacy of his entire family.

What could be more important or carry more weight than a man's legacy? Before that moment, his children would have carried the stigma of being the *son of a swindler*. They likely would have learned how to manipulate and exploit others by following their father's example, continuing the cheating cycle of deception for generations. But with one encounter with Jesus—and one man's decision to surrender and change—a new legacy was written. Jesus didn't just forgive Zacchaeus; He transformed the future of his family. He made all things new.

Revelation 21:5a (AMPC)
5 And He Who is seated on the throne said, See! I make all things new.

Religion Rejects Jesus Redeems

Too often, those who are the instruments of *Post-Traumatic Church Disorder* prioritize rules over relationship or discipline over true discipleship—those same people, bound by a religious spirit—also choose rejection over redemption. The story of Zacchaeus is a perfect example. The moment Jesus stepped into his home; the religious crowd didn't celebrate the possibility of transformation—they responded with criticism and judgment.

Luke 19:7 (AMPC) Emphasis by the author
And when the people saw it, they all muttered among themselves and indignantly complained, He (Jesus) has gone in to be the guest of and lodge with a man who is devoted to sin and preeminently a sinner

(Zacchaeus).

Where the religious people were content to reject and write off Zacchaeus, Jesus was intent on redeeming and rewriting his life's story.

Redemption under the new covenant is an amazing and beautiful thing. Under the old covenant, when you touched the unclean thing, you became unclean. But under the new covenant, Jesus modeled that when you, redeemed by the power of God, touched the unclean thing, it becomes clean! Under the old covenant, the leper was deemed unclean, rejected, and ostracized; anyone who came in contact with them also became unclean, rejected, and ostracized. But Jesus touched them, and their uncleanness was redeemed, healed, and made whole.[lx]

Just like Zacchaeus, the woman caught in the act of adultery was shamed, rejected, and despised—yet a single encounter with Jesus' redeeming grace completely altered the course of her life. Or take the example of the prostitute who poured expensive perfume on Jesus' feet and wiped them with her hair. Though those in the room were appalled by her presence, Jesus didn't turn her away. He embraced her and received her gift. Again and again, throughout the Gospels, we don't see Jesus rejecting the broken or unclean— we see Him redeeming them. Religion may reject, but Jesus always redeems.

As I've listened to countless stories of rejection tied to *Post-Traumatic Church Disorder*, one truth keeps standing out: religion rejects, but Jesus redeems. As we pointed out in the last chapter, even Jesus Himself was rejected by the very religious leaders who claimed to represent His Father. So let me encourage you—don't let the rejection of religion keep you from receiving the redemption that only Jesus can offer.

Maybe you didn't look like they did. You didn't act like they did. You listened to the music with the *demonic drum beat and electric guitars* and not that southern gospel music that they so adored. Every generation has had its sacred traditions and idols of rejection that were postured above the redeeming commandments in God's Word.

Did you know that at different times in church history, singing in harmony was considered to be of the devil because Gregorian chants were the norm, and later, the introduction of the pipe organ split the church? – It's true…foolish…but true.[lxi]

Understanding that our enemy prowls like a roaring lion, seeking whom he may devour, it's both sobering and heartbreaking to recognize that, far too often, the church itself has unintentionally become one of his most effective allies in attacking the children of God.

Let me explain. As mentioned in an earlier chapter, one of a lion's most successful strategies is to isolate its prey—separating it from the strength and safety of the pack before striking. In the same way, when Satan influences the church to *reject like religion* rather than *redeem like Jesus*, that rejection leaves people vulnerable and exposed. Those who were meant to be protected and empowered by spiritual family find themselves isolated, weakened, and easy targets. Instead of being surrounded with love and covered in grace, they are sacrificed by the very community that was meant to strengthen them. Godly leadership shelters and lifts up—satanic strategy isolates to tear down.

In John 14, Jesus tells His disciples in verses 12–14 that those who truly love Him will keep His commandments and do the works He did. The very word *"Christian"* means *"Christ-like"* or *"little Christ,"* emphasizing our call to reflect Him. In Matthew 7, Jesus echoes this message by teaching that the world will recognize His followers by their love for one another. His words leave little room for confusion or compromise—when it comes to following Jesus, love and obedience aren't optional; they're essential.

His Dying Declaration

There's a legal principle known as a *"dying declaration"* which gives unique weight to a person's final words. The idea is simple but profound: when someone knows their death is near, their words are often seen as deeply honest and reflective of their truest priorities. Because of this, courts will allow such declarations as evidence, even when they would normally be considered hearsay.

Many of us have, at some point, imagined the question: *"What would I do if I knew today was my last day on earth?"* While our answers may differ depending on personal values, one theme remains consistent—we would speak and act in ways that reflect what matters most. We'd focus on legacy, on love, and on leaving behind something meaningful for the people closest to us.

For me, I know exactly where I'd want to be: with my family. I'd make sure they knew how deeply I loved them. I'd speak life into my son, passing down the most important truths I've learned—lessons I'd want him to carry long after I'm gone. Those final words wouldn't be wasted on anything trivial. They'd matter because I would want him to remember every single one of them.

That's why John chapter 13 strikes me so powerfully. On the night before His crucifixion—knowing what was ahead—Jesus chose to model something unforgettable. As the Son of God and the leader of His disciples, His final actions and words weren't random or rushed. They were deliberate. They were weighty. They were, in essence, His *dying declaration*. And what He chose to do and say in that moment offers us one of the clearest pictures of what leadership in the Kingdom of God is meant to look like.

John 13:1-17 (TPT – Emphasis by the author)
1 Jesus knew that the night before Passover would be his last night on earth before leaving this world to return to the Father's side. All throughout his time with his disciples, Jesus had demonstrated a deep and tender love for them. And now he longed to show them the full measure of his love. 2 Before their evening meal had begun, the accuser had already deeply embedded betrayal into the heart of Judas Iscariot, the son of Simon.
3 Now Jesus was fully aware that the Father had placed all things under his control, for he had come from God and was about to go back to be with him. 4 So he got up from the meal and took off his outer robe, and took a towel and wrapped it around his waist. 5 Then he poured water into a basin and began to wash the disciples' dirty feet and dry them with his towel.
6 But when Jesus got to Simon Peter, he objected and said, "I can't let you wash my dirty feet—you're my Lord!"
7 Jesus replied, "You don't understand yet the meaning of what I'm doing, but soon it will be clear to you."
8 Peter looked at Jesus and said, "You'll never wash my dirty feet—never!"
"But Peter, if you don't allow me to wash your feet," Jesus responded, "then you will not be able to share life with me."
9 So Peter said, "Lord, in that case, don't just wash my feet, wash my hands and my head too!"
10 Jesus said to him, "You are already clean. You've been washed completely and you just need your feet to be cleansed—but that can't be said of all of you." For Jesus knew which one was about to betray him, 11 and that's why he told them that not all of them were clean.
12 After washing their feet, he put his robe on and returned to his place at the table. **"Do you understand what I just did?"** *Jesus said. 13* **"You've called me your teacher and lord, and you're right, for that's who I am. 14-15 So if I'm your teacher and lord and have just washed your dirty feet, then you should follow the example that I've set for you and wash one another's dirty feet.** *Now, do for each other what I have just done for you. 16 I speak to you timeless truth: a servant is not superior to his master, and an apostle is never greater than the one who sent him. 17 So now put into practice what I have done for you, and you will experience a life of happiness enriched with untold blessings!"*

In verse 1, we're told that Jesus was fully aware this was His final night on earth before His death. And in those final moments—as His dying declaration—He chose to model preference and humility. He revealed what mattered most to Him, set the standard for what should matter to us, and then demonstrated it by lovingly washing the feet of those who called Him their leader… even Judas, the very one He knew would soon betray Him. Afterward, He instructed His disciples to follow His example—to lead by serving one another from that same posture of humility and love.

There's no mistaking the message Jesus was teaching—even though it stands in stark contrast to the *Power Pyramid* model that many Christian leaders have adopted as their leadership standard. Jesus flipped that model on its head. He didn't lead from the top, placing others beneath Him and asserting authority over them. Instead, He led by humbly and lovingly prioritizing and serving the very people He created.

This is why the next generation of leaders must be intentional about doing things differently. I'm under no illusion that a large number of leaders from past generations—those who have built their ministries on *Power Pyramid* structures rather than the *Kingdom Pyramid* model or who have led for decades with a heavy-handed, legalistic approach that rejected people instead of redeeming them—will suddenly read this book, have a change of heart, and spend their remaining years leading in a new way. While it's possible that a few may shift course, the reality is that if years of reading God's Word and stories about Jesus washing feet haven't compelled them to reevaluate their leadership style, I don't imagine my words alone will be the tipping point.

But if you're reading this and are still willing to step onto the potter's wheel—allowing God to shape and mold you into the leader He created you to be—then maybe something within these pages has stirred your heart. Maybe it's challenged the paradigms and leadership norms you've seen modeled and inspired you to become the kind of leader you once longed for.

Perhaps you're like Zacchaeus—called by God but caught in a pattern of doing things the wrong way and now sensing a call to change. Maybe you relate more to David, having served under a leader who, instead of nurturing your anointing, tried to destroy it out of jealousy and fear. Or maybe you're like Joseph—someone who once had a dream, only to see it crushed by betrayal and abandonment from the people closest to you. And for some, you've never even seen healthy leadership modeled, but deep down, you know that when it's your time to lead, you want to do it God's way.

To every single one of you, I want to encourage you with this truth: God makes all things new.

Isaiah 43:19a (AMPC)
19 Behold, I am doing a new thing! Now it springs forth; do you not perceive and know it and will you not give heed to it?

Revelation 21:5 (AMPC)
5 And He Who is seated on the throne said, See! I make all things new.

Also, He said, Record this, for these sayings are faithful (accurate, incorruptible, and trustworthy) and true (genuine). [Isa. 43:19.]

For Zacchaeus, repentance was the turning point that allowed him to leave behind his old ways and step into the identity God had for him. For David, it was unwavering faithfulness that carried him through years of hardship and into the role God anointed him to fulfill. And for Joseph, it was perseverance that ultimately brought him into the realization of the dream God planted in his heart as a young boy. In each story, God began the work—and it was God who faithfully brought it to completion.

You may be reflecting on your own life right now, feeling the weight of a *Post-Traumatic Church Disorder* experience and the pain that came from the inconsistencies, disappointments, or abuse you encountered. But maybe, just maybe, after reading this book, you're beginning to recognize the enemy's hand in it all—how he tried to use pain, manipulation, and disillusionment to sever your connection to the body of Christ and even rob you of the calling God placed on your life, but you realize now there is more that God has for you!

No matter how painful or traumatic, what you've been through has shaped a perspective that's uniquely yours. And if you allow God to redeem it, that perspective can become a powerful gift—one that brings hope and direction to others who are walking similar roads but feel lost and unseen. As Renay Crouse, Executive Director of the Bair Foundation—a remarkable organization that helps children find loving foster and adoptive families—shared with me recently: *"The benefit of having the experience of not being seen is that you actually learn to see people."*

Your journey—every wound, every scar—has qualified you to lead in places others have never been and may never otherwise go. And when you begin to view your pain through the lens of legacy and purpose, you might begin to see how the very experiences that left you marked have equipped you to lead this next generation better than anyone led you.

Like a battle-tested lieutenant, you carry hard-earned wisdom that younger soldiers—those who haven't yet stepped onto the battlefield—can draw from. Your survival is not just your own testimony; it's the training manual that might help them live and thrive. After all, what didn't destroy you could become the very thing that saves someone else—if you're willing to step into the role God created you for.

By now, you should recognize that your PTCD pain was never God's doing. It was always the enemy—manipulating people and circumstances—strategically working to isolate you, steal your purpose, and derail your destiny. But here's the powerful truth: **you're still here.** Yes, the enemy may have won a few battles, but the war is far from over. And as long as you don't quit, God has promised you the victory.

Through His Word—and even through your pain—God has equipped you with the wisdom and insight needed to help raise up a generation of leaders who can go farther, lead better, and love deeper than any generation before them.

In my book *Dad's Letters: Wisdom for Sons on Faith, Identity, and Becoming the Man God Created You to Be*, I expressed a similar thought through a spiritual father's letter to sons:

Somewhere out there is a David standing alone in a field, completely unaware that he carries the heart of a king. And he will need someone— maybe you—to see what others overlooked and call out the greatness that was always inside him[lxii].

So many leaders miss this. They think their calling is about their own success, their own recognition, their own ascent. But the greatest aspect of leadership is often this: being the reason someone else rises into the fullness of what God created them to be.

David's own father and brothers stood close enough to influence him, yet failed to recognize the king right in front of them. They prioritized wrongly. They judged by appearances. They looked for outward qualifications instead of seeing the heart.

Son, don't ever be that kind of leader. See people with God's eyes. Look for the hidden potential others overlook. Call out greatness where it has never been spoken.

When you build a team without needing the credit... when you celebrate others' victories as if they were your own... when you choose empowerment over comparison... you create an exponential legacy that insecure leaders will never experience. Because insecurity chokes destiny, but encouragement unleashes it.

Here's what I want you to remember: When you play a role in someone else's success, their victory becomes part of your legacy. When you empower the greatness in another for the sake of the Kingdom, the whole team wins.

So when God puts people under your leadership, be intentional. Speak life into them. Call out their gifting. Affirm their purpose. Your words matter more than you know.

Ask God to show you what they cannot yet see in themselves. And when He does, declare it boldly. Sometimes one encouragement from the right person at the right time can change the entire trajectory of someone's life.

And son—don't stop there. Teach the ones you lead to do the same. Encourage the giant-slayers you raise to become legacy-minded—men and women who will one day identify and empower other giant-slayers after them.

That's how Kingdom legacy is built. That's how generations are shaped. That's how kings are discovered in fields.[lxiii]

Dale Mast expresses a parallel thought on leadership and calling powerfully in his book *And David Perceived He Was King*:

"When we observe and become emotionally attached to outcomes of injustice, God will often use us to be a part of the solution. We will only change what we desire or what disturbs us. Normally, they are intricately connected as one." [lxiv]

God is calling you to be that solution. This is the Leadership Edition of *PTCD*, and as a leader in the Kingdom of God, you are positioned to make a difference in your own leadership. Whether you have been in leadership your entire life and are now recognizing areas that need to change, or you have not yet stepped into the fullness of being the leader God created you to be, you are being strategically positioned and challenged to become more. There is NO CONDEMNATION for those who are in Christ Jesus, so be resolved to walk in grace toward yourself and toward others who may have failed in the past. You cannot change yesterday, but you have every opportunity to impact tomorrow. You can pour into the next generation and give them more teaching and insight than you may have received yourself, using the influence you still have to shape the future and your leadership legacy with real intentionality.

Whether the burden you carry comes from injustice you have witnessed or endured, or from the sobering realization that some of your own leadership may have contributed to unhealthy outcomes, it is likely connected to the next phase of your calling. In this season, God is inviting you to face that honestly, receive His grace fully, and step boldly into the kind of leadership that reflects His heart.

The Body of Christ is waiting for you to step into your place, because when you are not there, something vital is missing. Your children, and even your spiritual children, are depending on you to shift your thinking and establish a legacy they can confidently follow. And at the end of it all, what is at stake is your own fulfillment, being able to say with confidence that you ran the race God set before you and did not allow people, pain, failure, or even Satan himself to stop you from becoming who God created you to be, even when everything inside of you may have wanted to give up.

How we continue despite the resistance we encounter shapes the legacy we leave.[lxv]

It no longer matters how long you have been off course, how deep the wound went, or how far you feel you have strayed. What matters is this moment, this opportunity to step into a redeemed perspective, a restored identity, and a different future. No amount of PTCD, pain, failure, or rejection has the power to override the redemption available to you in Jesus.

Deuteronomy 30:19-20a (AMPC – Emphasis by the author)
*19 I call heaven and earth to witness this day against you that I have set before you life and death, the blessings and the curses; therefore **choose life, that you and your descendants may live***
20 And may love the Lord your God, obey His voice, and cling to Him. For He is your life and the length of your days, that you may dwell in the land which the Lord swore to give to your fathers.

So as we close the final chapter of *Post-Traumatic Church Disorder: Addressing the Elephant in the Sanctuary*, I want you to hear this with absolute clarity: God's redemption was never just about recovering what was lost. It is about transforming what was broken into something far more beautiful than you ever imagined. He does not just heal your past. He prepares you for a future filled with purpose, influence, and the kind of impact that only comes from having walked through the fire and survived.

Every scar you carry is a testimony waiting to speak life into someone else. Every tear you have shed has watered the soil of a legacy that can touch generations.

And for those reading this through leadership lenses, hear me clearly: this is not just your invitation to heal. It is your call to lead differently. To lead with greater wisdom. To lead with greater humility. To lead with greater courage, integrity, and intentionality than perhaps you have seen modeled before. Whether you are just stepping into leadership, serving faithfully under another leader, or carrying the weight of senior leadership, God is calling you higher, not into performance, but into alignment with His heart.

This is your commissioning moment. Not just to heal, but to lead God's way. Not just to survive, but to thrive in His strength and grace. Not just to rebuild, but to help pioneer a better path forward for those who are still silently suffering. You have been seen. You have been shaped. And now, you have been sent.

So, walk forward with courage and intentionality. Refuse to live in the shadow of what hurt you. And remember: God does not waste a thing. In His hands, even the most painful chapters can become the most powerful ones.

All things new is not a distant hope. It is the reality you step into the moment you say yes.

Aaron D. Davis

ABOUT THE AUTHOR

Aaron D. Davis is a 4x best-selling author, speaker, pastor, and former law enforcement officer with a unique and powerful story of resilience, faith, and redemption. A medically retired Detective Sergeant and S.W.A.T. team officer, Aaron survived an attempt on his life in the line of duty—an experience that forever shaped his passion for healing trauma, restoring hope, and helping others walk in freedom.

Aaron is the author of the #2 Best-selling book, *Quantum Christianity: Believe Again*, the #1 Best-selling book, *Limitless: You Can Experience the Freedom, Power, and Potential You Were Created For,* The #2 Best-selling book, *PTCD – Post-traumatic Church Disorder: Addressing the Elephant in the Sanctuary*, and the #3 Best-selling book, *Dad's Letters: Wisdom for Sons on Faith, Identity, and becoming the Man God Created You to Be*—books that have resonated with readers around the world. He's also the author of the *Limitless Freedom* curriculum and training seminar, designed to be used in churches, offering a biblically grounded framework for personal and spiritual freedom and transformation.

Whether through writing, speaking, coaching, or consulting, Aaron is committed to equipping people and organizations with practical tools for lasting breakthrough and meaningful impact.

He lives in Nashville, Tennessee, with his wife, Lisa, to whom he has been happily married for nearly 30 years. Together, they are the proud parents of their son, Rocky. Aaron's life and message are a testimony to God's power to redeem even the most painful chapters—and to make all things new.

Other Books and Resources by Aaron D. Davis

To explore more books and audiobooks by Aaron D. Davis, visit his Author Central page at: amazon.com/author/tattoopreacher, his official website at TattooPreacher.com, or connect with him on social media where he's known as The Tattooed Preacher or @Tattoopreacher (X, LinkedIn, Instagram, Facebook, YouTube). You can also search "Tattoo Preacher" on YouTube to access his teaching series and a wide range of impactful video content.

Quantum Christianity: Believe Again

In *Quantum Christianity,* Aaron Davis explores the questions that often lead people away from faith—questions born from the gap between what we've been taught and what we've experienced. By uncovering the intersection between science and Scripture, he offers a deeper understanding of belief, challenging partial truths and revealing the surprising, hope-filled answers that await those who dare to ask, "There has to be more." (Available in paperback, hardcover and audiobook).

Limitless: You Can Experience the Freedom, Power, and Potential You Were Created For

In *Limitless*, Aaron Davis tackles the real struggles so many believers face—the frustration of battling the same sins, setbacks, and strongholds again and again. Through practical wisdom and biblical truth, he shows that you don't have to stay stuck in cycles of defeat. You were created for freedom, victory, and the limitless potential God designed for your life. (Available in adult, young adult, Spanish, and audiobook).

Dad's Letters: Wisdom for Sons on Faith, Identity, and Becoming the Man God Created You to Be

Dad's Letters is a collection of 152 short, heartfelt letters written from the perspective of a loving father (the Father) to a son. Blending biblical truth, life experience, and practical wisdom, Aaron D. Davis offers guidance for men seeking stronger faith, clearer identity, and the courage to become who God created them to be. With a tone that is direct, compassionate, honest, and affirming, each letter speaks to character, discipline, integrity, emotional resilience, leadership, repentance, and purpose. Whether placed in the hands of a son, read by a man searching for direction, or given by a parent who wants to pass on lasting wisdom, Dad's Letters is a trusted voice of love, truth, and encouragement for the journey into manhood. (Available in paperback, hardcover and audiobook).

Bibliography

i Miller, Craig A. - Breaking Emotional Barriers to Healing: Understanding the Mind-Body Connection to Your Illness (p. 23). Whitaker House. Kindle Edition.

ii Miller, Craig A. - Breaking Emotional Barriers to Healing: Understanding the Mind-Body Connection to Your Illness (p. 25). Whitaker House. Kindle Edition.

iii Howard-Browne, Rodney
https://www.instagram.com/p/DF7ocBeMm6s/?img_index=2

iv Tyler, Darren
https://www.instagram.com/reel/DE5sEb7yH3r/?utm_source=ig_web_copy_link&igsh=MzRlODBiNWFlZA==

v Maxwell, John C https://www.instagram.com/p/DFT3SmzIyqQ/

vi Dr. Rodney Howard-Browne
https://www.instagram.com/p/DEhgnhlvZ9Y/?img_index=2 Paraphrased by the author.

vii https://substack.com/@adamgrant/note/c-172137973

viii @TruthTheory https://www.instagram.com/p/DEp4OhqqERa/

ix @Truththeory https://www.instagram.com/p/DF0A70rpuEI/

x Acuff, Jon - ATG Episode #230 Leaders Who Can't Be Questioned:
https://jonacuff.com/atg230#:~:text=%E2%80%9CLeaders%20who%20can't%20be,spoiler%3A%20everyone%20lied%20and%20said

xi @iamsimkins https://www.instagram.com/p/DFQjKnVh-VE/?img_index=14

xii – Dr. Rodney Howard-Browne
https://www.instagram.com/p/DFNSIbFBx6t/?img_index=2

xiii @bishoppitts https://www.instagram.com/p/DF8Y0HWz07W/

xiv @leadersonlyco https://www.instagram.com/p/DFqO-0VSMzA/?img_index=1

xv December 2 Leadership Principle #337
https://www.instagram.com/p/DDEz_5yoNUB/

xvi Mast, Dale L. - And David Perceived He Was King: IDENTITY - the Key to Your DESTINY (p. 47). Xulon Press. Kindle Edition.

xvii @Colbyfmaier https://www.instagram.com/p/DEqtM3LPzrZ/

xviii @PastorMauryD https://www.instagram.com/p/DEFuTM2unQN/

xix @DerwinLGray https://www.instagram.com/p/DEKcVUXqAWs/

xx @Iamsmithfitness https://www.instagram.com/p/DFvVSPXv__X/

xxi Galatians 6:7-8
xxii @TheDarrenScott https://www.instagram.com/p/DD5yOpkvfKO/

xxiii Quote reference – footnote F from 2 Corinthians 12:7 in The Passion Translation of the Bible (TPT)

xxiv Dooley, Phil https://www.instagram.com/p/DEAAICPR5WC/

xxv – Warren and David Wiersbe
https://www.dailychristianquote.com/warren-and-david-wiersbe/#:~:text=When%20ministry%20becomes%20performance%2C%20then,presence%20moves%20into%20the%20sanctuary

xxvi @Garrettnogan https://www.instagram.com/p/DE8GpVLSc2m/

xxvii Mast, Dale L.. And David Perceived He Was King: IDENTITY - the Key to Your DESTINY (p. 46). Xulon Press. Kindle Edition.

xxviii @moisfearless (small revisions added by the author)
https://www.instagram.com/p/DEh-ALpo0S5/

xxix Davis, Aaron. Limitless: You Can Experience the Freedom, Power and Potential You Were Created For . Rosa_Penn@Fiverr. Kindle Edition.

xxx https://www.goodreads.com/quotes/685059-the-greatest-gift-you-can-give-somebody-is-your-own

[xxxi] Rogan, Joe. *The Joe Rogan Experience* (podcast), quoted statement on leadership, reposted on https://www.instagram.com/roganfans - later removed and unable to cite exactly

[xxxii] https://x.com/purposologist/status/540627549668519936?lang=en - @purposologist – Alexander den Heijer

[xxxiii] https://www.christianpost.com/news/survey-reasons-why-people-leave-the-church.html

[xxxiv] https://relevantmagazine.com/culture/study-young-people-are-leaving-the-church-due-to-perceived-hypocrisy-and-judgment/ **While these studies indicate that negative perceptions and experiences—including moments of offense—contribute to individuals leaving church communities, they do not pinpoint an exact percentage of departures caused solely by offensive events.

[xxxv] https://www.instagram.com/reel/DHTSRmHODDt/?utm_source=ig_web_copy_link&igsh=MzRlODBiNWFlZA==

[xxxvi] @chriswinelandcomedy
https://www.instagram.com/reel/DBwPcRguXT0/?utm_source=ig_web_copy_link&igsh=MzRlODBiNWFlZA==

[xxxvii] Thomas, Clint - The Disciples Blueprint - Section 4 - Page 147
[xxxviii] Mast, Dale L.. And David Perceived He Was King: IDENTITY - the Key to Your DESTINY (p. 46). Xulon Press. Kindle Edition.

[xxxix] https://www.forbes.com/sites/robasghar/2014/02/25/ranking-the-9-toughest-leadership-roles/

[xl] https://www.soulshepherding.org/pastors-under-stress/
All these surveys are of Protestant pastors from a variety of denominations in America: (1) David Ross and Rick Blackmon's "Soul Care for Servants" workshop reported the results of their Fuller Institute of Church Growth research study in 1991 and other surveys in 2005 and 2006. (2) Francis A Schaeffer Institute of Church Leadership Development research studies in 1998 and 2006. (3) Leadership Magazine's research for their article on "Marriage Problems Pastors Face," Fall 1992 issue. (4) Grey Matter Research, 2005 scientific study of pastors from every city in America. (5) Pastors at Greater Risk by H.B. London and Neil B. Wiseman, Regal

Books, 2003. (6) Focus on the Family 2009 survey of 2,000 pastors. (7) Leadership Journal poll of readers, 2013.

[xli] @pastormauryd https://www.instagram.com/p/DEkTmIFO7Cw/

[xlii] Bishop Dale Bronner

[xliii] Footnote John 5:18 https://www.bible.com/bible/1849/JHN.5.18

[xliv] - Mast, Dale L.. And David Perceived He Was King: IDENTITY - the Key to Your DESTINY (p. 45). Xulon Press. Kindle Edition.

[xlv] @library4success https://www.instagram.com/p/DDR4a_vTCAQ/

[xlvi] @James.a.murray
https://www.instagram.com/p/DDFsSm6TWk_/?img_index=7

[xlvii] Rephrased from – Dr. Rodney Howard-Browne
https://www.instagram.com/p/DFIIjJaIhKe/?img_index=2.

[xlviii] Footnote e John 8:31-32 TPT.

[xlix] -Davis, Aaron. Quantum Christianity: Believe Again (pp. 133-134). amazon.com. Kindle Edition.

[l] Davis, Aaron. Quantum Christianity: Believe Again (pp. 87-88). amazon.com. Kindle Edition.

[li] Davis, Aaron. Quantum Christianity: Believe Again (p. 92). amazon.com. Kindle Edition. Additional sentence added for PTCD.

[lii] - Davis, Aaron. Limitless: You Can Experience the Freedom, Power and Potential You Were Created For . Rosa_Penn@Fiverr. Kindle Edition.

[liii] Jentezen Franklin https://www.instagram.com/p/DFoPIHsSsEn/

[liv] @Jimmybelloso https://www.instagram.com/p/DFdKkzbuMue/

[lv] Nehemiah 4:1

[lvi] @iansimkins https://www.instagram.com/p/DFh9JLWO0Fg/

[lvii] @shane_pruitt78 https://www.instagram.com/p/DEXufcOpcHp/

[lviii] Mast, Dale L. - And David Perceived He Was King: IDENTITY - the Key to Your DESTINY (pp. 46-47). Xulon Press. Kindle Edition.

[lix] – C.S. Lewis (attributed, though exact source debated)

[lx] Bill Johnson– Washed by the Word – Bethel Church
https://www.youtube.com/watch?v=qXUS1OQc5kA

[lxi] Davis, Aaron. Quantum Christianity: Believe Again (p. 78). amazon.com. Kindle Edition.

[lxii] Mast, Dale L.. And David Perceived He Was King: IDENTITY - the Key to Your DESTINY (pp. 52-53). (Function). Kindle Edition. (Paraphrased Reference)

[lxiii] Davis, Aaron, Dad's Letters: Wisdom for Son's on Faith, Identity, and Becoming the Man God Created You to Be (pages 174-175)
[lxiv] Mast, Dale, And David Perceived He Was King (page 89)

[lxv] Goff, Bob Instagram @bobgoff (December 12, 2024)